THE OFFICIAL U.S. ARMY
LEADERSHIP
HANDBOOK
CURRENT EDITION

Including:
Army Leadership
Counseling
Training Units & Developing Leaders

ADRP 6-22 (FM 6-22), ATP 6-22.1, ADRP 7-0

Headquarters,
Department of the Army

The Official U.S. Army Leadership Handbook - Current Edition

Full-Size 8.5" x 11" Format - For Leaders Everywhere: Includes "Counseling" and "Training Units and Developing Leaders" (ADRP 6-22 (FM 6-22), ATP 6-22.1, ADRP 7-0)

U.S. Army

This edition first published 2017 by Carlile Military Library. "Carlile Military Library" and its associated logos and devices are trademarks. All rights reserved.
Published in the United States of America.

ISBN-13: 978-1-9763-2450-5
ISBN-10: 1976324505

Change No. 1

ADRP 6-22, C1

Headquarters
Department of the Army
Washington, DC, 10 September 2012

Army Leadership

1. This change replaces the cover to align with Doctrine 2015 standards.

2. ADRP 6-22, 1 August 2012, is changed as follows:

Remove Old Pages	**Insert New Pages**
cover	cover

3. File this transmittal sheet in front of the publication for reference purposes.

DISTRIBUTION RESTRICTION: Approved for public release; distribution is unlimited.

ADRP 6-22, C1
10 September 2012

By order of the Secretary of the Army:

RAYMOND T. ODIERNO
General, United States Army
Chief of Staff

Official:

JOYCE E. MORROW
Administrative Assistant to the
Secretary of the Army
1224210

DISTRIBUTION:
Active Army, Army National Guard, and United States Army Reserve: To be distributed in accordance with the initial distribution number (IDN) 110180, requirements for ADRP 6-22.

PIN: 103008-001

ADRP 6-22 (FM 6-22)

Army Doctrine Reference Publication
No. 6-22

Headquarters
Department of the Army
Washington, DC, 1 August 2012

Army Leadership

Contents

	Page
PREFACE	iv
INTRODUCTION	v

PART ONE   THE BASIS OF LEADERSHIP

Chapter 1   **FUNDAMENTALS OF LEADERSHIP** 1-1
- Leadership Defined 1-1
- Foundations of Army Leadership 1-2
- Civilian-Military Linkage 1-3
- Leadership and Command Authority 1-3
- Mission Command 1-3
- Formal and Informal Leadership 1-4
- Army Leadership Requirements Model 1-4
- Attributes 1-5
- Core Leader Competencies 1-5

Chapter 2   **ROLES AND LEVELS OF LEADERSHIP** 2-1
- Roles and Relationships 2-1
- Levels of Leadership 2-4
- Collective Leadership 2-6

PART TWO   THE ARMY LEADER: PERSON OF CHARACTER, PRESENCE AND INTELLECT

Chapter 3   **CHARACTER** 3-1
- Foundations of Army Leader Character 3-1
- Army Values 3-1
- Empathy 3-3
- The Warrior Ethos and Service Ethos 3-4
- Discipline 3-5
- Character Development 3-5
- Character and Beliefs 3-6
- Character and Ethics 3-6

DISTRIBUTION RESTRICTION: Approved for public release; distribution is unlimited.

*This publication supersedes FM 6-22 (except Appendix B, Counseling), dated 12 October 2006.

Contents

Chapter 4	PRESENCE	4-1
	Basics of Army Leader Presence	4-1
	Military and Professional Bearing	4-1
	Fitness	4-1
	Confidence	4-2
	Resilience	4-2

Chapter 5	INTELLECT	5-1
	Basics of an Army Leader's Intellect	5-1
	Mental Agility	5-1
	Sound Judgment	5-1
	Innovation	5-2
	Interpersonal Tact	5-2
	Expertise	5-3

PART THREE COMPETENCY-BASED LEADERSHIP FOR DIRECT THROUGH STRATEGIC LEVELS

Chapter 6	LEADS	6-1
	Leads Others	6-1
	Builds Trust	6-7
	Extends Influence Beyond the Chain of Command	6-8
	Leads by Example	6-10
	Communicates	6-12

Chapter 7	DEVELOPS	7-1
	Overview of Develops	7-1
	Creates a Positive Environment/Fosters Esprit de Corps	7-1
	Prepares Self	7-6
	Develops Others	7-8
	Developing on the Job	7-12
	Stewards the Profession	7-15

Chapter 8	ACHIEVES	8-1
	Gets Results	8-1
	Providing Direction, Guidance, and Priorities	8-1
	Monitoring Performance	8-3
	Competencies Applied for Success	8-3

Chapter 9	LEADERSHIP IN PRACTICE	9-1
	Challenges of the Operational Environment	9-1
	Combat and Operational Stress	9-3
	Stress in Training and Operations	9-4
	Stress of Change	9-4
	Tools for Adaptability	9-4

PART FOUR LEADING AT ORGANIZATIONAL AND STRATEGIC LEVELS

Chapter 10	ORGANIZATIONAL LEADERSHIP	10-1
	Leading	10-1
	Developing	10-4
	Achieving	10-6

Chapter 11	STRATEGIC LEADERSHIP	11-1
	Overview of Strategic Leadership	11-1
	Leading	11-2
	Developing	11-6
	Achieving	11-9
	GLOSSARY	**Glossary-1**
	REFERENCES	**References-1**
	INDEX	**Index-1**

Figures

Figure 1-1. The Army leadership requirements model 1-5
Figure 2-1. Army leadership levels 2-4
Figure 3-1. The Soldier's Creed 3-4
Figure 3-2. The Army Civilian Corps Creed 3-4

Tables

Introductory Table-1. Rescinded Army terms v
Introductory Table-2. Modified Army terms vi
Table 3-1. Summary of the attributes associated with *Character* 3-5
Table 4-1. Summary of the attributes associated with *Presence* 4-2
Table 5-1. Summary of the attributes associated with *Intellect* 5-5
Table 6-1. Summary of the competency *Leads others* 6-7
Table 6-2. Summary of the competency *Builds trust* 6-8
Table 6-3. Summary of the competency *Extends influence beyond the chain of command* 6-10
Table 6-4. Summary of the competency *Leads by example* 6-12
Table 6-5. Summary of the competency *Communicates* 6-14
Table 7-1. Summary of the competency *Creates a positive environment* 7-5
Table 7-2. Summary of the competency *Prepares self* 7-8
Table 7-3. Counseling—Coaching—Mentoring Comparison 7-12
Table 7-4. Summary of the competency *Develops others* 7-15
Table 7-5. Summary of the competency *Stewards the profession* 7-16
Table 8-1. Summary of the competency *Gets results* 8-4

Preface

Army doctrine reference publication (ADRP) 6-22 expands on the leadership principles established in Army doctrine publication (ADP) 6-22. ADRP 6-22 describes the Army's view of leadership, outlines the levels of leadership (direct, organizational, and strategic), and describes the attributes and core leader competencies across all levels.

The principal audience for ADRP 6-22 is all leaders, military and civilian. Trainers and educators throughout the Army will also use this publication.

Commanders, staffs, and subordinates ensure their decisions and actions comply with applicable United States, international, and, in some cases, host-nation laws and regulations. Commanders at all levels ensure their Soldiers operate in accordance with the law of war and the rules of engagement (see Field Manual [FM] 27-10).

ADRP 6-22 uses joint terms where applicable. Selected joint and Army terms and definitions appear in both the glossary and the text. For definitions shown in the text, the term is italicized and the number of the proponent publication follows the definition. The use of the term influence throughout this publication reflects the definition of common English usage "the act or power of producing an effect without apparent exertion of force or direct exercise of command," as distinct from the usage outlined in FM 3-13. It is contrary to law for DOD to undertake operations intended to influence a domestic audience; nothing in this publication recommends activities in contravention of this law.

ADRP 6-22 applies to the Active Army, Army National Guard/Army National Guard of the United States, and United States Army Reserve unless otherwise stated.

This publication incorporates copyrighted material.

The proponent of ADRP 6-22 is Headquarters, U.S. Army Training and Doctrine Command. The preparing agency is the Center for Army Leadership, Combined Arms Center - Leader Development and Education, United States Army Combined Arms Center. Send comments and recommendations on DA Form 2028 (Recommended Changes to Publications and Blank Forms) to Center for Army Leadership ATTN: ATZL-CLR (ADP/ADRP 6-22), 290 Stimson Avenue, Fort Leavenworth, KS 66027-1293; by e-mail to usarmy.leavenworth.tradoc.mbx.6-22@mail.mil; or submit an electronic DA Form 2028.

Acknowledgments

These copyright owners have granted permission to reproduce material from their works.

Leading Change, by John P. Kotter. Reproduced with permission of Harvard Business School Press. Copyright © 1996.

Making Partnerships Work, by Jonathan Hughes and Jeff Weiss. Reproduced with permission of Vantage Partners, LLC. Copyright © 2001. All rights reserved.

Leadership in Organizations, 8th ed by Gary Yukl. Reproduced with permission of the author. Copyright © 2012.

"Assessing the Construct Validity and Utility of Two New Influence Tactics", by Gary Yukl, Carolyn Chavez, and Charles F. Seifert. *Journal of Organizational Behavior* Reproduced with permission of the author. Copyright © 2005.

"Consequences of Influence Tactics Used With Subordinates, Peers, and the Boss," by Gary Yukl and J. Bruce Tracey. *Journal of Applied Psychology*. Reproduced with permission of the author. Copyright © 1992.

Introduction

ADRP 6-22 establishes and describes the leader attributes and core leader competencies that facilitate focused feedback, education, training, and development across all leadership levels.

An ideal Army leader has strong intellect, physical presence, professional competence, moral character and serves as a role model. An Army leader is able and willing to act decisively, within the intent and purpose of superior leaders and in the best interest of the organization. Army leaders recognize that organizations, built on mutual trust and confidence, successfully accomplish missions.

Everyone in the Army is part of a team and functions in the role of leader and subordinate. Being a good subordinate is part of being a good leader. All Soldiers and Army Civilians must serve as leaders and followers. It is important to understand that leaders do not just lead subordinates—they also lead other leaders. Leaders are not always designated by position, rank, or authority.

ADRP 6-22 describes the attributes and core competencies required of contemporary leaders. ADRP 6-22 addresses the following topics necessary to become a competent, multiskilled, and agile Army leader:

- Understand the Army definitions of leader and leadership.
- Use the Army leadership requirements model as a common basis for thinking and learning about leadership and associated doctrine.
- Become knowledgeable about the roles and relationships of leaders, including the role of subordinate or team member.
- Discover what makes a good leader: a person of character with presence and intellect.
- Learn how to lead, develop, and achieve through competency-based leadership.
- Identify the influences and stresses in our changing environment that affect leadership.
- Understand the basics of leading at the direct, organizational, and strategic levels.

ADRP 6-22 contains four parts comprised of 11 chapters that describe the Army's view on leadership:

Part One defines leadership, describes the foundations of Army leadership, and introduces the Army Leadership Requirements Model in Chapter 1. It addresses the various roles of Army leaders and the levels of leadership in Chapter 2.

Part Two describes the leader attributes of character, presence, and intellect. Chapter 3 on leader character covers the Army Values, empathy and the Warrior Ethos, as well as the role of ethics. Chapter 4 on leader presence discusses military bearing, physical fitness, confidence, and resilience. Chapter 5 on leader intellect describes mental agility, sound judgment, innovation, interpersonal tact, and expertise.

Part Three describes the core leader competencies and their application. Chapter 6 addresses the category of *leads*: leads others, extends the influence beyond the chain of command, leads by example, and communicates. Chapter 7 describes the category of *develops*: creating a positive environment, prepares self, and develops others. Chapter 8 describes the category of *achieves*. Chapter 9 discusses the challenges of the operational environment, stress, and change.

Part Four addresses the roles and responsibilities of organizational leaders in Chapter 10 and strategic leaders in Chapter 11.

Based on current doctrinal changes, certain terms have been rescinded or modified for the purposes of ADRP 6-22. The glossary contains acronyms and defines terms. See introductory tables 1 and 2 for specific changes.

Introductory Table-1. Rescinded Army terms

Term	*Remarks*
leader teams	Rescinded.
officership	Rescinded.
shared leadership	Rescinded.
virtual team	Rescinded.

Introductory Table-2. Modified Army terms

Term	Remarks
adaptability	No longer a formally defined term.
Army Values	No longer a formally defined term.
attribute	No longer a formally defined term.
climate	No longer a formally defined term.
coaching	No longer a formally defined term.
core leader competencies	No longer a formally defined term.
counseling	No longer a formally defined term.
critical thinking	No longer a formally defined term.
culture	No longer a formally defined term.
direct leadership	No longer a formally defined term.
domain knowledge	No longer a formally defined term.
ethical reasoning	No longer a formally defined term.
Informal leadership	No longer a formally defined term.
leadership	Modified definition.
lifelong learning	No longer a formally defined term.
mental agility	No longer a formally defined term.
military bearing	No longer a formally defined term.
multisource assessment	No longer a formally defined term.
organizational leadership	No longer a formally defined term.
profession of arms	No longer a formally defined term.
resilience	No longer a formally defined term.
responsibility	No longer a formally defined term.
role	No longer a formally defined term.
self-awareness	No longer a formally defined term.
self-development	No longer a formally defined term.
self-efficacy	No longer a formally defined term.
strategic leadership	No longer a formally defined term.
well-being	No longer a formally defined term.

PART ONE

The Basis of Leadership

All Army team members, Soldiers and Army Civilians alike, must understand what leadership is and does. The military is set apart from other professions because Soldiers must be prepared to use deadly force and have the courage to overcome hostile forces. Army leaders exercise a profound responsibility because the consequences of their decisions and actions affect the lives of Soldiers, their families, the enemy and non-combatants. Leaders draw from deep-rooted values and professional competence to demonstrate resolve to do what is right at the right time for the right reason. National and Army values and expectations inspire professional development, instilling a desire to acquire the essential knowledge to lead. Leaders apply this knowledge across established competencies to achieve mission success. The roles and functions of Army leaders apply to the three interconnected levels of leadership: direct, organizational and strategic. Excellence occurs when leadership operates cohesively across levels. The Army profession is a calling for the professional American Soldier and Army Civilian from which leaders inspire and influence others to carry out the missions entrusted to them.

Chapter 1

Fundamentals of Leadership

LEADERSHIP DEFINED

1-1. *Leadership* is the process of influencing people by providing purpose, direction, and motivation to accomplish the mission and improve the organization (ADP 6-22). As an element of combat power, leadership unifies the other elements of combat power (information, mission command, movement and maneuver, intelligence, fires, sustainment and protection). Confident, competent, and informed leadership intensifies the effectiveness of the other elements of combat power.

INFLUENCING

1-2. Influencing is getting people—military and civilian, governmental and non-governmental partners, or even bystanders such as a local populace—to do what is required. Influencing entails more than simply passing along orders. Through words and personal example, leaders communicate purpose, direction, and motivation.

PURPOSE

1-3. Purpose gives subordinates the reason to achieve a desired outcome. Leaders should provide clear purpose for their followers. Leaders can use direct means of conveying purpose through requests or orders.

Direction

1-4. Providing clear direction involves communicating what to do to accomplish a mission: prioritizing tasks, assigning responsibility for completion, and ensuring subordinates understand the standard. Although subordinates want and need direction, they expect challenging tasks, quality training, and adequate resources. They should have appropriate freedom of action. Providing clear direction allows followers to adapt to changing circumstances through modifying plans and orders through disciplined initiative within the commander's intent.

Motivation

1-5. Motivation supplies the will and initiative to do what is necessary to accomplish a mission. Motivation comes from within, but others' actions and words affect it. A leader's role in motivation is to understand the needs and desires of others, to align and elevate individual desires into team goals, and to inspire others to accomplish those larger goals. Some people have high levels of internal motivation to get a job done, while others need more reassurance, positive reinforcement, and feedback.

1-6. Indirect approaches to motivation can be as successful as direct approaches. Setting a personal example can sustain the drive in others. This becomes apparent when leaders share the hardships. When a unit prepares for a deployment, all key leaders should share in the hard work. This includes leadership presence at night, weekends, and in any conditions or location where subordinates are working.

Improve the Organization

1-7. Improving for the future means capturing and acting on important lessons of ongoing and completed projects and missions. Improving is an act of stewardship, striving to create effective, efficient organizations. Developmental counseling is crucial for helping subordinates improve performance and prepare for future responsibilities. Counseling should address strong areas as well as weak ones. Part Three provides information on counseling. Two proven techniques that involve subordinates in assessing for improvement are in-progress reviews and after action reviews (AAR).

FOUNDATIONS OF ARMY LEADERSHIP

1-8. The foundations of Army leadership are grounded in history, loyalty to the nation and the Constitution, accountability to authority, and evolving Army doctrine. To enable leaders to become competent at all levels of leadership, the Army identifies three categories of core leader competencies: lead, develop, and achieve. These categories and their subsets represent the roles and functions of leaders. Leaders embrace the responsibilities to lead others to achieve mission and organizational outcomes. They do so while taking care of Soldiers and Army Civilians and ensuring they prepare to assume greater leadership responsibilities. Through education, training and experience leaders develop into competent and disciplined professionals of the Army.

1-9. The Army and its leadership requirements are based on the nation's democratic foundations, defined values, and standards of excellence. The Army recognizes the importance of preserving the time-proven standards of competence that distinguished leaders throughout history. Leadership doctrine acknowledges that societal change, evolving security threats, and technological advances require adaptability.

1-10. Although America's history and cultural traditions derive from many parts of the world, the Declaration of Independence and the Constitution establish common values, goals, and beliefs. These documents explain the purpose of our nationhood and detail inherent rights and responsibilities. Every Soldier and leader should be familiar with these documents.

1-11. On 4 July 1776, the Declaration of Independence formally stated America's separation from British rule and asserted its right as an equal participant in dealings with other sovereign nations. In 1787, the Constitution of the United States formally established the functions of our government. It clearly explains the functions and the checks and balances between the three branches of government: executive, legislative, and judicial. The Constitution sets the parameters for the creation of our national defense establishment, including the basis for the formation, funding, and command of the Army.

Fundamentals of Leadership

CIVILIAN-MILITARY LINKAGE

1-12. The Constitution grants Congress the power to raise and support armies. Subsequently, the armed forces have the task of defending the United States and its territories. A special status in law marks membership in the Army and the other Services. Distinctive uniforms and insignia reflect that status. To function effectively, the Army and other Services organize into hierarchies of authority. The Army's hierarchy begins with the President of the United States, the civilian leadership comprised of the Secretary of Defense and the Secretary of the Army, and then extends to the individual Soldier.

1-13. To formalize ties to the nation and to affirm subordination to its laws, members of the Army—Soldiers and Army Civilians—swear or affirm an oath to support and defend the Constitution of the United States against all enemies, foreign and domestic. Soldiers simultaneously acknowledge the authority of the President as Commander in Chief and officers as the President's agents. The purpose of the oath is to affirm military subordination to civilian authority. The Army Values link tightly with the oaths.

1-14. The oaths and values emphasize that the Army's military and civilian leaders are instruments of the people of the United States. Soldiers should recognize that in or out of uniform, they represent their units, the Army, and the nation. Every Soldier must balance official duties with the civil responsibilities afforded by the laws of the nation. They must function as ambassadors for the nation in peace and war. Similarly, the Army expects honorable behavior by Army Civilians.

LEADERSHIP AND COMMAND AUTHORITY

1-15. Command is a prescribed responsibility established by pertinent official directives, policies, and precedents. The key elements of command are authority and responsibility (see AR 600-20).

1-16. *Command* is the authority that a commander in the armed forces lawfully exercises over subordinates by virtue of rank or assignment. Command includes the authority and responsibility for effectively using available resources and for planning the employment of, organizing, directing, coordinating, and controlling military forces for the accomplishment of assigned missions. It also includes responsibility for health, welfare, morale, and discipline of assigned personnel (JP 1-02).

1-17. Commanders and subordinates rely on each other to perform their duties with competence and integrity. Leaders have to answer for how subordinates live and act beyond duty hours. Society and the Army look to leaders to ensure that Soldiers and Army Civilians receive the proper training and care, uphold expected values, and accomplish missions.

1-18. In Army organizations, commanders establish standards and policies for achieving and rewarding superior performance, as well as for punishing misconduct. Military commanders enforce lawful orders under the Uniform Code of Military Justice. Consequently, organizations are profoundly shaped by the personality of their commanders. Army leaders selected to command are expected to lead beyond the mere exercise of formal authority. They should lead by example and serve as role models; their personal example and actions carry tremendous moral force. For that reason, people inside and outside the Army recognize leaders as the embodiment of the Army's commitment to readiness and good stewardship of its resources and personnel.

MISSION COMMAND

1-19. *Mission command* is the exercise of authority and direction by the commander using mission orders to enable disciplined initiative within the commander's intent to empower agile and adaptive leaders in the conduct of unified land operations (ADP 6-0). Mission command calls for leaders with the ability to build a collaborative environment, the commitment to develop subordinates, the courage to trust, the confidence to delegate, the patience to overcome adversity, and the restraint to allow lower echelons to develop the situation. Specifically, mission command requires that leaders receive training, education, and experience to become—

- Critical and creative problem solvers, agile and able to make decisions in operational environments with uncertainty, complexity, and change.
- Skilled at applying the Army Design Methodology and the operations process.

- Skilled communicators able to create shared understanding and support for the mission.
- Practitioners able to integrate their efforts with unified action partners, sensitive to the operational and strategic implications of their actions.
- Inspirational leaders who are able to engender utmost trust and confidence with and among subordinates and fellow leaders.
- Lifelong students of the Army profession.
- Adaptive leaders skilled in the art and science of influence, including negotiation and mediation.

FORMAL AND INFORMAL LEADERSHIP

1-20. To be effective team builders, organizational leaders and commanders must be able to identify and interact with both formal and informal teams, including—
- The traditional chain of command.
- Coordination directing unified action partners.
- Technical channels combining commanders and staff officers.

1-21. Formal leadership is granted to individuals by virtue of assignment to positions of responsibility and is a function of rank and experience. The Uniform Code of Military Justice supports military leaders in positions of legitimate authority. Formal leader impose their authority over subordinates through lawful orders and directives.

1-22. Informal leadership exists throughout organizations, must support legitimate authority, and plays an important role in mission accomplishment. Informal leadership is not based on rank or position in the organizational hierarchy. It can arise from knowledge, experience, or technical expertise and may require initiative on the part of the individual to assume responsibility. When leading without designated authority, informal leaders need to appreciate potential impacts and contribute to the team's success. As the final decisionmaker, the formal leader is ultimately responsible for legitimizing an informal leader's advice.

1-23. Although leading through other leaders is a decentralized process, it does not imply a commander or supervisor cannot step in and temporarily take active control if the need arises. However, bypassing the chain of command should be by exception and focused on solving an urgent problem or guiding an organization back on track with the leader's original guidance.

1-24. Informal networks often arise both inside and outside formal organizations. Although leaders occupy positions of legitimate authority, groups form to share information and lessons gained from experience. When informal groups form, they often take on the same characteristics as formally designed organizations. As such, they develop norms unique to their network and seek legitimacy through their actions.

EMPOWERING SUBORDINATES AND RISK

1-25. Competent leaders know the best way to create a solid organization is to empower subordinates. Empowering subordinates does not mean omitting checks and only making necessary corrections. Leaders help subordinates in identifying successes and mistakes by ensuring they sort out what happened and why. A quality AAR will help them learn from their successes and mistakes in a positive manner.

1-26. Because subordinates learn best by doing, leaders should be willing to take prudent risks and accept the possibility that less-experienced subordinates will make mistakes. Risk assessment and risk management help determine existing risks and mitigation strategies. If subordinate leaders are to grow and develop trust, it is best to let them learn through experience. Effective leaders allow space for subordinates to experiment within the bounds of intent-based orders and plans.

ARMY LEADERSHIP REQUIREMENTS MODEL

1-27. The Army exists to serve the American people, to protect enduring national interests and to fulfill the nation's military responsibilities. This requires values-based leadership, impeccable character, and professional competence. The requirements are for leaders at all levels and are common to all cohorts. The model informs leaders of the enduring capabilities needed regardless of the level of leadership, mission, or assignment. All model components are interrelated and relate to the Department of Defense (DOD) civilian leader development framework established by DODI 1430.16 (see figure 1-1).

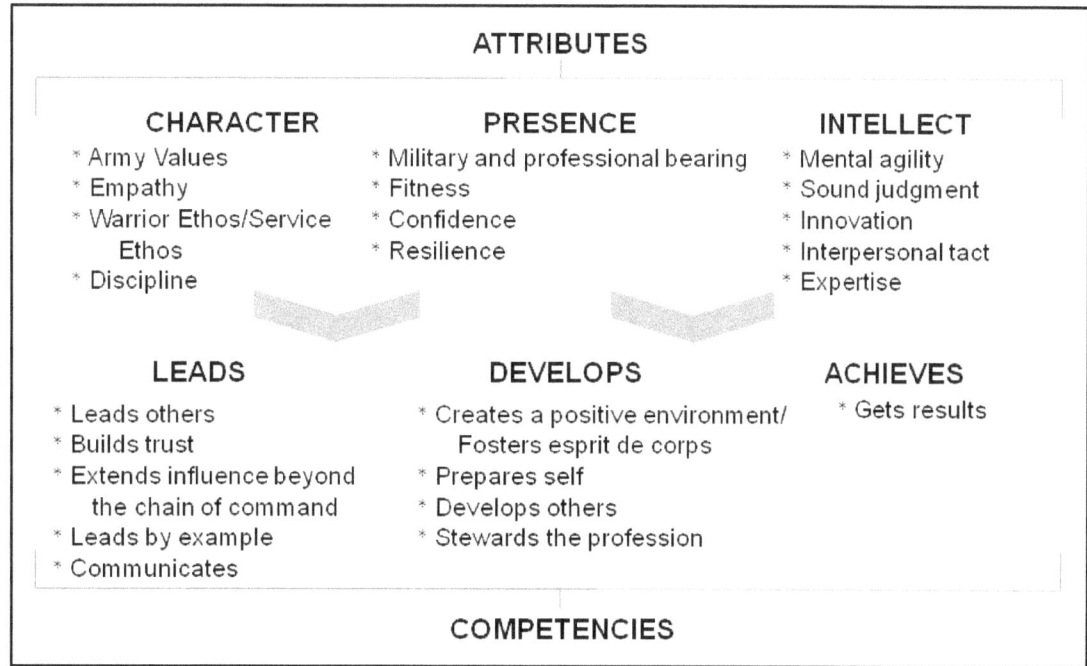

Figure 1-1. The Army leadership requirements model

1-28. The model's components center on what a leader is (attributes) and what a leader does (competencies). The leader's character, presence, and intellect enable the leader to master the core leader competencies. The Army leader is responsible to lead others; to develop the environment, themselves, others, and the profession as a whole; and to achieve organizational goals.

1-29. Effective leadership and leader development require mutual recognition and acceptance of leader and follower roles. Leadership is a reciprocal influence process between leaders and followers.

ATTRIBUTES

1-30. Attributes describe the leaders that the Army wants. Attributes describe how an individual behaves and learns within an environment. The leader attributes are character, presence, and intellect. These attributes represent the values and identity of the leader (character) with how the leader is perceived by followers and others (presence), and with the mental and social faculties the leader applies in the act of leading (intellect). Character, a person's moral and ethical qualities, helps a leader determine what is right and gives a leader motivation to do what is appropriate, regardless of the circumstances or consequences. Actions, words, and the manner in which leaders carry themselves convey presence. Presence is not just a matter of showing up; it involves the example that the leader projects to inspire others to do their best and follow their lead. An Army leader's intelligence draws from conceptual abilities and is applied to one's duties and responsibilities. Conceptual abilities enable effective problem-solving and sound judgment.

CORE LEADER COMPETENCIES

1-31. Leader competence develops from a balanced combination of institutional schooling, self-development, realistic training, and professional experience. Building competence follows a systematic and gradual approach, from mastering individual competencies to applying them in concert and tailoring them to the situation at hand. Leading people by giving them a complex task helps them develop the confidence and will to take on progressively more difficult challenges.

1-32. Competencies provide a clear and consistent way of conveying expectations for Army leaders. Current and future leaders want to know how to be successful leaders. The core leader competencies apply across all levels of leader positions and throughout careers, providing a good basis for evaluation and focused multisource assessment and feedback. A spectrum of leaders and followers (superiors, subordinates, peers, and mentors) can observe and assess competencies demonstrated through behaviors.

1-33. Leader competencies can be developed. Leaders acquire the basic competencies at the direct leadership level. As the leader moves to organizational and strategic level positions, the competencies provide the basis for leading through change. Leaders continuously refine and extend the ability to perform these competencies proficiently and learn to apply them to increasingly complex situations.

1-34. Performing missions develops, sustains, and improves these competencies. Leaders do not wait until deployments to develop their leader competencies. They use every training opportunity to assess and improve their ability to lead.

1-35. To improve their proficiency, Army leaders can take advantage of chances to learn and gain experience in the leader competencies. They should look for new learning opportunities, ask questions, seek training opportunities, conduct self-assessments, and request performance critiques. This lifelong approach to learning ensures leaders remain viable as professionals.

Chapter 2
Roles and Levels of Leadership

ROLES AND RELATIONSHIPS

2-1. Army leaders of character lead by personal example and consistently serve as role models through a dedicated lifelong effort to learn and develop. They achieve excellence when disciplined followers do their duty, commit to the Army Values, and feel empowered to accomplish any mission while simultaneously improving their organizations with focus towards the future.

2-2. The Army cannot accomplish its mission unless all Army leaders, Soldiers, and Army Civilians accomplish their mission—whether filing status reports, repairing vehicles, planning budgets, packing parachutes, maintaining pay records, or standing guard duty. The Army relies on dedicated Soldiers and Army Civilians across all components to accomplish missions worldwide.

2-3. Each role and responsibility is unique, yet there are common ways in which leaders interact. Every individual in the Army is a member of a team – as leaders or followers.

2-4. When the Army speaks of Soldiers, it refers to officers, noncommissioned officers (NCOs), and enlisted men and women. Army Civilians are employees of the Department of the Army and, like Soldiers, are members of the executive branch of the federal government. All Army Soldiers and Army Civilians are charged to support and defend the Constitution against all enemies, foreign and domestic, by providing effective Army landpower to combatant commanders and to accomplish the organization's mission.

2-5. The roles and responsibilities of Army leaders overlap and complement each other. Formal Army leaders come from three different categories: commissioned officers, noncommissioned officers, and Army Civilians. Collectively, these groups work toward a common goal and follow a shared value system.

OFFICERS

2-6. Officers (including warrant officers) hold their grade and office under a commission issued under the authority of the President of the United States or the Secretary of the Army. Granted on the basis of special trust and confidence placed in the officer's patriotism, valor, fidelity, and abilities, an officer's commission grants authority to direct subordinates and subsequently, an obligation to obey superiors.

2-7. Officers are essential to the Army's organization to command units, establish policy, and manage resources while balancing risks and caring for their people and families. They integrate collective, leader, and Soldier training to accomplish the Army's missions. They serve at all levels, from focusing on unit operations to leading change at the strategic levels. Command makes officers responsible and accountable for everything their command does or fails to do.

2-8. Serving as an officer differs from other forms of Army leadership by the quality and breadth of expert knowledge required, in the measure of responsibility attached, and in the magnitude of the consequences of inaction or ineffectiveness. An enlisted leader swears an oath of obedience to lawful orders, while an officer promises to, "well and faithfully discharge the duties of the office." This distinction establishes a different expectation for disciplined initiative. Officers maintain the momentum of operations. They must possess the courage to deviate from standing orders when required and be willing to accept the responsibility for their actions. While officers depend on the counsel, technical skill, maturity, and experience of subordinates to translate their orders into action, the ultimate responsibility for mission success or failure resides with the officer in charge.

2-9. As with all Army leaders, the Army Values guide officers in their daily actions. These values manifest themselves as principles of action. As a Soldier and leader of Soldiers, an officer adheres to the Soldier's Creed and the Warrior Ethos. An officer's responsibility as a public servant is first to the nation, then to the Army, and then to the unit and Soldiers. As a professional, the officer is obligated to be competent and stay abreast of changing requirements. The Army expects officers to live the Army Values as leaders of character.

2-10. Warrant officers possess a high degree of specialization in a particular field in contrast to the more general assignment pattern of other officers. Warrant officers command aircraft, maritime vessels, and special units. Warrants provide quality advice, counsel, and solutions to support their unit or organization. They maintain, administer, and manage the Army's equipment, support activities, and technical systems. Their extensive professional experience and technical knowledge qualifies warrant officers as invaluable role models and mentors for junior officers and NCOs.

2-11. While warrant positions are usually functionally oriented, they lead and direct Soldiers the same as other leaders and staff officers. Senior warrants provide the commander with the benefit of years of tactical and technical experience. Warrant officers functioning at higher levels become systems experts rather than equipment experts. As such, they must have a firm grasp of the environment and know how to integrate the systems they manage into complex operational environments.

NONCOMMISSIONED OFFICERS

2-12. The Army relies on NCOs capable of conducting daily operations, executing complex tactical operations, and making intent-driven decisions. Soldiers look to their NCOs for solutions, guidance, and inspiration. Soldiers count on leaders they trust and admire. Soldiers can relate to NCOs since NCOs advanced through the junior enlisted ranks. They expect them to convey information and provide day-to-day guidance to get the job done. To answer the challenges of the operational environment, NCOs must train Soldiers to cope, prepare, and perform regardless of situation. In short, the Army NCO is a leader of strong character, comfortable in every role.

2-13. NCO leaders are responsible for setting and maintaining high-quality standards and discipline. They are standard-bearers and role models critical to training, educating, and developing subordinates. NCOs are accountable for caring for Soldiers and setting the example for them.

2-14. While preparing Soldiers for missions, NCOs stress fieldcraft and physical hardening. The NCO knows that the tools provided by technology will not reduce the need for mentally and physically fit Soldiers. Soldiers will continue to carry heavy loads, convoy for hours or days, and clear enemy forces from rural and urban strongholds. Tactical success relates directly to the Soldiers' level of tactical and technical training, as well as their fitness and resiliency. Taking care of Soldiers ensures they are prepared for whatever challenges lie ahead.

2-15. NCOs have roles as trainers, mentors, communicators, and advisors. When junior officers first serve in the Army, their NCO helps to train and mold them. Doing so ensures Soldier safety while forming professional and personal bonds with the officers based on mutual trust and common goals. "Watching each other's back" is a fundamental step in team building and cohesion.

2-16. Commanders at all levels have senior enlisted advisors who are an important source of knowledge and discipline for all enlisted matters. At the highest level, the Sergeant Major of the Army is the Army Chief of Staff's personal advisor who recommends policy to support Soldiers throughout the Army.

ARMY CIVILIANS

2-17. Army Civilians are experienced personnel committed to serving the nation as an integral part of the Army team. They provide mission-essential capability, stability, and continuity during war and peace to support Soldiers. Army Civilians take their support mission seriously and are committed to selfless service in the performance of their duties. The Army Civilian Corps Creed affirms their role as a member of the Army team and their special contribution to organizational stability and continuity.

2-18. Major roles and responsibilities of Army Civilians include establishing and executing policy; managing Army programs, projects, and systems; and operating activities and facilities for Army equipment, support, research, and technical work. These roles support the organizational Army as well as Soldiers based around the world.

2-19. Selection of Army Civilians depends on their eligibility to hold the position. Their credentials reflect the expertise with which they enter a position. Proficiency derives from education and training they have obtained, prior experiences, and career-long ties to special professional fields. Army Civilians hold the grade of the position in which they serve. Except for the Commander in Chief (the President of the United States) and Secretary of Defense, Army Civilians do not exercise military command; however, they may be designated to exercise general supervision over an Army installation or activity under the command of a military superior. Army Civilians primarily exercise authority based on the position held, not their grade.

2-20. Civilian personnel have functional proponents for career fields that ensure provisions exist for career growth. Army Civilians are free to pursue positions and promotions as they desire. Personnel policies generally state that Army Civilians should be in positions that do not require military personnel for reasons of law, training, security, discipline, rotation, or combat readiness. Army Civilians, many with uniformed military experience, bring a wealth of knowledge and experience to the Army team.

2-21. While most Army Civilians historically support military forces at home stations, Army Civilians also deploy with military forces to sustain theater operations. As evidenced by the increasing demands of recent deployments, Army Civilians have served at every level and location, providing expertise and support wherever needed. Army Civilians support their military counterparts and often remain for long periods within the same organization, providing continuity and stability that the highly mobile personnel management system used for the military rarely allows. However, when the position or mission dictates, Army Civilians may transfer or deploy to meet the needs of the Army.

UNIFIED ACTION PARTNERS

2-22. The Army team may include members of other government agencies, intergovernmental organizations, and coordination with nongovernmental organizations and the private sector. When added to an organization, members of these groups change both the makeup and the capabilities of the combined team. While leaders may exercise formal authority over joint servicemembers attached to a unit, there are different cultures within the services. Understanding these differences will make coordination easier. Typically, leaders will not have formal authority over interagency, intergovernmental, and multinational partners. Leaders must exercise a different form of leadership more focused on collaboration to influence and guide the behavior of members of multinational forces. Leaders must foster a command climate that includes and respects all members.

2-23. Developing teams within organizations begins early in the operations process and continues throughout execution. Leaders develop understanding by training and planning with unified action partners. Sustained engagement with host nation governments and forces enhances the developed understanding. Integrating capabilities during unified land operations requires interaction and preparation before commanders commit forces. Integration occurs through training exercises, exchange programs, and training events resulting in greater collaboration in developing systems and equipment for the forces involved.

LEVELS OF LEADERSHIP

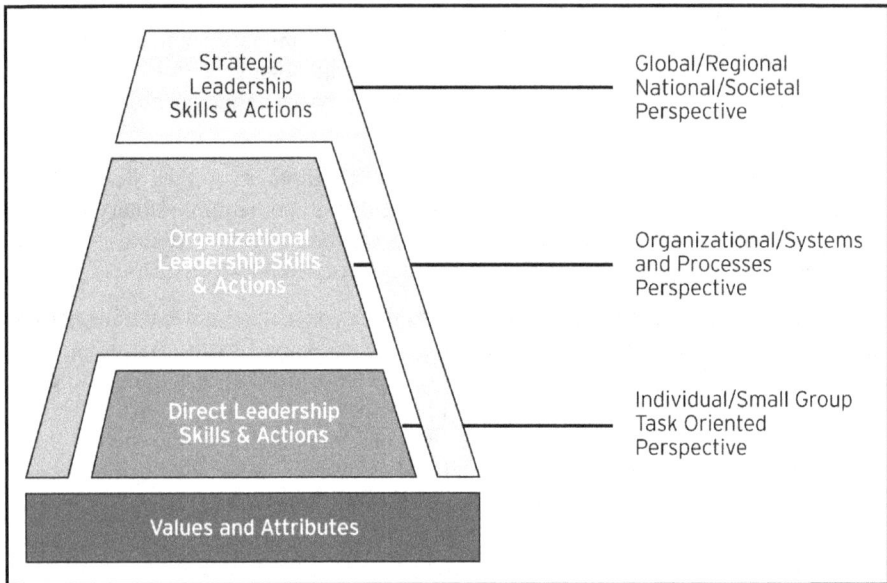

Figure 2-1. Army leadership levels

2-24. Figure 2-1 shows the three levels of Army leadership: direct, organizational, and strategic. Factors determining a position's leadership level can include the position's span of control, its headquarters level, and the degree of control exerted or autonomy granted by the leader holding the position. Other factors include the size of the unit or organization, the type of operations it conducts, and its planning horizon.

2-25. Most NCOs, company grade officers, and Army Civilian leaders serve at the direct leadership level. Some senior NCOs, most field grade officers, and higher-grade Army Civilians serve at the organizational leadership level. Primarily, general officers and equivalent senior executive service Army Civilians serve at the organizational or strategic leadership levels.

2-26. Often, the rank or grade of the leader holding a position does not indicate the position's leadership level. A sergeant first class serving as a platoon sergeant works at the direct leadership level. If the same NCO holds a headquarters job dealing with issues and policy affecting a brigade-sized or larger organization, that NCO works at the organizational leadership level. However, if the sergeant's primary duty is running a staff section that supports leaders who run the organization, the NCO is a direct leader.

2-27. It is important to realize that the headquarters echelon alone does not determine a position's leadership level. For example, leaders of all ranks and grades serve in strategic-level headquarters, but they are not all strategic-level leaders. Likewise, an Army Civilian at a range control facility with a dozen subordinates works at the direct leadership level. An Army Civilian deputy garrison commander with a span of influence over several thousand people is an organizational-level leader.

DIRECT LEVEL LEADERSHIP

2-28. Direct leadership is face-to-face or first-line leadership. It generally occurs in organizations where subordinates see their leaders all the time: teams, squads, sections, platoons, departments, companies, batteries, and troops. The direct leader's span of influence may range from a few to dozens of people.

2-29. Direct leaders develop their subordinates one-on-one and influence the organization indirectly through their subordinates. For instance, a company commander is close enough to the Soldiers to exert direct influence when observing training or interacting with subordinates during other scheduled functions.

2-30. Direct leaders generally experience more certainty and less complexity than organizational and strategic leaders. Mainly, they are close enough to the action to determine or address problems. Examples of direct leadership tasks are monitoring and coordinating team efforts, providing clear and concise mission intent, and setting expectations for performance.

ORGANIZATIONAL LEVEL LEADERSHIP

2-31. Organizational leaders influence several hundred to several thousand people. They do this indirectly, generally through more levels of subordinates and staffs than do direct leaders. The additional levels of subordinates can make it more difficult for them to see and judge immediate results. Organizational leaders have staffs to help them lead their people and manage their organizations' resources. They establish policies and the organizational climate that support their subordinate leaders.

2-32. Organizational leaders generally include military leaders at the battalion through corps levels, military and civilian leaders at directorate through installation levels, and Army Civilians at the assistant through undersecretary of the Army levels. Their planning and focus generally ranges from two to ten years. Some examples of organizational leadership are setting policy, managing multiple priorities and resources, or establishing a long-term vision and empowering others to perform the mission.

2-33. While the same core leader competencies apply to all levels of leadership, organizational leaders usually works with more complexity, more people, greater uncertainty, and a greater number of unintended consequences. Organizational leaders influence people through policymaking and systems integration in addition to face-to-face contact.

2-34. Getting out of the office and visiting remote parts of their organizations is important for organizational leaders. They make time to verify if their staff's reports and briefings match their own perceptions of the organization's progress toward mission accomplishment. Organizational leaders use personal observation and visits by designated staff members to assess how well subordinates understand the commander's intent and to determine if there is a need to reinforce or reassess the organization's priorities.

STRATEGIC LEVEL LEADERSHIP

2-35. Strategic leaders include military and civilian leaders at the major command through DOD levels. Strategic leaders are responsible for large organizations and influence several thousand to hundreds of thousands of people. They establish force structure, allocate resources, communicate strategic vision, and prepare their commands and the Army for future roles.

2-36. Strategic leaders work in uncertain environments that present highly complex problems affecting or affected by events and organizations outside the Army. The actions of a combatant commander often have critical impacts on global politics. They command very large, joint organizations with broad, continuing missions. (JP 3-0 discusses combatant commands.)

2-37. Strategic leaders apply all core leader competencies they acquired as direct and organizational leaders, while further adapting them to the more complex realities of their strategic environment. Strategic leader decisions must consider congressional hearings, Army budgetary constraints, new systems acquisition, civilian programs, research, development, and inter-service cooperation.

2-38. Strategic leaders, like direct and organizational leaders, process information quickly, assess alternatives based on incomplete data, make decisions, and generate support. However, strategic leaders' decisions can affect more people, commit more resources, and have wider-ranging consequences in space, time, and political impact, than those of organizational and direct leaders.

2-39. Strategic leaders are important catalysts for change and transformation. Because they follow a long-term approach to planning, preparing, and executing, they often do not see their ideas come to fruition during their limited tenure. The Army's transformation to more flexible, more rapidly deployable, and more lethal unit configurations, such as brigade combat teams, is a good example of long-range strategic planning. While the Army relies on many leadership teams, it depends predominantly on organizational leaders to endorse the long-term strategic vision to reach all of the Army. Because they exert influence primarily through staffs and trusted subordinates, strategic leaders must develop strong skills in selecting and developing talented and capable leaders for critical duty positions.

COLLECTIVE LEADERSHIP

2-40. When leaders of different elements with different roles align to a collective effort, they create the greatest amount of synergy to achieve the desired results. Successful leadership depends on the alignment of purpose, direction, and motivation. Leaders who work in isolation produce only limited results at best and—at worst—will unhinge other efforts. Coordinated actions of teams and units working toward the same purpose accomplish missions. Leaders working collectively are not only coordinating and synchronizing actions across the range of military operations but they have a shared mindset as to how to create and maintain a positive climate. This unifying and collective aspect of leadership is undeniably an essential element of militaries all the way down to small teams. Collective leaders—

- Recognize that cohesive leadership has a greater impact than an individual leader has alone.
- Consciously contribute to unifying beliefs, attitudes, and actions up and down and across units.
- Concede personal power and control to subordinates, peers, and superiors when doing so will enhance a collective focus.
- Sacrifice self-interest and personal or unit accomplishments in favor of mutual goals.
- Create and groom relationships with others inside and outside the organization that contribute to advancing goals.
- Become aware of sources of expertise across a unit and draw on it when needed.

PART TWO

The Army Leader: Person of Character, Presence, and Intellect

Army leadership doctrine addresses all aspects of leadership, the most important being the Army leader. Part Two examines that person and highlights critical attributes all Army leaders can use to reach their full professional potential from direct leader to strategic leader. When Soldiers and Army Civilians begin as leaders, they bring certain values and attributes, such as family-ingrained values, and the aptitude for certain sports or intellectual abilities, such as learning foreign languages. Education, training and experience aim at using these existing qualities and potential to develop well-rounded leaders. Development of the desired attributes associated with character, presence and intellect requires acknowledgement through consistent self-awareness and lifelong learning.

Chapter 3

Character

FOUNDATIONS OF ARMY LEADER CHARACTER

3-1. Character, comprised of a person's moral and ethical qualities, helps determine what is right and gives a leader motivation to do what is appropriate, regardless of the circumstances or consequences. An informed ethical conscience consistent with the Army Values strengthens leaders to make the right choices when faced with tough issues. Army leaders must embody these values and inspire others to do the same.

3-2. Character is essential to successful leadership. It determines who people are, how they act, helps determine right from wrong, and choose what is right. Elements internal and central to a leader's core are—
- Army Values.
- Empathy.
- Warrior Ethos and Service Ethos.
- Discipline.

ARMY VALUES

3-3. Soldiers and Army Civilians enter the Army with personal values developed in childhood and nurtured over years of personal experience. By taking an oath to serve the nation and the institution, one agrees to live and act by a new set of values—Army Values. The Army Values consist of the principles, standards, and qualities considered essential for successful Army leaders. They are fundamental to helping Soldiers and Army Civilians make the right decision in any situation. Teaching values is an important leader responsibility by creating a common understanding of the Army Values and expected standards.

3-4. The Army recognizes seven values that all Army members must develop. When read in sequence, the first letters of the Army Values form the acronym "LDRSHIP":

- Loyalty.
- Duty.
- Respect.
- Selfless service.
- Honor.
- Integrity.
- Personal courage.

LOYALTY: BEAR TRUE FAITH AND ALLEGIANCE TO THE U.S. CONSTITUTION, THE ARMY, YOUR UNIT AND OTHER SOLDIERS.

3-5. All Soldiers and Army Civilians swear an oath to support and defend the Constitution of the United States. The Constitution established the legal basis for the Army in Article I, Section 8, where it outlines congressional responsibilities regarding America's armed forces. Consequently, leaders—as members of the armed forces or Army Civilians—have an obligation to be faithful to the Army and its people.

3-6. To create strong organizations, superiors, subordinates, and peers must embrace loyalty. Good units build loyalty and trust through training. Leaders earn subordinates' loyalty by training them well, treating them fairly, and living the Army Values. Loyalty and trust are extremely critical for the successful day-to-day operations of all organizations. Ultimately, loyalty extends to other Services and agencies. The reality of modern operations shows that unified action partners are essential to successful mission outcomes.

DUTY: FULFILL YOUR OBLIGATIONS.

3-7. Duty extends beyond law, regulation, and orders. Professionals consistently strive to do their best. Army leaders exercise initiative when they fulfill the purpose, not merely the letter, of received orders. With initiative, leaders take responsibility for their actions and those of their subordinates. Conscientiousness is a human trait that internalizes duty. Conscientious leaders have a sense of responsibility for personal contributions to the Army, demonstrated through dedicated effort, organization, thoroughness, reliability, and practicality. Conscientiousness guides leaders to do what is right.

RESPECT: TREAT PEOPLE AS THEY SHOULD BE TREATED.

3-8. Respect for the individual is the basis for the Geneva Convention; this body of law codifies the ideal that Soldiers, even in the most trying of circumstances, are bound to treat others with dignity and respect. Army leaders must work with people from a wide range of backgrounds. An Army leader should prevent misunderstandings arising from cultural differences. Actively seeking to learn about different cultures and being sensitive to other cultures will aid in mentoring, coaching, and counseling subordinates. Leaders must actively seek opportunities to better understand other cultures, see other perspectives, and appreciate what others find important.

3-9. Army leaders should consistently foster a climate that treats everyone with dignity and respect, regardless of race, gender, sexual orientation, creed, or religious belief. Fostering a positive climate begins with a leader's personal example.

SELFLESS SERVICE: PUT THE WELFARE OF THE NATION, THE ARMY AND YOUR SUBORDINATES BEFORE YOUR OWN.

3-10. People often refer to the military as "the Service." Selfless service means doing what is right for the nation, the Army, the organization, and subordinates. While the needs of the Army and the nation should come first, it does not imply leaders should neglect their Families or themselves. To the contrary, such neglect weakens a leader and can cause the Army more harm than good.

HONOR: LIVE UP TO ARMY VALUES.

3-11. Honor provides the moral compass for character and personal conduct for all members of the Army. Honor holds the Army Values together. Honor requires a person to demonstrate an understanding of what is right. Military ceremonies recognizing individual and unit achievements demonstrate and reinforce the importance the Army places on honor. Living honorably, in line with the Army Values, sets an example for every member of the organization and contributes to an organization's positive climate and morale.

3-12. How leaders conduct themselves and meet obligations define them as persons and leaders. In turn, how the Army meets the nation's commitments defines the Army as an institution. Honor demands putting the Army Values above self-interest and above career and personal comfort. Honor gives the strength of will to live according to the Army Values, especially in the face of personal danger. It is not coincidence that our military's highest award is the Medal of Honor. Its recipients clearly go beyond the call of duty.

INTEGRITY: DO WHAT IS RIGHT, LEGALLY AND MORALLY.

3-13. Leaders of integrity consistently follow clear principles. The Army relies on leaders of integrity who possess high moral standards and are honest in word and deed. Leaders are honest to others by not presenting themselves or their actions as anything other than what they are, remaining committed to truth.

3-14. Leaders of integrity do the right thing because their character permits nothing less. To instill the Army Values in others, leaders must demonstrate them. Personal values inevitably extend beyond the Army Values, including such things as political, cultural, or religious beliefs. However, as an Army leader and a person of integrity, these values should reinforce, not contradict, the Army Values. Conflicts between personal and Army Values should be resolved before a leader can expect to become a morally complete Army leader. If in doubt, a leader may consult a mentor with respected values and judgment.

PERSONAL COURAGE: FACE FEAR, DANGER, OR ADVERSITY (PHYSICAL AND MORAL).

3-15. Personal courage is not the absence of fear. It is the ability to put fear aside and do what is necessary. Personal courage takes two forms: physical and moral. Effective leaders demonstrate both. Physical courage requires overcoming fears of bodily harm and doing one's duty. It triggers bravery that allows a Soldier to take risks in combat in spite of the fear of wounds or even death.

3-16. Moral courage is the willingness to stand firm on values, principles, and convictions. It enables all leaders to stand up for what they believe is right, regardless of the consequences. Leaders, who take full responsibility for their decisions and actions even when things go wrong, display moral courage. Moral courage also expresses itself as candor. Candor means being frank, honest, and sincere with others. It requires impartiality and fairness.

EMPATHY

3-17. Army leaders show empathy when they genuinely relate to another person's situation, motives, and feelings. Empathy does not necessarily mean sympathy for another, but identification that leads to a deeper understanding. Empathy allows the leader to anticipate what others are experiencing and to try to envision how decisions or actions affect them. Leaders with a strong tendency for empathy can apply it to understand Army Civilians, Soldiers and their Families, local populations, and enemy combatants. The ability to see something from another person's point of view, to identify with, and enter into another person's feelings and emotions, enables the Army leader to better interact with others.

3-18. Leaders take care of Soldiers and Army Civilians by giving them the training, equipment, and support needed to accomplish the mission. During operations, empathetic Army leaders share hardships to gauge if their plans and decisions are realistic. They recognize the need to provide Soldiers and Army Civilians with reasonable comforts and rest periods to maintain good morale and mission effectiveness.

3-19. Army leaders recognize that empathy includes nurturing a close relationship between the Army and Army Families. To build a strong and ready force, Army leaders at all levels promote healthy Families. Empathy for Families includes allowing Soldiers recovery time from difficult missions, protecting leave periods, and supporting events that allow information exchange and family team building.

3-20. The requirement for leader empathy extends beyond Army Civilians, Soldiers, and their Families. Within the operational environment, leader empathy is helpful when dealing with local populations, victims of natural disasters, and prisoners of war. Essentially, empathy produces better cultural understanding of people, missions, and operations and how they connect.

THE WARRIOR ETHOS AND SERVICE ETHOS

3-21. The Warrior Ethos refers to the professional attitudes and beliefs that characterize the American Soldier. It reflects a Soldier's selfless commitment to the nation, mission, unit, and fellow Soldiers. Army Civilians, while not warfighters, embody the principles of the Warrior Ethos through a service ethos that suffuses their conduct of duty with the same attitudes, beliefs, and commitment. The Warrior Ethos is developed and sustained through discipline, commitment to the Army Values, and pride in the Army's heritage. Lived by Soldiers and supported by Army Civilians, the Warrior Ethos is the foundation for the winning spirit that permeates the institution (see figures 3-1 and 3-2).

I AM AN AMERICAN SOLDIER.

I AM A WARRIOR AND A MEMBER OF A TEAM.

I SERVE THE PEOPLE OF THE UNITED STATES, AND LIVE THE ARMY VALUES.

I WILL ALWAYS PLACE THE MISSION FIRST.
I WILL NEVER ACCEPT DEFEAT.   WARRIOR ETHOS
I WILL NEVER QUIT.
I WILL NEVER LEAVE A FALLEN COMRADE.

I AM DISCIPLINED, PHYSICALLY AND MENTALLY TOUGH, TRAINED AND PROFICIENT IN MY WARRIOR TASKS AND DRILLS.

I ALWAYS MAINTAIN MY ARMS, MY EQUIPMENT AND MYSELF.

I AM AN EXPERT AND I AM A PROFESSIONAL.

I STAND READY TO DEPLOY, ENGAGE, AND DESTROY, THE ENEMIES OF THE UNITED STATES OF AMERICA IN CLOSE COMBAT.

I AM A GUARDIAN OF FREEDOM AND THE AMERICAN WAY OF LIFE.

I AM AN AMERICAN SOLDIER.

Figure 3-1. The Soldier's Creed

I AM AN ARMY CIVILIAN – A MEMBER OF THE ARMY TEAM.

I AM DEDICATED TO THE ARMY, OUR SOLDIERS AND CIVILIANS.

I WILL ALWAYS SUPPORT THE MISSION.

I PROVIDE STABILITY AND CONTINUITY DURING WAR AND PEACE.

I SUPPORT AND DEFEND THE CONSTITUTION OF THE UNITED STATES AND CONSIDER IT AN HONOR TO SERVE OUR NATION AND ITS ARMY.

I LIVE THE ARMY VALUES OF LOYALTY, DUTY, RESPECT, SELFLESS SERVICE, HONOR, INTEGRITY, AND PERSONAL COURAGE.

I AM AN ARMY CIVILIAN.

Figure 3-2. The Army Civilian Corps Creed

3-22. The Warrior Ethos requires unrelenting and consistent determination to do what is right across the range of military operations. Understanding what is right requires respect for everyone involved in complex missions, such as stability or defense support of civil authorities operations. Ambiguous situations, such as when to use lethal or nonlethal force, are a test for the leader's judgment and discipline. The Warrior Ethos helps create a collective commitment to succeed with honor.

3-23. The Warrior Ethos is crucial but perishable. It connects American Soldiers of today with those whose sacrifices have sustained America's existence. Consequently, the Army must continually affirm, develop, and sustain it. The key to the Warrior Ethos is not only physical, tactical, and technical training but a mindset developed through purposeful mental preparation. Building key mental and emotional attributes such as confidence, composure, mental agility, and resilience are central behaviors of the Warrior Ethos.

DISCIPLINE

3-24. Discipline at the individual level is primarily self-discipline, the ability to control one's own behavior. Discipline expresses what the Army Values require—willingly doing what is right.

3-25. Discipline is a mindset for a unit or an organization to practice sustained, systematic actions to reach and sustain a capability to perform its military function. Often this involves attending to the details of organization and administration, which are less urgent than an organization's key tasks, but necessary for efficiency and long-term effectiveness. Examples include an effective Command Supply Discipline Program, Organizational Inspection Programs, and training management.

Table 3-1. Summary of the attributes associated with *Character*

Factors internal and central to a leader that constitute an individual's core.	
Army Values	• Values are principles, standards, or qualities considered essential for successful leaders. • Values are fundamental to help people discern right from wrong in any situation. • The Army has seven values to develop in all Army individuals: loyalty, duty, respect, selfless service, honor, integrity, and personal courage.
Empathy	• The propensity to experience something from another person's point of view. • The ability to identify with and enter into another person's feelings and emotions. • The desire to care for and take care of Soldiers and others.
Warrior Ethos/ Service Ethos	• The internal shared attitudes and beliefs that embody the spirit of the Army profession for Soldiers and Army Civilians alike.
Discipline	• Control of one's own behavior according to Army Values; mindset to obey and enforce good orderly practices in administrative, organizational, training, and operational duties.

CHARACTER DEVELOPMENT

3-26. Soldiers and Army Civilians are shaped by their background, beliefs, education, and experience. An Army leader's job would be simpler if merely checking the team member's personal values against the Army Values and developing a simple plan to align them sufficed. Reality is much different. Becoming a person and leader of character is a process involving day-to-day experience, education, self-development, developmental counseling, coaching, and mentoring. While individuals are responsible for their own character development, leaders are responsible for encouraging, supporting and assessing the efforts of their people. Leaders of character develop through continual study, reflection, experience, and feedback. Leaders hold themselves and subordinates to the highest standards.

3-27. Doing the right thing is good. Doing the right thing for the right reason and with the right goal is better. People of character must possess the desire to act ethically in all situations. One of the Army leader's primary responsibilities is to maintain an ethical climate that supports development of such character. When an organization's ethical climate nurtures ethical behavior, people will think, feel, and act ethically. They will internalize the aspects of sound character. Leaders who are excessively negative, do not value people's worth, and berate followers are not setting a good example.

3-28. Effective leadership begins with developing and maintaining a leader identity. Identity refers to one's self-concept. People possess many self-definitions, such as female, strong, smart, or Soldier. Leader identity refers to an individual's awareness of self as a leader. Leader identity forms because one—

- Self-identifies as a leader.
- Is perceived as a leader by others.
- Is a leader in relation to another person.
- Is collectively endorsed by the organization as a leader.

3-29. Character development affects an individual's leader identity. Leaders lacking self-awareness will have difficulty influencing others or attaining goals related to leader growth and development. Leaders lacking a clear sense of leader identity will not want to develop or improve their leadership skills. An incomplete or inaccurate sense of identity hinders the growth of leaders. The ability to lead and inspire others begins with an understanding of oneself, which ultimately determines a leader's character.

CHARACTER AND BELIEFS

3-30. Beliefs derive from upbringing, culture, religious backgrounds, and traditions. Therefore, diverse religious and philosophical traditions have, and will, continue to shape different moral beliefs. Army leaders serve a nation that protects the fundamental principle that people are free to choose their own beliefs. America's strength derives, and benefits, from that diversity. Effective leaders are careful not to require their people to violate their beliefs by ordering or encouraging unlawful or unethical actions.

3-31. Beliefs matter because they help people understand their experiences. Those experiences provide a start point for what to do in everyday situations. Beliefs are convictions people hold as true. Values are deep-seated personal beliefs that shape a person's behavior. Values and beliefs are central to character.

3-32. The Constitution reflects national principles, such as the guarantee of freedom of religion. The Army places a high value on the rights of its Soldiers and Army Civilians to observe their respective faiths while respecting individual differences in moral background and personal conviction. While religious beliefs and practices remain a decision of individual conscience, leaders are responsible for ensuring Soldiers and Army Civilians have the opportunity to practice their faith. Commanders, according to regulatory guidance, approve requests for accommodation of religious practices unless they have an adverse impact on unit readiness, individual readiness, unit cohesion, morale, discipline, safety, and/or health. However, no leader may apply undue influence, coerce, or harass subordinates with reference to matters of religion. Chaplains are personal staff officers with specialized training and responsibilities for ensuring the free exercise of religion and are available to advise and help leaders at every level.

CHARACTER AND ETHICS

3-33. Adhering to the principles the Army Values embody is essential to upholding high ethical standards of behavior. Unethical behavior quickly destroys organizational morale and cohesion—it undermines the trust and confidence essential to teamwork and mission accomplishment. Consistently doing the right thing forges strong character in individuals and expands to create a culture of trust throughout the organization.

3-34. Ethics indicate how a person should behave. Values represent the beliefs that a person has. The seven Army Values represent a set of common beliefs that leaders are expected to uphold and reinforce by their actions. The translation from desirable ethics to internal values to actual behavior involves choices.

3-35. Ethical conduct must reflect genuine values and beliefs. Soldiers and Army Civilians adhere to the Army Values because they want to live ethically and profess the values because they know what is right. Adopting good values and making ethical choices are essential to produce leaders of character. Leaders seen as abusive or toxic (such as intimidating and insulting subordinates) have higher rates of non-combatant mistreatment and misconduct in their units.

3-36. The Soldier's Rules codify the law of war and outline ethical and lawful conduct in operations (see AR 350-1). They distill the essence of the law of war, Army Values, and ethical behavior: Army leaders must consistently focus on shaping ethics-based organizational climates in which subordinates and organizations can achieve their full potential. Leaders who adhere to applicable laws, regulations, and unit standards build credibility with their subordinates and enhance trust with the American people they serve.

ETHICAL REASONING

3-37. To be an ethical leader requires more than knowing the Army Values. Leaders must be able to apply them to find moral solutions to diverse problems. Ethical reasoning must occur during the operations process. Leaders consider ethics in planning, preparing, executing, and assessing operations.

3-38. Ethical choices may be between right and wrong, shades of gray, or two rights. Some problems center on an issue requiring special consideration of what is most ethical. Leaders use multiple perspectives to think about ethical concerns, applying the following perspectives to determine the most ethical choice. One perspective comes from the view that desirable virtues such as courage, justice, and benevolence define ethical outcomes. A second perspective comes from the set of agreed-upon values or rules, such as the Army Values or Constitutional rights. A third perspective bases the consequences of the decision on whatever produces the greatest good for the greatest number as most favorable.

3-39. Army leaders are expected to do the right things for the right reasons. It is why followers count on their leaders to be more than just technically and tactically proficient. They rely on them to make ethical decisions. Determining what is right and ethical can be difficult.

3-40. Ethical concerns are not new for leaders. Leaders should not intentionally issue vague or ambiguous orders or instructions to avoid responsibility in the event a subordinate commits misconduct. Vague orders may foster a climate of indiscipline, permitting subordinates to act outside the framework of the Army Values in pursuit of mission accomplishment. Nothing is more dangerous from an ethical perspective and could do more harm to the reputation of the Army and its mission. Leaders have a responsibility to research relevant orders, rules, and regulations and to demand clarification of orders that could lead to criminal misinterpretation or abuse. Ultimately, Army leaders must accept responsibility for the consequences of their actions.

3-41. Ethical reasoning is complex in practice. If time allows in particularly ill-defined situations, using concepts from the Army Design Methodology (see ADRP 5-0) can help to frame the right problem and consider ethical implications in detail. Resolving ethical problems requires critical thinking based on the Army Values. No formula will work every time. By embracing the Army Values to govern personal actions, developing an understanding of regulations and orders, learning from experiences, and applying ethical reasoning, leaders will be better prepared to face tough decisions.

ETHICAL ORDERS

3-42. Making the right choice and acting on it when faced with an ethical question can be difficult. Sometimes it means standing firm and disagreeing with the boss on ethical grounds. These occasions test character. Situations in which a leader thinks an unlawful order is issued can be the most difficult.

3-43. Under normal circumstances, a leader executes a superior leader's decision with enthusiasm. Unlawful orders are the exception: a leader has a duty to question such orders and refuse to obey them if clarification of the order's intent fails to resolve his objections. If a Soldier perceives an order is unlawful, the Soldier should fully understand the details of the order and its original intent. The Soldier should seek immediate clarification from the person who gave it before proceeding.

3-44. If the question is more complex, seek legal counsel. If it requires an immediate decision, as may happen in the heat of combat, make the best judgment possible based on the Army Values, personal experience, critical thinking, previous study, and reflection. There is a risk when a leader disobeys what may be an unlawful order, and it may be the most difficult decision that Soldier ever makes. Nonetheless, it is what competent, confident, and ethical leaders should do.

3-45. While a leader may not be completely prepared for complex situations, spending time to reflect on the Army Values, studying, and honing personal leadership competencies will help. Talk to superiors, particularly those who have done the same. It is up to Army leaders to make values-based, ethical choices for the good of the Army and the nation. Army leaders should have the strength of character to make the right choices.

This page intentionally left blank.

Chapter 4
Presence

BASICS OF ARMY LEADER PRESENCE

4-1. The impression a leader makes on others contributes to his success in leading them. This impression is the sum of a leader's outward appearance, demeanor, actions, and words.

4-2. Leaders illustrate through their presence that they care. There is no greater inspiration than leaders who routinely share in team hardships and dangers. Being where subordinates perform duties allows the leader to have firsthand knowledge of the real conditions Soldiers and Army Civilians face. Presence is a critical attribute leaders need to understand. It is not just a matter of showing up; actions, words, and the manner in which leaders carry themselves convey presence. A leader's effectiveness is dramatically enhanced by understanding and developing the following areas—
- Military and professional bearing: projecting a commanding presence, a professional image of authority.
- Fitness: having sound health, strength, and endurance, which sustain emotional health and conceptual abilities under prolonged stress.
- Confidence: projecting self-confidence and certainty in the unit's ability to succeed in whatever it does; able to demonstrate composure and outward calm through steady control over emotion.
- Resilience: the psychological and physical capacity to bounce back from life's stressors repeatedly to thrive in an era of high operational tempo.

4-3. The Army recognizes a holistic emphasis on fitness prevents unnecessary harm whether from dangerous missions, routine operations, or a family outing. Holistic fitness recognizes that individual well-being depends on multiple areas including physical fitness, medical health, resilience, preparation for adverse environments, nutrition, psychological, spiritual (self identity, beliefs, and life purpose beyond self), behavioral (healthy practices related to substance abuse, eating, rest, and hygiene), and social (positive connection with others). Leaders follow policies and adopt practices to maintain total fitness. Leaders pay special attention to fitness when preparing for demanding deployments and for the restoration, sustainment, and enhancement of total health during redeployments.

MILITARY AND PROFESSIONAL BEARING

4-4. Army leaders are expected to look and act as professionals. Soldiers and Army Civilians displaying an unprofessional appearance do not send a message of professionalism. Skillful use of professional bearing—fitness, courtesy, and proper military appearance—can help overcome difficult situations. A professional appearance and competence command respect.

FITNESS

4-5. Unit readiness begins with physically fit Soldiers and leaders; operations drain physically, mentally, and emotionally. Physical fitness, while crucial for success in battle, is important for all members of the Army team, not just Soldiers. Physically fit people feel more competent and confident, handle stress better, work longer and harder, and recover faster. These attributes provide valuable payoffs in any environment.

4-6. The physical demands of leadership, deployments, and continuous operations can erode more than physical attributes. Physical fitness and adequate rest support cognitive functioning and emotional stability, both essential for sound leadership. If not physically fit before deployment, the effects of additional stress compromise mental and emotional fitness as well. Operations in difficult terrain, extreme climates, and high altitude require extensive physical conditioning; once in the area of operations there must be continued efforts to sustain physical readiness.

Chapter 4

4-7. Preparedness for operational missions must be a primary focus of the unit's physical fitness program. The forward-looking leader develops a balanced physical fitness program that enables Soldiers to execute the unit's mission-essential task list. The Army revised the Army Physical Readiness Training program to prepare Soldiers and units for the physical challenges of fulfilling decisive action missions facing a wide range of threats in complex operational environments and with emerging technologies.

4-8. Since leaders' decisions affect their organizations' effectiveness, health, and safety, it is an ethical and practical imperative for leaders to remain healthy and fit. Staying healthy and physically fit protects Soldiers from disease and strengthens them to cope with the psychological effects of extended operations. Leaders and Soldiers need exercise, sufficient sleep, nutritional food, and water to enable peak performance.

4-9. Health fitness maintains good health. It includes routine physical exams; practicing good dental hygiene, personal grooming, and cleanliness; keeping immunizations current; as well as considering psychological stresses. Healthy Soldiers perform better in extreme operational environments. Health fitness includes avoiding things that can degrade personal health, such as substance abuse, obesity, and tobacco use, as well as overuse of caffeine and other stimulants.

CONFIDENCE

4-10. Confidence is important for leaders and teams. Confidence is the faith leaders place in their abilities to act properly in any situation, even under stress or with little information. Self-confidence grows from professional competence. The confidence of an effective leader is contagious and permeates the entire organization. Confident leaders help Soldiers control doubt while reducing team anxiety. Excessive confidence can be as detrimental as too little confidence. Both extremes impede learning and adaptability.

RESILIENCE

4-11. Resilient leaders can recover quickly from setbacks, shock, injuries, adversity, and stress while maintaining their mission and organizational focus and they foster this capacity in followers. Resilient leaders learn and grow from those situations, incorporating changes into positive outcomes for mission accomplishment. Resilience helps leaders and their organizations to carry difficult missions to conclusion.

4-12. Resilience and the will to succeed help leaders during adversity. Competence and knowledge guide the energies of a strong will to pursue courses of action that lead to success. Leaders instill resilience and a winning spirit in subordinates though leading by example and with tough and realistic training.

4-13. Resilience is essential when pursuing mission accomplishment. Regardless of the working conditions, a strong personal attitude helps prevail over adverse external conditions. All Army members will experience situations when it would seem easier to accept defeat rather than finish the task. During those times, everyone needs an inner source of energy to press on to mission completion. When things go badly, a leader must draw on inner reserves to persevere.

Table 4-1. Summary of the attributes associated with *Presence*

How others perceive a leader based on the leader's outward appearance, demeanor, actions and words.	
Military and professional bearing	• Possessing a commanding presence. • Projecting a professional image of authority.
Fitness	• Having sound health, strength, and endurance that support one's emotional health and conceptual abilities under prolonged stress.
Confidence	• Projecting self-confidence and certainty in the unit's ability to succeed in its missions. • Demonstrating composure and outward calm through control over one's emotions.
Resilience	• Showing a tendency to recover quickly from setbacks, shock, injuries, adversity, and stress while maintaining a mission and organizational focus.

Chapter 5
Intellect

BASICS OF AN ARMY LEADER'S INTELLECT

5-1. An Army leader's intellect draws on the mental tendencies and resources that shape conceptual abilities applied to one's duties and responsibilities. Conceptual abilities enable effective problem solving and sound judgment before implementing concepts and plans. They help one think creatively and reason analytically, critically, ethically, and with cultural sensitivity to consider unintended as well as intended consequences. Leaders must anticipate the second- and third-order effects of their actions.

5-2. The conceptual components affecting an Army leader's intellect include—
- Mental agility.
- Sound judgment.
- Innovation.
- Interpersonal tact.
- Expertise.

MENTAL AGILITY

5-3. Mental agility is a flexibility of mind, an ability to anticipate or adapt to uncertain or changing situations. Agility enables thinking through second- and third-order effects when current decisions or actions are not producing the desired results. Mental agility provides organizations with operational adaptability to develop situational understanding to seize, retain, and exploit the initiative.

5-4. Mental agility relies upon inquisitiveness and the ability to reason critically. Inquisitive leaders are eager to understand a broad range of topics and keep an open mind to multiple possibilities before reaching an optimal solution. Critical thinking is a thought process that aims to find facts, to think through issues, and solve problems. Central to decisionmaking, critical thinking enables understanding of changing situations, arriving at justifiable conclusions, making good judgments, and learning from experience. Critical and creative thinking are the basis for the Army Design Methodology to understand, visualize, and describe complex, ill-structured problems and develop approaches to solve them. Critical thinking captures the reflection and continuous learning essential to applying Army Design Methodology concepts. Creative thinking involves thinking in innovative ways while capitalizing on imagination, insight, and novel ideas.

5-5. Critical thinking examines a problem in depth from multiple points of view. This is an important skill for Army leaders—it allows them to influence others and shape organizations. The first and most important step in finding an appropriate solution is to isolate the main problem. A leader's mental agility to quickly isolate a problem and identify solutions generates initiative to adapt during operations. Leaders must instill agility and initiative within subordinates by creating a climate that encourages participation and trust. Identifying and accepting honest mistakes in training makes subordinates more likely to develop initiative. These qualities are necessary in the generating force and the operational Army.

SOUND JUDGMENT

5-6. Judgment requires the capacity to assess situations shrewdly and to draw rational conclusions. Consistent good judgment enables leaders to form sound opinions and make reliable estimates and sensible decisions. Leaders acquire experience through trial and error and by observing others. Learning from others can occur through mentoring and coaching by superiors, peers, and even subordinates (see Part Three).

5-7. Often, leaders must juggle facts, questionable data, and intuitive feelings to arrive at a quality decision. Good judgment informs the best decision for the situation. It is a key attribute of transforming knowledge into understanding and quality execution.

5-8. Judgment contributes to an ability to determine possible courses of action and decide what action to take. Before choosing, leaders consider the consequences. Some sources that aid judgment are senior leaders' intents, desired outcomes, laws, regulations, experience, and values. Good judgment includes the ability to assess subordinates, peers, and the enemy for strengths and weaknesses to create appropriate solutions and action. Like mental agility, it is a critical part of problem solving and decisionmaking.

INNOVATION

5-9. Innovation describes the ability to introduce something new when needed or as opportunities exist. Innovative leaders tend to be inquisitive and good problem solvers. Being innovative includes creativity in producing original and worthwhile ideas. Leaders should seize such opportunities to think creatively and to innovate. A key concept for creative thinking is developing new ideas and approaches to accomplish missions. Creative thinking uses adaptive approaches (drawing from previous circumstances) or innovative approaches (developing completely new ideas).

5-10. Leaders think creatively to adapt to new environments. Innovative leaders prevent complacency by finding new ways to challenge subordinates with forward-looking approaches and ideas. To be innovators, leaders rely on intuition, experience, knowledge, and input from subordinates. Innovative leaders reinforce team building by making everybody responsible for, and stakeholders in, the innovation process.

INTERPERSONAL TACT

5-11. Effectively interacting with others depends on knowing what others perceive. It relies on accepting the character, reactions, and motives of oneself and others. Interpersonal tact combines these skills, along with recognizing diversity and displaying self-control, balance, and stability in situations.

RECOGNIZING DIVERSITY

5-12. Background, schooling, race, religion, and other factors shape Soldiers and Army Civilians. Personal perspectives vary within societal groups. By acknowledging differences, qualifications, contributions, and potential, Army leaders further strengthen the team effort by creating an environment where subordinates know they are valued for their talents, contributions, and differences. A leader's job is to employ the different capabilities and talents brought to the team to build the best possible team.

5-13. Army leaders should remain open to cultural diversity; it is unknown how the talents of individuals or groups will contribute to mission accomplishment. During World War II, Marines from the Navajo Nation formed a group of radio communications specialists called the Navajo Code Talkers. They handled command radio traffic in their native language—a unique talent. This significantly contributed to successful operations because the Japanese code breakers could not decipher their messages.

SELF-CONTROL

5-14. Effective leaders control their emotions. Leaders should display the right amount of sensitivity and passion to tap into subordinates' emotions, instead of hysterics or lack of emotion. Maintaining self-control inspires calm confidence in the team. Self-control encourages feedback from subordinates that can expand understanding of what is really happening. Self-control in combat is especially important for Army leaders. Leaders who lose their self-control cannot expect those who follow to maintain theirs.

EMOTIONAL FACTORS

5-15. An Army leader's self-control, balance, and stability greatly affect their ability to interact with others. People have hopes, fears, concerns, and dreams. Understanding that emotional energy sparks motivation and endurance is a powerful leadership tool. Giving constructive feedback helps mobilize the team's emotional energies to accomplish difficult missions.

Intellect

5-16. Self-control, balance, and stability enable making ethical choices. An ethical leader successfully applies ethical principles to decisionmaking. It is critical for leaders to remain calm under pressure and expend energy on things they can positively influence and not worry about things they cannot.

BALANCE

5-17. Emotionally balanced leaders are able to display the right emotion for a given situation and can read others' emotional state. They draw on experience to provide subordinates the proper perspective on unfolding events. They have a range of attitudes, from relaxed to intense, with which to approach diverse situations. They know how to choose what is appropriate for the circumstances. Balanced leaders know how to convey urgency without throwing the entire organization into chaos.

STABILITY

5-18. Effective leaders are steady, levelheaded when under pressure and fatigued, and calm in the face of danger. These characteristics stabilize subordinates who are always looking to their leader's example—
- Model the emotions for subordinates to display—calm and rational under pressure.
- Do not give in to the temptation to do what personally feels good.
- If under great stress, it might feel better to vent—but will that help the organization?

EXPERTISE

5-19. Expertise is the special knowledge and skill developed from experience, training, and education. Domain knowledge is what leaders know about application areas used in their duties and positions. Leaders create and use knowledge in at least four domains. Tactical knowledge relates to accomplishing a designated objective through military means. Technical knowledge consists of the specialized information associated with a particular function or system. Joint knowledge is an understanding of joint organizations, their procedures, and roles in national defense. Cultural and geopolitical knowledge is awareness of cultural, geographic, and political differences and sensitivities.

TACTICAL KNOWLEDGE

5-20. Army leaders know fundamentals, tactics, techniques, and procedures (TTP). Their tactical knowledge allows them to employ individuals, teams, and organizations effectively with the activities of systems (combat multipliers) to fight and win engagements and battles or to achieve other objectives. Competent readiness-focused leaders try to replicate actual operational conditions during training to develop tactical knowledge. Unfortunately, leaders cannot always take the entire unit to the field for full-scale maneuvers. They must achieve maximum readiness by training parts of a scenario or a unit on the ground, while exercising larger echelons with simulations.

5-21. Fieldcraft describes the skills Soldiers require for self-sustainment during operations. Understanding and excelling at fieldcraft sets conditions for mission success and reduces the likelihood of casualties. Likewise, Army leaders ensure their Soldiers take care of themselves and provide the means to do so. Leaders gain proficiency in fieldcraft through formal training, study, and practice. They must enforce tactical discipline and ensure Soldiers practice fieldcraft to prevent future casualties.

TECHNICAL KNOWLEDGE

5-22. Technical knowledge relates to equipment, weapons, and systems—from individual weapons to systems that give leaders technical means to execute decisive action. Closer to their equipment than organizational and strategic leaders, direct leaders have a greater need to know how it works and how to use it. Subordinates expect their first-line leaders to be experts in the applicable technical skills.

5-23. Leaders ensure their subordinates know how to operate the organizations' equipment. They often set an example with a hands-on approach. When new equipment arrives, direct leaders learn how to use it and train their subordinates to do the same. Once individuals are trained, teams, and, in turn, units train together. Army leaders know understanding equipment strengths and weaknesses is critical.

5-24. Leaders need to know what value the equipment has for their operations and how to employ the item. At higher levels, the technical knowledge requirement shifts from understanding how to operate single items to employing entire systems. Higher-level leaders have a responsibility to understand capabilities and the organizational impact. Some organizational and strategic level leaders have general oversight responsibility for new system development. Their interests lay in understanding how systems affect doctrine, organizational design, training, related materiel, personnel, and facilities. They must provide the necessary resources to properly field, train, maintain, operate, inventory, and turn-in equipment.

JOINT KNOWLEDGE

5-25. Leaders acquire joint knowledge through formal training in the Joint Professional Military Education program and assignments in joint organizations. Army leaders acknowledge all Services possess certain strengths and limitations. Only close cooperation of the Services can assure swift mission accomplishment in the complex operational environment.

CULTURAL AND GEOPOLITICAL KNOWLEDGE

5-26. Culture consists of shared beliefs, values, and assumptions about what is important. Army leaders are mindful of cultural factors in three contexts:

- Sensitive to the different backgrounds of team members to best use their talents.
- Aware of the culture of the country in which the organization is operating.
- Consider and evaluate the possible implications of partners' customs, traditions, doctrinal principles, and operational methods.

5-27. The operational environment requires cultural and geopolitical awareness. Leaders ensure the organization is properly prepared to deal with the population of particular areas—as partners, neutrals, or adversaries. These are important factors when Army leaders attempt to extend influence beyond the chain of command.

5-28. Success in decisive action requires understanding unified action partner cultures. Multiple organizational cultures exist within the DOD. Typically, the Army is solution-oriented, focused on accomplishing the mission efficiently. Other agencies may be process-oriented and unconcerned about the speed of mission accomplishment. Leaders must bridge the cultures to accomplish the mission.

5-29. Cultural understanding is crucial to the success of unified action operations. Leaders should learn the customs, traditions, operational procedures, and doctrine of their unified action partners. To operate successfully in a multinational setting, Army leaders must understand differences in doctrinal terminology and the interpretation of orders and instructions. They must learn how and why others think and act as they do. A multicultural environment requires leaders to keep plans and orders as simple as possible to prevent misunderstandings and needless losses. Dedicated liaison teams and linguists provide a cultural bridge between partners to mitigate some differences, but they cannot eliminate them.

Table 5-1. Summary of the attributes associated with *Intellect*

The mental resources or tendencies that shape a leader's conceptual abilities and effectiveness.		
Mental agility		• Flexibility of mind; the ability to break habitual thought patterns. • Anticipating or adapting to uncertain or changing situations; to think through outcomes when current decisions or actions are not producing desired effects. • The ability to apply multiple perspectives and approaches.
Sound judgment		• The capacity to assess situations shrewdly and draw sound conclusions. • The tendency to form sound opinions, make sensible decisions and reliable guesses. • The ability to assess strengths and weaknesses of subordinates, peers, and enemy to create appropriate solutions and action.
Innovation		• The ability to introduce new ideas based on opportunity or challenging circumstances. • Creativity in producing ideas and objects that are both novel and appropriate.
Interpersonal tact		• The capacity to understand interactions with others. • Being aware of how others see you and sensing how to interact with them effectively. • Conscious of character, reactions and motives of self and others and how they affect interactions. • Recognizing diversity and displaying self-control, balance, and stability.
Expertise		• Possessing facts, beliefs, logical assumptions and understanding in relevant areas.

This page intentionally left blank.

PART THREE

Competency-based Leadership for Direct through Strategic Levels

Leaders serve to provide purpose, direction, and motivation. Army leaders work to lead others; to develop themselves, their subordinates, and organizations; and to accomplish missions. The competencies take on different nuances and complexities as leaders move from direct leadership positions to the organizational and strategic leader levels.

Continuously refining values and attributes, as well as acquiring professional knowledge, is only part of becoming a competent leader. Leadership succeeds when the leader effectively acts and applies the core leader competencies.

Chapter 6

Leads

LEADS OTHERS

6-1. Army leaders apply character, presence, and intellect to the core leader competencies while guiding others toward a common goal and mission accomplishment. Direct leaders influence others person-to-person, such as a team leader who instructs, encourages hard work, and recognizes achievement. Organizational and strategic leaders guide their organizations using indirect means of influence. At the direct level, a platoon leader knows what a battalion commander wants done, because the lieutenant understands the commander's intent two levels up. The intent creates a critical link between the organizational and direct leadership levels. At every level, leaders take advantage of formal and informal processes to extend influence beyond the traditional chain of command.

6-2. All of the Army's core leader competencies, especially leading others, involve influence. The motivation behind influence should align to the mission of the organization and of those influenced. Positive and genuine intentions are more likely to produce successful outcomes. Army leaders can draw on a variety of methods to influence others and can use one or more methods to fit to the specifics of any situation. These outcomes range from obtaining compliance to building commitment to achieve. Compliance is the act of conforming to a requirement or demand. Commitment is willing dedication or allegiance to a cause or organization. Active opposition to influence denotes resistance.

USING COMPLIANCE AND COMMITMENT

6-3. Compliance is appropriate for short-term, immediate requirements and for situations with little risk tolerance. Compliance methods are appropriate for leaders to use with others who are relatively unfamiliar with the tasks or unwilling or unable to commit fully to the request. If a task has little time for delay, and there is not a great need for a subordinate to understand why the request occurs, then compliance is an acceptable approach. Compliance is not particularly effective when a leader's greatest aim is to create initiative and high esteem within the team.

6-4. Commitment generally produces longer lasting and broader effects. Whereas compliance only affects a follower's behavior, commitment reaches deeper—changing attitudes, beliefs, and behavior. For example, when a leader builds responsibility among followers, they will likely demonstrate more initiative, personal involvement, and creativity. Commitment grows from an individual's desire to gain a sense of control and develop self-worth by contributing to the organization. Depending on the influence objective, leaders can strengthen commitment by reinforcing followers' identification with the nation (loyalty), the Army (professionalism), the unit or organization (selfless service), the leadership in a unit (respect), and to the job (duty).

Methods of Influence

6-5. Influence is the essential element of leadership. Influence refers to how people create and relay their messages, behaviors, and attitudes to affect the intentions, beliefs, behaviors, and attitudes of another person or group of people. Influence depends upon relationships where leaders build positive rapport and a relationship of mutual trust, making followers more willing to support requests. Examples include showing personal interest in a follower's well-being, offering praise, and understanding a follower's perspective. Army leaders have choices in methods of influence based on audience, intent, and expected reaction.

6-6. *Pressure* is applied when leaders use explicit demands to achieve compliance, such as establishing task completion deadlines with negative consequences imposed for unmet completion. This method should be used infrequently since it tends to trigger resentment from followers, especially if the pressure becomes severe. When followers perceive that pressures are not mission-related but originate from their leader's attempt to please superiors for personal recognition, resentment can quickly undermine an organization's morale, cohesion, and quality of performance. Pressure is a good choice when the stakes are high, time is short, and previous attempts at achieving commitment have not been successful.

6-7. *Legitimating* occurs when leaders establish their authority as the basis for a request when it may not be obvious. In the military, certain jobs must be done regardless of circumstances when subordinate leaders receive legitimate orders from higher headquarters. Reference to one's position suggests to those being influenced that there is the potential for official action if the request is not completed.

6-8. *Exchange* is an influence method that leaders use when they make an offer to provide some desired item or action in trade for compliance with a request. Exchange requires that the leaders control certain resources or rewards valued by those being influenced. A four-day pass as reward for excelling during a maintenance inspection is an example of exchange.

6-9. *Personal appeals* occur when the leader asks the follower to comply with a request based on friendship or loyalty. This may be useful in a difficult situation when mutual trust is the key to success. The leader appeals to the follower by highlighting special talents and professional trust for encouragement before taking on a tough mission. An S3 might ask a staff officer to brief at an important commander's conference if the S3 knows the staff officer will do the best job conveying information.

6-10. *Collaboration* occurs when the leader cooperates in providing assistance or resources to carry out a directive or request. The leader makes the choice more attractive by being prepared to step in and resolve problems. A major planning effort before a deployment for humanitarian assistance would require possible collaboration with unified action partners.

6-11. *Rational persuasion* requires the leader to provide evidence, logical arguments, or explanations showing how a request is relevant to the goal. This is often the first approach to gaining compliance or commitment from followers and is likely to be effective if the leader is recognized as an expert in the specialty area in which the influence occurs. Leaders often draw from their own experience to give reasons why some task can be accomplished because the leader has tried it and done it.

6-12. *Apprising* happens when the leader explains why a request will benefit a follower, such as giving greater satisfaction in their work or performing a task a certain way that will save time. In contrast to exchange, the benefits are out of the control of the leader. A commander may use the apprising method to inform a newly assigned NCO that serving in a staff position, before serving as a platoon sergeant, could provide invaluable experience. The commander points out that the additional knowledge may help the NCO achieve higher performance and possibly lead to an accelerated promotion.

6-13. *Inspirational appeals* occur when the leader fires up enthusiasm for a request by arousing strong emotions to build conviction. A leader may stress to a fellow leader that without help, the safety of the team may be at risk. By appropriately stressing the results of stronger commitment, a unit leader can inspire followers to surpass minimal standards and reach elite performance status.

6-14. *Participation* occurs when the leader asks others to take part in his processes to address a problem or meet an objective. Active participation leads to an increased sense of worth and recognition. It provides value to the effort and builds commitment to execute. By involving key leaders at all levels during planning, senior leaders ensure that their followers take stock in the vision. These subordinates will later be able to pursue critical intermediate and long-term objectives, even after senior leaders have moved on.

Application of Influence

6-15. To succeed and create true commitment, subordinates should perceive influencing methods as authentic and sincere. Positive influence comes from leaders who do what is right for the Army, the mission, the team, and each individual Soldier. Negative influence—real and perceived—emanates from leaders who primarily focus on personal gain and lack self-awareness. Even honorable intentions, if wrongly perceived by followers as self-serving, will yield mere compliance. False perception may trigger unintended side effects such as resentment of the leader and the deterioration of unit cohesion.

6-16. The nature of the mission determines which influence method or combination of methods is appropriate. When a situation is urgent and greater risk is involved, eliciting follower compliance may be desirable. Direct-level leaders often use compliance to coordinate team activities in an expedient manner. In comparison, organizational leaders typically use indirect influence to build strong commitment.

6-17. When influencing their followers, Army leaders should consider—
- The objectives for the use of influence should be in line with the Army Values, ethics, the Uniform Code of Military Justice, the Soldier's Creed, and the Civilian Creed.
- Compliance-seeking influence focuses on meeting and accounting for task demands.
- Commitment-encouraging influence emphasizes empowerment and long-lasting trust.

Resistance

6-18. Diagnosis of the nature of the relationship and cause of opposition is a leader's first response to resistance. Leaders should consider the nature of the relationship and degree of good will. If a negative rapport exists, resistance may show a lack of trust and need additional effort to establish a positive relationship. If a positive relationship exists, then resistance may reflect different interests or perceived pressure on well-being or autonomy. Resistance may stem from perceived threats associated with possible reduction in personal freedoms. This reaction occurs in instances when heavy pressure is applied and it can strengthen resistance to influence and more generally to any requests from the same source.

6-19. Leaders need to ensure all parties focus on a common understanding. Overt acknowledgement of resistance can help reduce it. Leaders increase receptivity to messages and build support for achieving goals by interrupting the other party's focus on resistance. Refocusing on intended positive outcomes may sway negative mindsets and consume some of the energy fueling resistance.

6-20. Leaders may need to clarify misperceptions or correct false beliefs stemming from claims of illegitimate sources or outright adversaries. Increasing the amount and quality of evidence can improve the effect of rational persuasion. Broadening the extent of personal appeal or better informing the followers of benefits is another way of refining the methods of influence. Leaders can lessen resistance by indicating concerns with their own position or requests. This demonstrates that the leaders recognize both the positives and negatives of a given request and that they are approaching the issue even-handedly and fairly.

6-21. Repeated, consistent requests can signal that the leaders are intent on reaching agreement on the requests. For instance, if an Army leader wants the local police to participate in patrols, they may be asked a dozen times on different occasions to participate. Eventually the number and detail of the requests may wear down resistance. However, this may have the opposite effect of entrenching the original negative position, signaling the need for a different method. Perhaps embedding the desired outcome into a narrative illustrates the ease of accommodating the request and the benefits to all parties. Regardless of approach taken, leaders should not risk their integrity nor wander from their mission to be perceived as influential.

PROVIDING PURPOSE AND MOTIVATION

6-22. Leaders influence others to achieve some purpose. To be successful at exerting influence, Army leaders have an end or goal in mind. Sometimes the goal will be very specific, while many are less distinct and unmeasurable, but are still valid and meaningful.

6-23. Leaders in command positions use commander's intent to convey purpose. Commander's intent is a concise expression of the purpose of the operation and the desired end state. Leaders communicate purpose with implied or explicit instructions so others may exercise initiative while maintaining focus. This is important for situations when unanticipated opportunities arise or the original solution no longer applies.

6-24. In addition to purpose, leaders provide direction. Direction deals with how to achieve a goal, task, or mission. Subordinates do not always need to receive guidance on the details of execution. The skilled leader will know when to provide detailed guidance and when to focus only on purpose.

6-25. Mission command conveys purpose without providing detailed direction. It provides the greatest possible freedom of action to subordinates, facilitating their abilities to develop the situation, adapt, and act decisively in dynamic conditions within the commander's intent. It focuses on empowering subordinate leaders and sharing necessary information. For effective mission command, leaders must engage senior leaders, subordinate leaders, and their staffs in collaboration and dialogue that leads to enhanced situational understanding and decisionmaking.

6-26. Motivation is the reason for doing something or the level of enthusiasm for doing it. Army leaders use the knowledge of what motivates others to influence those they lead. Understanding how motivation works provides insight into why people may take action and how strongly they are driven to act.

6-27. It is important for the leader to define 'what' and 'why' clearly. Subordinates should be able to start the process with the end in mind by knowing what success looks like and how they can track progress. Motivation increases when subordinates understand how their role relates to larger and more important outcomes. This is important because such links are not always obvious to subordinates.

6-28. Goal setting is a way of shaping motivation. The key is to set achievable goals. Larger goals can be broken into smaller goals to keep individuals engaged. To work, the individual must have the necessary skills and abilities to perform the task, have some reason to be committed to the goal, and receive feedback to gauge progress. Task assignment and goal setting account for the characteristics and limitations of those performing the task. Finally, framing performance goals positively produces better persistence and performance than negative framing.

6-29. Leaders can encourage subordinates to set goals on their own and to set goals together. When goals are accepted, they focus attention and action, increase the effort and persistence expended even in the face of failure, and develop strategies to help in goal accomplishment.

6-30. Positive reinforcement such as tangible incentives (such as monetary rewards or time off) as well as intangible rewards (such as praise or recognition) can enhance motivation. Leaders can use healthy competition to renew intensity, such as recognition for the most improved score, the top five finishes, or those working together best. Punishment can be used when there is an immediate need to discontinue dangerous or otherwise undesirable behavior. It can send a clear message about behavioral expectations and the consequences of violating those expectations. One caution is that punishment should be used sparingly and only in extreme cases because it can lead to resentment.

6-31. People often want the opportunity to be responsible for their own work and to be creative—they want to be empowered. Leaders empower subordinates by training them to do a job and providing them with necessary task strategies; give them the necessary resources, authority, and clear intent; and then step aside to let them accomplish the mission. Empowering subordinates is a forceful statement of trust and one of the best ways of developing leaders. Empowerment implies accepting the responsibility for the freedom to act and create.

Building and Sustaining Morale

6-32. Military historians describing great armies often focus on weapons and equipment, training, and the national cause. They may mention numbers or other factors to analyze, measure, and compare. Many historians place great emphasis on one critical factor that cannot be easily measured: morale.

6-33. Morale is the Army's most important intangible human element. It is a measure of how people feel about themselves, their team, and their leaders. Units achieve high morale through effective leadership, shared effort, trust, and mutual respect. High morale results in a cohesive team striving to achieve common goals. Competent leaders know that morale holds the team together and sustains it during operations.

6-34. Leaders can boost morale in the face of extreme danger by providing their Soldiers the means and support for successful operations. Units with high morale are usually more effective in operations and respond to hardships and losses better. Not surprisingly, these units often conduct reunions and maintain close friendships for decades after they have served together.

RESOLVING CONFLICTS

6-35. Conflict is the process in which one individual or group perceives that another individual or group negatively affects their interests. Conflict does not require the involvement of two people, nor is it necessarily founded in reality based on actual circumstances. One person may be in conflict with another, without the second person even realizing it or being at fault. As a leader, it is important to identify and resolve conflict before it affects personal and organizational functioning and effectiveness.

6-36. Conflicts can be categorized as work-based such as clarifying roles, competing for resources, or generating different solutions to the same problem, or individual-based such as personality differences, annoyances, and tension. Work-based conflicts can be beneficial to organizations resulting in improved decisionmaking, elimination of redundancies, and increased commitment; however, individual-based conflicts can result in lower morale and effectiveness of the individuals as well as the organization.

ENFORCING STANDARDS

6-37. To lead others and gauge task completion correctly, the Army has established standards. Standards are formal, detailed instructions—describable, measurable, and achievable. They provide a mark for performance to assess execution of a task. To use standards effectively, leaders know, communicate, and enforce high but realistic standards. Effective leaders explain the standards that apply to their organizations and empower subordinates to enforce them.

6-38. When enforcing standards for unit activities, leaders must remain aware that not everything can be a number one priority. Striving for excellence in every area, regardless of how trivial, could be overwhelming. Leaders must prioritize tasks ensuring all tasks meet established standards. True professionals ensure the standard fits the task's importance.

6-39. A leader's ultimate goal is to train to the standards that ensure mission success. Leaders set intermediate goals to prepare the organization to meet the standards. To be successful, leaders use the Army training management model. Leaders use the training management process to set appropriate training goals and to plan, resource, execute, and evaluate training accordingly.

Performing Checks and Inspections

6-40. Thorough inspections ensure Soldiers, units, and systems are fully capable and ready to execute the mission. Focused checking minimizes the chance of neglect or mistakes that may derail a mission or cause needless casualties. It gives leaders a chance to recognize subordinates or make on-the-spot corrections as necessary. Training subordinates for independent action is vital. To foster independence and initiative, direct leaders give instructions and clear mission intent with mission orders. They allow subordinates to complete missions without constantly looking over their shoulders.

Instilling Discipline

6-41. Leaders who consistently enforce standards simultaneously instill discipline that will pay-off in critical situations. True discipline demands habitual and reasoned obedience. An effective leader instills discipline by training to standard, using rewards and punishment judiciously, instilling confidence, building trust among team members, and ensuring they have the necessary technical and tactical expertise. Confidence, trust, and team effort are crucial for success in operational settings.

BALANCING MISSION AND WELFARE

6-42. Considering the needs of subordinates is a function of all Army leaders. Having genuine concern for follower well-being accompanies motivation, inspiration, and influence. Soldiers and Army Civilians will be more willing to go the extra mile for leaders whom they respect. Sending Soldiers or Army Civilians in harm's way to accomplish the mission seems to contradict the emphasis on taking care of people. How can a leader truly care for comrades and send them on missions that might get them killed?

Taking Care of Soldiers and Army Civilians

6-43. Taking care of Soldiers demands individuals perform their duties even at risk to their lives. Preparing for the realities of combat is a direct leader's most important duty. It entails creating a disciplined environment for learning and growth and enforcing high standards in training. Training must be rigorous and simulate operational environments as much as possible while keeping safety in mind. Leaders use risk management to balance risk cost with mission benefits. Unit leaders must recognize the need to provide reasonable comforts to bolster morale and maintain long-term combat effectiveness.

6-44. Many leaders connect at a personal level with their followers to anticipate and understand individual circumstances and needs. As discussed previously, building relationships is a way to encourage commitment from followers. Knowing others is the basis many successful leaders use to treat personnel well. It ranges from ensuring a subordinate has time for an annual dental exam to finding out about a person's preferred hobbies and pastimes. Leaders should provide an adequate family support and readiness network that helps Families, whether they are working at home station or deployed.

Identifying High Risk Behavior

6-45. Leaders identify subordinates who exhibit high-risk behavior. High-risk behavior is a behavioral pattern that intentionally or unintentionally increases the individual's probability of negative consequences. Examples of high-risk behavior include driving under the influence, failing to wear proper protective equipment, criminal activity, illegal use of drugs, and other dangerous activities. Data suggests there is a link between these behaviors and suicides as well as accidental deaths. Studies suggest there is a direct link to increased life stressors and increased risk behavior. High-risk behaviors can ruin careers.

6-46. The Army regulates good order and discipline through enforcement of statutes (e.g., the Uniform Code of Military Justice) and policy. Misconduct represents a conscious decision to accept both the risk associated with a prohibited activity (such as riding a motorcycle without a helmet) and the risk of being caught while violating the standard (the Army's helmet policy). Leaders identify Soldiers as high-risk when they violate standards.

6-47. A commander's primary responsibility for unit sustainment is to ensure the readiness, health, morale, welfare, and discipline of the unit. Every leader has a role in supporting that responsibility. Leaders must identify at-risk Soldiers, mitigate their stress, and intervene to help them.

Table 6-1. Summary of the competency *Leads others*

Leaders motivate, inspire, and influence others to take initiative, work toward a common purpose, accomplish critical tasks, and achieve organizational objectives. Influence focuses on compelling others to go beyond their individual interests and to work for the common good.	
Uses appropriate methods of influence to energize others	Uses methods ranging from compliance to commitment (pressure, legitimate requests, exchange, personal appeals, collaboration, rational persuasion, apprising, inspiration, participation, and relationship building).
Provides purpose, motivation and inspiration	<ul><li>Inspires, encourages, and guides others toward mission accomplishment.</li><li>Emphasizes the importance of organizational goals.</li><li>Determines the course of action necessary to reach objectives and fulfill mission requirements.</li><li>Communicates instructions, orders, and directives to subordinates.</li><li>Ensures subordinates understand and accept direction.</li><li>Empowers and delegates authority to subordinates.</li><li>Focuses on the most important aspects of a situation.</li></ul>
Enforces standards	<ul><li>Reinforces the importance and role of standards.</li><li>Performs individual and collective tasks to standard.</li><li>Recognizes and takes responsibility for poor performance and addresses it appropriately.</li></ul>
Balances mission and welfare of followers	<ul><li>Assesses and routinely monitors effects of mission fulfillment on mental, physical, and emotional attributes of subordinates.</li><li>Monitors morale, physical condition, and safety of subordinates.</li><li>Provides appropriate relief when conditions jeopardize success of the mission or present overwhelming risk to personnel.</li></ul>

BUILDS TRUST

6-48. Trust enables influence and mission command. When high levels of trust exist, people are more willing and naturally accepting of influence and influence is more likely to occur in multiple directions.

6-49. Trust encompasses reliance upon others, confidence in their abilities, and consistency in behavior. Trust builds over time through mutual respect, shared understanding, and common experiences. Communication contributes to trust by keeping others informed, establishing expectations, and developing commitments. Sustaining trust depends on meeting those expectations and commitments. Leaders and subordinates earn or lose trust through everyday actions and attitudes.

6-50. It is important for leaders to promote a culture and climate of trust. To establish trust, leaders create a positive command climate that fosters trust by identifying areas of common interest and goals. Teams develop trust through cooperation, identification with other members, and contribution to the team effort. Leaders build trust with their followers and those outside the organization by adhering to the leadership competencies and demonstrating good character, presence, and intellect. Leaders need to be competent and have good character to be trusted.

6-51. Leaders who coach, counsel, and mentor subordinates establish close relationships that foster trust. These relationships built on trust enable leaders to empower subordinates, encourage initiative, reinforce accountability, and allow for open communication. Further, these relationships establish predictability and cohesion within the team.

6-52. Failure to cultivate a climate of trust or a willingness to tolerate discrimination or harassment on any basis erodes unit cohesion and breaks the trust subordinates have for their leaders. Unethical behavior, favoritism, personal biases, and poor communication skills erode trust. Broken trust often creates suspicion, doubt, and distrust. Restoring broken trust is not a simple process – it requires situational awareness and significant effort on the part of all parties affected.

Table 6-2. Summary of the competency *Builds trust*

\	\
Leaders build trust to mediate relationships and encourage commitment among followers. Trust starts from respect among people and grows from common experiences and shared understanding.	
Sets personal example for trust	• Is firm, fair, and respectful to gain trust. • Assesses degree of own trustworthiness.
Takes direct actions to build trust	• Fosters positive relationship with others. • Identifies areas of commonality (understanding, goals, and experiences). • Engages other members in activities and objectives. • Corrects team members who undermine trust with their attitudes or actions.
Sustains a climate of trust	• Assesses factors or conditions that promote or hinder trust. • Keeps people informed of goals, actions, and results. • Follows through on actions related to expectations of others.

EXTENDS INFLUENCE BEYOND THE CHAIN OF COMMAND

6-53. While Army leaders traditionally exert influence within their unit and its established chain of command, multiskilled leaders must be capable of extending influence to others beyond the chain of command. Extending influence beyond the chain of command is the second leader competency. In today's politically- and culturally-charged operational environments, even direct leaders may work closely with unified action partners, the media, local civilians, political leaders, police forces, and nongovernmental agencies. Extending influence requires special awareness about the differences in how influence works.

6-54. When extending influence beyond the traditional chain of command, leaders often have to influence without authority designated or implied by rank or position. Civilian and military leaders often find themselves in situations where they must build informal teams to accomplish organizational tasks. Leaders must engage and communicate via multiple means (face-to-face, print media, broadcast media, social media, and other emerging collaboration technologies) to influence the perceptions, attitudes, sentiments, and behaviors of key actors and agencies. Leaders establish themes and messages and may personally engage key players to ensure the themes and messages are transmitted and received as intended.

6-55. The key element of extending influence and building teams is the creation of a common vision among prospective team members. A unique aspect of extending influence is that those who are targets of influence outside the chain may not even recognize or willingly accept the authority of an Army leader. Often informal teams develop in situations where there are no official chains of authority. In some cases, it may require leaders to establish their credentials and capability for leading others. At other times, leaders may need to interact as a persuasive force but not from an obvious position and attitude of power.

6-56. Leading without authority requires adaptation to the environment and cultural sensitivities of the given situation. Leaders require cultural knowledge to understand different social customs and belief systems and to address issues in those contexts. When conducting operations, for example, even small-unit leaders must understand that their interaction with the local populace and their leaders can have dramatic impacts on the overall theater strategy. The manner in which a unit conducts house-to-house searches for insurgents can influence the local population's acceptance of authority or become a recruiting incentive for the insurgency.

BUILDING TRUST OUTSIDE LINES OF AUTHORITY

6-57. Forming effective, cohesive teams is often the first challenge of a leader working outside a traditional command structure. These teams usually form from disparate groups unfamiliar with military customs and culture. Successful teams develop an infectious winner's attitude. Problems are challenges rather than obstacles. Cohesive teams accomplish missions more efficiently than a loose group of individuals. While developing seamless teams is ideal, sometimes it will not be practical to bring disparate groups together.

6-58. Building alliances is similar to building teams, the difference being that groups maintain greater independence in alliances. Trust is a common ingredient in effective alliances. Alliances evolve by establishing contact with others, growing friendships, and identifying common interests.

6-59. Whether operating in focused teams or loose alliances, training and working together builds collective competence and mutual trust. A mutual trust relationship ultimately permeates the entire organization, embracing every member, regardless of gender, race, social origin, religion, or duty status.

6-60. The requirements for building trust and cohesion are valid for relationships extending beyond the organization and the chain of command. They apply when working with task-organized organizations, unified action partners, and noncombatants. If a special operations team promises critical air support and medical supplies to indigenous multinational forces for an upcoming operation, the personal reputation of the leader and trust in the United States as a respected, supportive nation, can be at stake.

UNDERSTANDING SPHERE, MEANS, AND LIMITS OF INFLUENCE

6-61. When operating within an established command structure and common procedures, the provisions and limits of roles and responsibilities are readily apparent. When leading outside an established organization, assessing the parties involved becomes another part of the operation. Identifying who is who, what role they have, over whom they have authority or influence, and how they are likely to respond to the Army leader's influence are important considerations. Sometimes this is viewed as understanding the limits to the Army's or the leader's influence.

6-62. Spanning the boundaries of disparate groups or organizations requires special attention. The key to extending influence outside the chain of command is learning about those organizations. By understanding their interests and desires, the leader will know what methods of influence are most likely to work.

6-63. Effective operations require commanders to establish information themes and integrate them with actions to achieve a desired end state. Information, as an element of combat power, is a critical and sometimes decisive factor in operations. Effectively employed, it shapes the operational environment and multiplies the effects of friendly successes while countering adversary or enemy information efforts.

NEGOTIATING, BUILDING CONSENSUS AND RESOLVING CONFLICTS

6-64. Leaders must often resolve conflicts between Army interests and local populations or others. One method is negotiation. Negotiation is a problem-solving process in which two or more parties discuss and seek to satisfy their interests on various issues through joint decisions. The desired end-state of the negotiation process is the creation of a good choice between a clear, realistic, and satisfactory commitment and a reasonable alternative to a negotiated agreement that better meets the leader's interests. Interests relate to each party's needs, fears, concerns, goals, and motivations. Parties' interests may be shared, different, or in conflict. Effective leaders negotiate around interests rather than positions that tend to be static and unyielding. Negotiation situations often involve multiple issues such as lives, security, resources, and alliances. They occur over time, often in cross-cultural settings with multiple parties, and can be extremely complex. Successful agreements frequently depend on positive relationships. While many approaches to negotiation exist, an appropriate strategy for the current operational environment is principled negotiation. The leader skilled in principled negotiation forms working relationships with the other parties while ensuring sound substantive outcomes that do not require either compromise or force to achieve organizational goals.

6-65. Successful negotiations involve several components. Leaders should—
- Understand and be willing to challenge assumptions about all parties involved, the desired outcome, the situation, and the negotiation itself.
- Consider the measures of success for negotiation and choose the right one for the right situation.
- Prepare thoroughly in a manner that supports the desired outcome and process for negotiation.
- Build effective working relationships based on genuine rapport, respect, and reputation. Separate relationship issues from substantive issues and address both on their own merits.

- Utilize meaningful communication among involved parties to inquire, acknowledge, and advocate while demonstrating active listening and understanding while shaping perceptions and emotions of all parties.
- Generate many options or creative solutions that meet the interests of all parties as well as possible. Creating options should be separate from evaluating and deciding.
- Use objective, balanced, and fair criteria, standards, and merit to evaluate options. Apply a test of reciprocity: would one party find this aspect fair if they proposed it?
- Determine alternatives to a negotiated agreement. Alternatives are ways that each party can meet their interests without creating an agreement in the current negotiation. What is each party's best alternative to a negotiated agreement?
- Commit to an agreement only if it is better than alternatives, is the best of many options, and meets interests based on fair criteria. A commitment should be clearly defined, well planned, and reasonable for implementing. Leaders must not promise what they cannot or will not deliver just to get an agreement.
- Review each negotiation systematically and use lessons to learn from one interaction to the next.

Table 6-3. Summary of the competency *Extends influence beyond the chain of command*

Leaders need to influence beyond their direct lines of authority and beyond chains of command to include unified action partners. In these situations, leaders use indirect means of influence: diplomacy, negotiation, mediation, arbitration, partnering, conflict resolution, consensus building, and coordination.	
Understands sphere, means and limits of influence	• Assesses situations, missions, and assignments to determine the parties involved in decisionmaking, decision support, and possible interference or resistance.
Negotiates, builds consensus and resolves conflict	• Builds effective working relationships. • Uses two-way, meaningful communication. • Identifies individual and group interests. • Identifies roles and resources. • Generates and facilitates generation of possible solutions. • Applies fair standards to assess options. • Creates good choices between firm, clear commitment and alternatives to a negotiated agreement.

LEADS BY EXAMPLE

DISPLAYING CHARACTER

6-66. Leaders operate on instinct that has evolved from what they have seen. What leaders see others do sets the stage for what they may do. Modeling these attributes of character defines the leaders to the people with whom they interact. A leader of sound character will exhibit that character at all times.

6-67. Living by the Army Values and the Warrior Ethos best displays character and leading by example. It means putting the organization and subordinates above personal self-interest, career, and comfort. For the Army leader, it requires putting the lives of others above a personal desire for self-preservation.

Leading with Confidence in Adverse Conditions

6-68. A leader who projects confidence is an inspiration to followers. Subordinates will follow leaders who are comfortable with their own abilities and will question the leader who shows doubt.

6-69. Displaying confidence and composure when things are not going well can be a challenge for anyone, but is important for the leader to lead others through a grave situation. Confidence is a key component of leader presence. A leader who shows hesitation in the face of setbacks can trigger a chain reaction among others. A leader who is over-confident in difficult situations may lack the proper degree of care or concern.

6-70. Leading with confidence requires a heightened self-awareness and ability to master emotions. Developing the ability to remain confident no matter what the situation involves—
- Having prior opportunities to experience reactions to severe situations.
- Maintaining a positive outlook when a situation becomes confusing or changes.
- Remaining decisive after discovering mistakes.
- Encouraging others when they show signs of weakness.

Displaying Courage

6-71. Projecting confidence in combat and other situations requires physical and moral courage. While physical courage allows Soldiers to defend their ground, moral courage empowers leaders to stand firm on values, principles, and convictions. Leaders who take responsibility for their decisions and actions display moral courage. Morally courageous leaders critically look inside themselves, consider new ideas, and change what caused failure.

6-72. Moral courage in daily operations is as important as physical courage in combat. Consider a Civilian test board director who has the responsibility to determine whether a new piece of military equipment performs to the established specifications. Knowing that a failed test may cause the possibility of personal pressure and command resistance from the program management office, a morally courageous tester will be prepared to endure that pressure and remain objective and fair in test procedures and conclusions. Moral courage is fundamental to living the Army Values of integrity and honor, whether civilian or military.

DEMONSTRATING COMPETENCE

6-73. It does not take long for followers to become suspicious of a leader who acts confident but does not have the competence to back it up. Having the appropriate levels of expertise is vital to prepare competent leaders who display confidence through their attitudes, actions, and words.

6-74. Leading by example demands that leaders stay aware of how subordinates execute their guidance and plans. Direct and organizational leaders cannot remain in safe headquarters designing complex plans without examining what their subordinates are experiencing. They must go to where the action is, whether the battlefield or shop floor. Effective leaders connect with their followers by sharing hardships and communicating openly to clearly see and feel what goes on from a subordinate's perspective.

6-75. Leaders at all levels must remember that graphics on a map symbolize Soldiers. To verify that a plan can succeed, true leaders lead from the front and share the experiences of their subordinates. Seeing the plan transform into action empowers the leader to better assess the situation and influence the execution by their immediate presence. Leaders who stay a safe distance from risk destroy their subordinates' trust and confidence. Military and civilian leaders must ask: would I readily do what I am asking them to do?

Table 6-4. Summary of the competency *Leads by example*

Leaders serve as role models. They maintain standards and provide effective examples through their actions. All Army leaders should model the Army Values. Modeling provides tangible evidence of desired behaviors and reinforces verbal guidance through demonstration of commitment and action.	
Displays character	<ul><li>Sets the example by displaying high standards of duty performance, personal appearance, military and professional bearing, physical fitness and ethics.</li><li>Fosters an ethical climate; shows good moral judgment and behavior.</li><li>Completes individual and unit tasks to standard, on time, and within the commander's intent.</li><li>Demonstrates determination, persistence, and patience.</li><li>Uses sound judgment and logical reasoning.</li></ul>
Exemplifies the Warrior Ethos	<ul><li>Removes or fights through obstacles, difficulties, and hardships to accomplish the mission.</li><li>Demonstrates the will to succeed.</li><li>Demonstrates physical and emotional courage.</li><li>Shares hardships with subordinates.</li></ul>
Leads with confidence in adverse situations	<ul><li>Provides leader presence at the right time and place.</li><li>Displays self-control, composure, and positive attitude.</li><li>Is resilient.</li><li>Remains decisive after discovering a mistake.</li><li>Acts in the absence of guidance.</li><li>Does not show discouragement when facing setbacks.</li><li>Remains positive when the situation becomes confusing or changes.</li><li>Encourages subordinates when they show signs of weakness.</li></ul>
Demonstrates technical and tactical competence	<ul><li>Meets mission standards, protects resources, and accomplishes the mission with available resources using technical and tactical skills.</li><li>Displays appropriate knowledge of equipment, procedures and methods; recognizes and generates innovative solutions.</li><li>Uses knowledgeable sources and subject matter experts.</li></ul>
Understands the importance of conceptual skills and models them to others	<ul><li>Displays comfort working in open systems.</li><li>Makes logical assumptions in the absence of facts.</li><li>Identifies critical issues to use as a guide in making decisions and taking advantage of opportunities.</li><li>Relates and compares information from different sources to identify possible cause-and-effect relationships.</li></ul>
Seeks diverse ideas and points of view	<ul><li>Encourages honest communications among staff and decisionmakers.</li><li>Explores alternative explanations and approaches for accompanying tasks.</li><li>Reinforces new ideas; demonstrates willingness to consider alternative perspectives to resolve difficult problems.</li><li>Discourages individuals from seeking favor through tacit agreement.</li></ul>

COMMUNICATES

6-76. Competent leadership depends on good communication. Although viewed as a process of providing information, communication as a competency ensures there is more than the simple transmission of information. It achieves a new understanding, creates new or better awareness. Communicating critical information clearly is an important skill to reach shared understanding of issues and solutions. It conveys thoughts, presents recommendations, bridges cultural sensitivities, and reaches consensus. Leaders cannot lead, supervise, build teams, counsel, coach, or mentor without the ability to communicate clearly.

LISTENING ACTIVELY

6-77. An important form of two-way communication to reach shared understanding is active listening. Although the most important purpose of listening is to comprehend the sender's message, listeners should provide an occasional indication to the speaker that they are attentive. Active listening involves avoiding interruption and keeping mental or written notes of important points or items for clarification. Good listeners will understand the message content and the urgency and emotion through how it is spoken.

6-78. It is critical to remain aware of barriers to listening that prevent hearing and absorbing what speakers say. Avoid formulating a response before hearing what the other person says. Do not allow distraction by anger, disagreement with the speaker, or other things to impede.

CREATE SHARED UNDERSTANDING

6-79. Competent leaders know themselves, the mission, and the message. They owe it to their organization and their subordinates to share information that directly applies to their duties. They should provide information that provides context and purpose. Additionally, sharing of information may prepare subordinates for future duties and greater responsibility.

6-80. Leaders keep their organizations informed because it builds trust. Shared information helps relieve stress and control rumors. Timely information exchange allows team members to determine requirements and adjust to changing circumstances. Informing subordinates of a decision and the supporting reasons shows appreciation and conveys the need for their support and input. Good information flow ensures the next leader in the chain is sufficiently prepared to take over, if required. Subordinates must clearly understand the leader's vision.

6-81. Leaders use a variety of means to share information: face-to-face talks, written and verbal orders, running estimates and plans, published memos, e-mail, Web sites, social media, and newsletters. When communicating to share information, the leader must acknowledge two critical factors:
- A leader is responsible for making sure the team understands the message.
- A leader must ensure that communication is not limited to the traditional chain of command but often includes lateral and vertical support networks.

6-82. The greater use and availability of e-mail, Web sites, and social media has increased the access and speed of information. The leader needs to be aware of misinformation and ensure accurate information is conveyed. Although electronic means of sharing data has made it easier, the leader needs to conduct face-to-face talks with subordinates to ensure they fully understand as well as receive feedback.

6-83. Communication also flows from bottom to top. Leaders find out what their people are thinking, saying, and doing by listening. Effective leaders observe their organizations by getting out to coach, to listen, and to clarify. They pass relevant observations to enable planning and decisionmaking.

6-84. Often, leaders communicate more effectively with informal networks than directly with superiors. Sometimes that produces the desired results but can lead to misunderstandings and false judgments. To run an effective organization and achieve missions without excessive conflict, leaders must figure out how to reach their superiors when necessary and to build a relationship of mutual trust. First, leaders must assess how the boss communicates and receives information. Some use direct and personal contact while others may be more comfortable with weekly meetings, e-mail, or memoranda. Knowing the boss's intent, priorities, and thought processes enhance organizational effectiveness and success. A leader who communicates well minimizes friction and improves the overall organizational climate.

6-85. To prepare organizations for inevitable communication challenges, leaders create training situations that force subordinates to act with minimum guidance or only the commander's intent. Leaders provide formal or informal feedback to highlight the things subordinates did well, what they could have done better and what they should do differently next time to improve information sharing and processing.

6-86. Open communication does more than share information. It shows leaders care about those they work with on a daily basis. Competent and confident leaders encourage open dialogue, listen actively to all perspectives, and ensure others can voice honest opinions without fear of negative consequences.

Table 6-5. Summary of the competency *Communicates*

Leaders communicate effectively by clearly expressing ideas and actively listening to others. By understanding the nature and importance of communication and practicing effective communication techniques, leaders will relate better to others and be able to translate goals into actions. Communication is essential to all other leadership competencies.	
Listens actively	<ul><li>Listens and watches attentively.</li><li>Makes appropriate notes.</li><li>Tunes in to content, emotion, and urgency.</li><li>Uses verbal and nonverbal means to reinforce with the speaker that you are paying attention.</li><li>Reflects on new information before expressing views.</li></ul>
Creates shared understanding	<ul><li>Shares necessary information with others and subordinates.</li><li>Protects confidential information.</li><li>Coordinates plans with higher, lower and adjacent organizations.</li><li>Keeps higher and lower headquarters, superiors and subordinates informed.</li><li>Expresses thoughts and ideas clearly to individuals and groups.</li><li>Recognizes potential miscommunication.</li><li>Uses appropriate means for communicating a message.</li></ul>
Employs engaging communication techniques	<ul><li>States goals to energize others to adopt and act on them.</li><li>Uses logic and relevant facts in dialogue; expresses well-organized ideas.</li><li>Speaks enthusiastically and maintains listeners' interest and involvement.</li><li>Makes appropriate eye contact when speaking.</li><li>Uses appropriate gestures.</li><li>Uses visual aids as needed.</li><li>Determines, recognizes, and resolves misunderstandings.</li></ul>
Is sensitive to cultural factors in communication	<ul><li>Maintains awareness of communication customs, expressions, actions, or behaviors.</li><li>Demonstrates respect for others.</li></ul>

Chapter 7
Develops

OVERVIEW OF DEVELOPS

7-1. Effective leaders strive to leave an organization better than they found it and expect other leaders to do the same. Leaders have the responsibility to create a positive organizational climate, prepare themselves to do well in their duties, and help others to perform well. Leaders look ahead and prepare talented Soldiers and Army Civilians to assume positions with greater leadership responsibility. They work on self-development to prepare for new challenges.

7-2. By living the core leader competencies and being a leader of character with presence and intellect, a leader can be effective over both the short- and long-term. A leader may be unaware of subordinate needs or that a self-focused agenda has harmful effects on organization development. Leaders need to honestly self-assess their behaviors and be alert to the potential negative outcomes of positive attributes. For example, being confident and decisive is important, but continuing with a failed plan or dismissing contradictory information will result in a rigid leader with an inability to adapt and get good results.

7-3. To have future focus and maintain balance in the present, Army leaders set priorities and weigh competing demands. They carefully steer their organizations' efforts to address short- and long-term goals, while continuing to meet requirements that could contribute directly to achieving those goals. The competing demands that vie for an organization's resources complicate a leader's job. Guidance from higher headquarters may help, but leaders have to make the tough calls to keep a healthy balance.

7-4. Developing people and the organization with a long-term perspective requires leaders who—
- Create a positive environment that fosters esprit de corps and teamwork, promotes cohesion, and encourages initiative and acceptance of responsibility. A leader maintains a healthy balance between caring for people and their families while focusing on the mission.
- Seek self-improvement. To master the profession at every level, a leader must make a full commitment to lifelong learning. Self-improvement requires self-awareness and leads to new skills necessary to adapt to changes in the leadership environment.
- Invest adequate time and effort to develop individual subordinates and build effective teams. Success demands a fine balance of teaching, counseling, coaching, and mentoring.
- Act as stewards of the profession, making choices and taking actions that ensure that leaders in the future sustain an Army capable of performing its core functions.

CREATES A POSITIVE ENVIRONMENT/FOSTERS ESPRIT DE CORPS

7-5. Climate and culture describe the environment in which a leader leads. The leader shapes the environment in which the leader and others operate. Culture refers to the environment of the Army as an institution and of major elements or communities within it. Strategic leaders shape the Army's culture, while organizational and direct leaders shape the climate of units and organizations.

7-6. Taking care of people and maximizing their performance largely determines how well the leader shapes the organization's climate. Climate is how members feel about the organization and comes from shared perceptions and attitudes about the unit's daily functioning. Climate affects motivation and the trust Soldiers and Army Civilians feel for their team and leaders. Climate is generally a short-term experience, depending upon a network of personalities within the organization that changes as people come and go.

7-7. Culture is a longer lasting and more complex set of shared expectations than climate. While climate is a reflection of how people think and feel about their organization now, culture consists of the shared attitudes, values, goals, and practices that characterize the larger institution over time. It is deeply rooted in long-held beliefs and customs. Leaders establish a climate consistent with the culture of the institution. Leaders use the culture to let members of the organization know they are part of something bigger than just themselves, that they have responsibilities to those who have gone before and those who will come after.

ESPRIT DE CORPS

7-8. Soldiers draw strength from knowing they are part of long-standing tradition. Many of the Army's everyday customs and traditions remind Soldiers they are the latest addition to a long line of Soldiers. The uniforms, official ceremony music, salutes, military titles, the organization's history, and the Army Values are reminders of tradition. This sense of belonging lives in many veterans long after they have left service. For many, service to the nation remains the single most significant experience of their lives.

7-9. Soldiers join the Army to become part of something greater than themselves. The Army Values help deepen existing personal values, such as family bonds, work ethic, and integrity. Unit history is an important bonding factor since Soldiers want to belong to organizations with distinguished service records. Unit names such as the Big Red One, All Americans, and Screaming Eagles carry an extensive history. To sustain tradition, leaders pass on the history that surrounds unit crests, awards, decorations, and badges. Upholding traditions ensures the Army's culture becomes integral to every member of the Army team.

SETTING THE CONDITIONS FOR POSITIVE CLIMATE

7-10. Climate and culture provide the context in which leaders and followers interact. Each element has an effect on the other. Research in military, government, and business organizations shows that positive environments lead to individuals who feel better about themselves, have stronger commitments, and produce better work. If leaders set the tone for a positive climate, others will respond in kind.

7-11. Leaders strive to establish a climate characterized as fair, inclusive, and ethical. To be fair, it must be applied consistently, be free from bias, be accurate, be correctable, and be based on ethical standards. Inclusive means that the organization integrates everyone, regardless of difference. Ethical means that actions throughout the organization conform to the Army Values and Warrior Ethos.

7-12. Many view leadership by default as only positive actions. However, some leaders use inappropriate strategies to obtain immediate results and mindless adherence to orders without concern for others. They may bully others, berate subordinates mercilessly, or make unlawful choices to get their way. Selfish leaders ignore ideas from others, micromanage events, hoard information, undermine peers, and work to look good to superiors. Extreme and consistent forms of these undesirable behaviors indicate a toxic or abusive leader. Leaders with a positive approach can be firm in exacting discipline and can do so with care and respect for those they lead and in the interest of the organization's future.

7-13. To create a positive climate, leaders have the challenge to identify the presence and effects of anyone who contributes to a negative climate. Some techniques for doing this include—

- Augmenting evaluations with information from peer and subordinate perspectives.
- Pursuing both evaluative and developmental approaches to correct negative behaviors.
- Using unit climate assessment reports to identify problems early.
- Focusing on long-term success by recognizing legitimate concerns from subordinates and making timely and candid feedback part of a leader's routine responsibility.

7-14. Part of being a steward of the profession is policing one's self and others in the organization. Leaders need to continually assess the organizational climate, realize the importance of development, and work to limit any zero-defect mentality. Recognizing the importance of long-term sustainability and sharing and encouraging feedback (both positive and negative) needs to be a priority for all unit members.

Fairness and Inclusiveness

7-15. Fair leaders use the same set of principles and values to avoid arbitrary treatment of others. All leaders are responsible for adhering to equal opportunity policies and preventing harassment. Creating a positive climate begins with encouraging diversity and inclusiveness. People have different capabilities and needs, so leaders should consider some differences while ignoring irrelevant differences. Leaders need to judge situations according to what is important in each case.

Open and Candid Communications

7-16. Effective leaders encourage open communications and candid observations. An open and candid environment is a key element in creating a unit poised to recognize and adapt to change. Approachable leaders show respect for others' opinions, even if contrary or out of the mainstream of thought. Some leaders specifically recognize others to provide a critical viewpoint to guard against groupthink. A positive leader remains calm and objective when receiving potentially bad news.

Learning Environment

7-17. The Army harnesses the experience of its people and organizations to improve the way it operates. Based on experiences, learning organizations adopt new techniques and procedures that complete jobs more efficiently or effectively. Likewise, they discard techniques and procedures that have outlived their purpose. Learning organizations create a climate that values learning in its members. Leaders actively identify and support opportunities for education, training, and experience.

7-18. Learning leaders use their experience to find better ways of doing things. It takes courage to create a learning environment. Leaders dedicated to a learning environment cannot be afraid to challenge how they and their organizations operate. When leaders ask, "why do we do it this way" and find the reason is, "because we've always done it that way," it is time for a closer look at the process. Unless leaders are willing to question how things operate now, no one will know what is possible.

7-19. Leaders who make it a priority to improve their subordinates lead learning organizations. They use effective assessment and training methods, motivate others to develop themselves, and help others obtain training and education to reach their potential. An upbeat climate encourages individuals to recognize the need for organizational change and supports a willing attitude of learning to work with change.

Assessing Climate

7-20. Leader behavior has significant impact on the organizational climate. Army leaders who adhere to the Army Values and Warrior Ethos create a healthy organizational climate. Leader behavior signals to every member of the organization what is or is not tolerated. The members' collective sense of the group—its organizational climate—is directly attributable to the leader's values, skills, and actions. Unit climate assessments help leaders understand the unit's climate (see AR 600-20).

Establishing a Positive Climate

7-21. After assessing the climate, leaders can monitor several key areas that indicate positive climate. Establishing clear and realistic goals for improvement is an important aspect. Communicating goals openly provides followers a clear vision to achieve. As subordinates meet these goals, leaders reward high performance that conforms to the proposed climate.

7-22. Communication between subordinates and leaders is essential to create a positive climate. Leaders empower subordinates to bring creative and innovative ideas forward, and they seek feedback from subordinates about the climate. The most effective action a leader can take to establish a positive climate is to demonstrate concern for their subordinates' welfare. Openly engaging in pro-unit or pro-organizational behaviors increases the likelihood that subordinates perceive leaders acting for the group's welfare and they know the leader has the group's best interests at heart.

Dealing with Ethics and Climate

7-23. A leader is the ethical standard-bearer for the organization, responsible for building an ethical climate that demands and rewards behavior consistent with the Army Values. Other staff specialists—the chaplain, staff judge advocate, inspector general, and equal employment opportunity specialist—help shape and assess the organization's ethical climate. Regardless of available expert help, the ultimate responsibility to create and maintain an ethical climate rests with the leader.

7-24. Setting a good ethical example does not necessarily mean subordinates will follow it. Some may feel that circumstance justifies unethical behavior. Therefore, the leader must monitor the organization's ethical climate and take prompt action to correct any discrepancies between the climate and the standard. To effectively monitor organizational climates, leaders can use the Ethical Climate Assessment Survey (see TC 1-05) combined with a focused leader plan of action as follows—

- Begin the plan of action by assessing the unit. Observe those in the unit and gather feedback from them or conduct formal assessments of the workplace.
- Analyze gathered information to identify what needs improvement. After identifying what needs improvement, begin developing courses of action to make the improvements.
- Develop a plan of action. Develop and consider several possible courses of action to correct identified weaknesses. Gather important information, assess the limitations and risks associated with the various courses, identify available key personnel and resources, and verify facts and assumptions. Attempt to predict the outcome for each possible course of action. Based on predictions, select several leader actions to address target issues.
- Execute the plan of action by educating, training, or counseling subordinates; instituting new policies or procedures; and revising or enforcing proper systems of rewards and punishment. Periodically reassess the unit to identify new matters of concern or to evaluate the effectiveness of the leader actions.

7-25. Leaders use this process for many areas of interest within the organization. It is important for subordinates to have confidence in the organization's ethical environment because much of what is necessary in combat goes against the grain of societal values that individuals bring into the Army. Strong commitment to the Army Values and Warrior Ethos by the commander fosters a unit's ethical climate.

BUILDING COHESION AND TRUST

7-26. Teamwork and cohesion are measures of climate. Selfless service is a requirement for effective teamwork. Effective teams and organizations work together for mission objectives. Leaders encourage others to work together while promoting group pride in accomplishments. Teamwork, based on commitment to the group, is built on trust. Trust means that others will act for the team and keep its interests ahead of their own. Leaders should integrate new team members with this commitment in mind.

7-27. Leaders shape cohesive teams by setting and maintaining high standards. Positive climates exist where good, consistent performance is the norm. This differs from a climate where perfectionism is the expectation. The team should appreciate a concentrated, honest effort even when the results are incomplete. They should feel that their leader recognizes value in every opportunity as a means to learn and improve. Effective leaders recognize that reasonable setbacks and failures occur whether the team does everything right or not. Leaders should express the importance of being competent and motivated, but understand weaknesses exist. Mistakes create opportunities to learn.

7-28. Soldiers and Army Civilians expect to be held to high but realistic standards. They gain confidence in leaders who help them achieve standards and lose confidence in leaders who do not know the standards or who fail to demand quality performance.

ENCOURAGING INITIATIVE

7-29. One of the greatest challenges for a leader is to encourage subordinates to exercise initiative. Soldiers and Army Civilians who are not in leadership positions are often reluctant to recognize that a situation calls for them to accept responsibility and step forward. This could involve speaking up when the Soldier has technical knowledge or situational information that the commander does not.

7-30. Climate largely determines the degree to which initiative and input is encouraged. Leaders can set the conditions for initiative by guiding others in thinking through problems for themselves. They can build confidence in the Soldier's or Army Civilian's competence and ability to solve problems.

DEMONSTRATING CARE FOR PEOPLE

7-31. Leaders who keep the well-being of their subordinates in mind create greater trust. Leaders who respect those with whom they work will likely garner respect in return. Simple actions can demonstrate respect and care, such as listening patiently or addressing Families' needs. Regular sensing of morale and actively seeking honest feedback about the health of the organization indicate care.

Table 7-1. Summary of the competency *Creates a positive environment*

\	\
Leaders establish and maintain positive expectations and attitudes to support effective work behaviors and healthy relationships. Leaders improve the organization while accomplishing missions. They should leave the organization better than it was when they arrived.	
Fosters teamwork, cohesion, cooperation and loyalty (esprit de corps)	• Encourages people to work together effectively. • Promotes teamwork and team achievement to build trust. • Draws attention to the consequences of poor coordination. • Integrates new members into the unit quickly.
Encourages fairness and inclusiveness	• Provides accurate evaluations and assessments. • Supports equal opportunity. • Prevents all forms of harassment. • Encourages learning about and leveraging diversity.
Encourages open and candid communications	• Shows others how to accomplish tasks while respectful and focused. • Displays a positive attitude to encourage others and improve morale. • Reinforces the expression of contrary and minority viewpoints. • Displays appropriate reactions to new or conflicting information or opinions. • Guards against groupthink.
Creates a learning environment	• Uses effective assessment and training methods. • Encourages leaders and their subordinates to reach their full potential. • Motivates others to develop themselves. • Expresses the value of interacting with others and seeking counsel. • Stimulates innovative and critical thinking in others. • Seeks new approaches to problems. • Communicates the difference between professional standards and a zero-defects mentality. • Emphasizes learning from one's mistakes.
Encourages subordinates to exercise initiative, accept responsibility and take ownership	• Involves others in decisions and informs them of consequences. • Allocates responsibility for performance. • Guides subordinate leaders in thinking through problems for themselves. • Allocates decisionmaking to the lowest appropriate level. • Acts to expand and enhance subordinate's competence and self-confidence. • Rewards initiative.
Demonstrates care for follower well-being	• Encourages subordinates and peers to express candid opinions. • Addresses subordinates' and families' needs (health, welfare, and development). • Stands up for subordinates. • Routinely monitors morale and encourages honest feedback.
Anticipates people's on-the-job needs	• Recognizes and monitors subordinate's needs and reactions. • Shows concern for how tasks and missions affect subordinate morale.
Sets and maintains high expectations for individuals and teams	• Clearly articulates expectations. • Creates a climate that expects good performance, recognizes superior performance, and does not accept poor performance. • Challenges others to match the leader's example.

PREPARES SELF

7-32. To prepare for increasingly more demanding operational environments, Army leaders must invest more time on self-study and self-development than before. Besides becoming multiskilled, Army leaders have to balance the demands of diplomat and Soldier. Acquiring these capabilities to succeed in decisive action is challenging, but critical. In no other profession is the cost of being unprepared as unforgiving, often resulting in mission failure and needless casualties.

BEING PREPARED FOR EXPECTED AND UNEXPECTED CHALLENGES

7-33. Successful self-development concentrates on the key components of the leader: character, presence, and intellect. While refining abilities to apply and model the Army Values, Army leaders maintain high levels of fitness and health, not only to earn the respect of others, but also to withstand the stresses of leading and maintaining their ability to think clearly.

7-34. While physical fitness is important, leaders must exploit every available opportunity to sharpen their intellectual capacity and relevant knowledge. The conceptual components affecting leader intelligence include mental agility, judgment, innovation, interpersonal tact, and expertise. A developed intellect helps the leader think creatively and reason analytically, critically, ethically, and with cultural sensitivity.

7-35. When faced with diverse operational settings, a leader draws on intellectual capacity, critical thinking abilities, and applicable expertise. Leaders create these capabilities by studying doctrine and putting the information into context with personal experiences, military history, and geopolitical awareness. Self-development should include learning languages, customs, belief systems, motivational factors, fundamentals, and TTP of unified action partners and potential adversaries.

7-36. Successful self-development is continuous and begins with the motivated individual, supplemented by a concerted team effort. Part of that team effort is quality feedback from multiple sources, including peers, subordinates, and superiors to establish self-development goals and self-improvement courses of action. These improve performance by enhancing previously acquired skills, knowledge, behaviors, and experience. Trust-based mentorship can help focus self-development efforts to achieve professional objectives.

7-37. Generally, self-development for junior leaders, specifically NCOs, is more structured and focused. The focus broadens as individuals do their own assessments, determine individual needs, and become more independent. While knowledge and perspective increase with age, experience, training, and operational assignments, goal-oriented self-development actions can accelerate and broaden skills and knowledge. Soldiers and Army Civilians can expect their leaders to enable in their self-development.

7-38. Civilian and military education is an important part of self-development. Leaders seek out education and training opportunities beyond required schooling. Leaders must develop themselves and help subordinates to acquire the individual attributes, intellectual capacities, and competencies to become great future leaders. To achieve leadership success in increasingly complex environments, leaders need to expand professional knowledge and develop a keen sense of self-awareness.

EXPANDING KNOWLEDGE

7-39. Leaders prepare themselves for leadership positions through lifelong learning and broadening experiences. Lifelong learning involves study and reflection to acquire new knowledge and to learn how to apply it when needed. Some leaders readily pick up strategies about how to learn new information faster and more thoroughly. Becoming a better learner involves several purposeful steps:
- Plan the approach to use to learn.
- Focus on achievable learning goals.
- Set aside time to study.
- Organize new information as it is encountered.
- Track how learning is proceeding.

7-40. Broadening consists of those education and training opportunities, assignments, and experiences that provide exposure outside the leader's branch or functional area competencies. Broadening allows development of a wider range of knowledge and skills, augments understanding of the spectrum of Army missions, promotes practical application of language training, or increases cross-cultural exposure and expands awareness of other governmental agencies, organizations, or environments.

7-41. Good learners focus on how to use new information as it relates to other information. To solidify new knowledge, leaders apply it and experience what it means. Leaders need to develop and expand knowledge of tactics and operational art, technical equipment and systems, diverse cultures, and geopolitical situations.

DEVELOPING SELF-AWARENESS

7-42. Self-awareness has the potential to help leaders become better adjusted and more effective. As a critical element of adaptability, self-awareness enables leaders to recognize their strengths and weaknesses across a range of environments and progressively employ strengths to correct these weaknesses. To be self-aware, leaders must be able to formulate accurate self-perceptions, gather feedback on others' perceptions, and change their self-concept as appropriate. Being self-aware ultimately requires leaders to develop a clear, honest picture of their capabilities and limitations.

7-43. To adapt, a leader's assessment of abilities and limitations must change as a given situation changes. This makes having an accurate and realistic evaluation of one's strengths and weaknesses essential to everything a leader does. Every leader has the ability to be self-aware. Competent leaders understand the importance of self-awareness—an on-going process whereby leaders take time to reflect upon their identity, values, goals and performance abilities. Self-aware leaders gain the trust of their subordinates by engaging in authentic actions that correspond to who they are and of what they are capable.

7-44. Subordinates see leaders who lack self-awareness as arrogant or disconnected. They may be technically competent but lack awareness as to how others see them. This may obstruct their readiness to learn and ability to adapt. Lacking awareness can keep them from creating a positive, learning work climate. Self-aware leaders sense how others react to their actions, decisions, and example.

7-45. Self-aware leaders are open to feedback and actively seek it. A leader's goal in obtaining feedback is to develop an accurate self-perception by understanding other people's perceptions. The Army provides the Multisource Assessment and Feedback program as a formal measure of peer, subordinate, superior, and self-impressions. It may provide critical feedback and insights that are not apparent otherwise. Another awareness tool is the AAR process to help units and individuals identify strengths and weaknesses. It is important to realize that feedback does not have to occur in formal counseling, surveys, or sensing sessions. Some of the best feedback comes from talking informally with Soldiers and Army Civilians.

7-46. Self-aware leaders analyze themselves and ask hard questions about experiences, events, and their actions. They examine their own behavior seriously. Competent and confident leaders make sense of their experience and use it to learn more about themselves. Journals and AARs are valuable tools to help gain an understanding of one's past experiences and reactions to the changes in the environment. Self-critique can be as simple as posing questions about one's own behavior, knowledge, or feelings or as formal as answering a structured set of questions about an event. Critical questions include—
- What happened?
- How did I react?
- How did others react and why?
- What did I learn about myself based on what I did and how I felt?
- How will I apply what I learned?

7-47. In rapidly changing environments, self-awareness is a critical factor in making accurate assessments of environmental changes and a leader's personal capabilities and limitations to operate in that environment. Self-awareness helps leaders translate prior training to a new environment and seek new information. Self-aware leaders are more responsive to situational and interpersonal cues regarding actions to take in a given situation. They are better informed and able to determine what assistance to seek to handle a given situation.

7-48. Self-regulation adjusts one's thoughts, feelings, and actions based on self-awareness. Proactive and logical, it follows self-awareness. When leaders determine a gap from actual to desired self, they should work to close the gap. Leaders can seek new perspectives and turn them into a leadership advantage.

Table 7-2. Summary of the competency *Prepares self*

Leaders prepare to execute their leadership responsibilities fully. They are aware of their limitations and strengths and seek self-development. Leaders maintain self-discipline, physical fitness, and mental well-being. They continue to improve the expertise required of their leadership roles and their profession.	
Maintains mental and physical health and well-being	• Recognizes imbalance or inappropriateness of one's own actions. • Removes emotions from decisionmaking. • Applies logic and reason to make decisions or when interacting with emotionally charged individuals. • Recognizes the sources of stress and maintains appropriate levels of challenge to motivate self. • Manages regular exercise, leisure activities, and time away. • Stays focused on life priorities and values.
Expands knowledge of technical, technological and tactical areas	• Seeks knowledge of systems, equipment, capabilities, and situations, particularly information technology systems. • Keeps informed about developments and policy changes inside and outside the organization.
Expands conceptual and interpersonal capabilities	• Understands the contribution of concentration, critical thinking, imagination, and problem solving in different task conditions. • Learns new approaches to problem solving. • Applies lessons learned. • Filters unnecessary information efficiently. • Reserves time for self-development, reflection, and personal growth. • Considers possible motives behind conflicting information.
Analyzes and organizes information to create knowledge	• Reflects on prior learning; organizes insights for future application. • Considers source, quality or relevance, and criticality of information to improve understanding. • Identifies reliable resources for acquiring knowledge. • Sets up systems of procedures to store knowledge for reuse.
Maintains relevant cultural awareness	• Learns about issues of language, values, customary behavior, ideas, beliefs, and patterns of thinking that influence others. • Learns about results of previous encounters when culture plays a role in mission success.
Maintains relevant geopolitical awareness	• Learns about relevant societies experiencing unrest. • Recognizes Army influences on unified action partners and enemies. • Understands the factors influencing conflict and peacekeeping, peace enforcing and peacemaking missions.
Maintains self-awareness: employs self understanding and recognizes impact on others	• Evaluates one's strengths and weaknesses. • Learns from mistakes to make corrections; learns from experience. • Seeks feedback; determines areas in need of development. • Determines personal goals and makes progress toward them. • Develops capabilities where possible but accepts personal limitations. • Seeks opportunities to use capabilities appropriately. • Understands self-motivation under various task conditions.

DEVELOPS OTHERS

7-49. *Leader development* is a deliberate, continuous, sequential, and progressive process grounded in the Army Values. It grows Soldiers and Army Civilians into competent, confident leaders capable of directing teams and organizations. Army leaders, as stewards of the Army profession, must place the needs of the Army as a whole above organizational or personal needs. This is particularly true in developing subordinates. Leader development occurs through the lifelong synthesis of education, training, and experience. Successful leaders balance the long-term needs of the Army, the near-term and career needs of their subordinates, and the immediate needs of their unit missions. The Army requires all its leaders to develop subordinates into leaders for the next level.

7-50. Leader development takes into consideration that military leaders are inherently Soldiers first and must be technically and tactically proficient as well as adaptive to change. Army leader development creates competent and confident leaders capable of leading trained and ready units. The concept acknowledges an important interaction that trains Soldiers now and develops leaders for the future.

7-51. The three developmental domains—institutional, operational, and self-development—shape the critical learning experiences throughout Soldiers' careers. The domains interact by using feedback and assessment from various sources and methods. Although leader development aims at producing competent leadership at all levels, it recognizes small-unit leaders must reach an early proficiency to operate in widely dispersed areas in combined arms teams and/or integrated with unified action partners. Army leaders must be self-aware and adaptive, comfortable with ambiguity, able to anticipate possible second- and third-order effects, and be multifunctional to exploit combined arms and joint integration.

7-52. The Army uses resident, distributed, and blended education (Professional Military Education and the Civilian Education System); training; and a mix of experiences and operational assignments. The effort requires improved individual assessment and feedback and increased development efforts at the organizational level such as mentoring, coaching, and counseling, as well as picking the right talent for assignments. These efforts instill in all Soldiers and leaders the desire and drive to improve their professional knowledge and competencies, thus improving current and future Army leaders' abilities to master the challenges of decisive action.

HELPING PEOPLE LEARN

7-53. In developmental relationships, it is the leader's responsibility to help subordinates learn. Leaders explain a subject's importance—how it will help individual and organizational performance. For instance, teaching someone how to drive with classroom instruction alone is not productive. Ultimately, the learner has to get behind the wheel. To maintain interest, minimize lectures and maximize hands-on training.

7-54. Learning from experience is not always possible—leaders cannot have every experience in training. Taking advantage of what others have learned provides the benefit without having the personal experience. Leaders should share their experiences with subordinates through counseling, coaching, and mentoring, such as combat veterans sharing experiences with Soldiers who have not been in combat.

ASSESSING DEVELOPMENTAL NEEDS

7-55. The first step in developing others is to understand how they develop best -- what areas are already strong and what areas should be stronger. Leaders who know their subordinates will have an idea where to encourage development. Leaders observe new subordinates under different task conditions to identify strengths and weaknesses and to see how quickly they pick up new information and skills.

7-56. Leaders often conduct an initial assessment before they enter a new position. They ask questions: How competent are new subordinates? What is expected in the new job? Leaders review the organization's policies, status reports, and recent inspection results. They ask the outgoing leader for an assessment and meet with key people outside the organization. They may reflect upon those initial impressions. Effective leaders update in-depth assessments since a thorough assessment helps implement changes gradually and systematically without causing damaging organizational turmoil.

7-57. To objectively assess subordinates, leaders—
- Observe and record subordinates' performance in the core leader competencies.
- Determine if the performances meet, exceed, or fall below expected standards.
- Share observations with subordinates and give an opportunity to comment.

7-58. Leaders provide honest feedback to others, discussing strengths and areas for improvement. Effective assessment results in an individual development plan designed to improve weaknesses and sustain strengths. These steps move planning to results—
- Design the plan together, to improve performance and encourage subordinates to take the lead.
- Agree on the required actions to improve leader performance in the core leader competencies. Subordinates must buy into this plan if it is going to work.
- Review the plan frequently, check progress, and modify the plan if necessary.

COUNSELING, COACHING AND MENTORING

7-59. Leaders have three principal ways of developing others. They can provide knowledge and feedback through counseling, coaching, and mentoring. Providing feedback is common to interacting with others during development. Feedback significantly contributes to development, accelerates learning in day-to-day experiences, and translates into better leader performance. Providing feedback starts with observation and accurate assessment of performance. Planning to make observations of a subordinate is the first step in feedback. The best observations occur when subordinates engage in critical performance, interact with their subordinates or other Soldiers, or address a challenging problem. Keeping observation notes is useful when tracking multiple subordinates.

Counseling

7-60. Counseling is central to leader development. Leaders who serve as designated raters have to prepare their subordinates to be better Soldiers or Army Civilians. Good counseling focuses on the subordinate's performance and issues with an eye toward tomorrow's plans and solutions. Leaders expect subordinates to be active participants seeking constructive feedback. Counseling cannot be an occasional event but should be part of a comprehensive program to develop subordinates. With effective counseling, no evaluation report—positive or negative—should be a surprise. A consistent counseling program includes all subordinates, not just the people thought to have the most potential.

7-61. Counseling is the process used by leaders to guide subordinates to improve performance and develop their potential. Subordinates are active participants in the counseling process. Counseling uses a standard format to help mentally organize and isolate relevant issues before, during, and after the counseling session. During counseling, leaders help subordinates to identify strengths and weaknesses and create plans of action. To make the plans work, leaders actively support their subordinates throughout the implementation and assessment processes. Subordinates invest themselves in the process by being forthright in their willingness to improve and being candid in their assessment and goal setting.

Coaching

7-62. While a mentor or counselor generally has more experience than the person being supported does, coaching relies primarily on teaching and guiding to bring out and enhance the capabilities already present. Coaching refers to the function of helping someone through a set of tasks or with general qualities. Those being coached may, or may not, have appreciated their potential. The coach helps them understand their current level of performance and guides them how to reach the next level of knowledge and skill.

7-63. Coaching is a development technique used for a skill, task, or specific behaviors. Coaches should possess considerable knowledge in the area in which they coach others.

7-64. An important aspect of coaching is identifying and planning for short- and long-term goals. The coach and the person being coached discuss strengths, weaknesses, and courses of action to sustain or improve. Coaches use the following guidelines—
- *Focus Goals*: This requires the coach to identify the purpose of the coaching session. Expectations of both the person being coached and the coach need to be discussed. The coach communicates to the individual the developmental tasks for the coaching session, which can incorporate the results of the individual's multisource assessment and feedback survey.
- *Clarify the Leader's Self-Awareness*: The coach works directly with the individual to define both strengths and developmental needs. During this session, the coach and the individual

communicate perceived strengths, developmental needs, and focus areas to improve performance. Both the coach and the individual agree on areas of developmental needs.

- *Uncover Potential*: The coach facilitates self-awareness of the individual's potential and developmental needs by guiding the discussion with questions. The coach actively listens to how the individual perceives potential. The aim is to encourage the free flow of ideas. The coach also assesses the individual's readiness to change and incorporates this into the session.
- *Eliminate Developmental Barriers*: The coach identifies developmental needs with the individual and those areas that may hinder self-development. It is during this step that the coach helps the individual determine how to overcome barriers to development and how to implement an effective plan to improve the leader's overall performance. The coach helps the individual identify potential sources of support for implementing an action plan.
- *Develop Action Plans and Commitment*: The coach and the individual develop an action plan defining actions that can improve performance within a given period. The coach utilizes a developmental action guide to communicate those self-directed activities the individual can accomplish to improve their performance in a particular competency.
- *Follow-Up*: After the initial coaching session, there should be a follow-up as part of a larger transition. After the initial coaching, participants should provide feedback concerning the effectiveness of the assessment, the usefulness of the information they received, and progress. Leaders who coach provide frequent informal feedback and timely, proactive, formal counseling to regularly inspire and improve subordinates.

Mentoring

7-65. Current and anticipated operations place additional pressures on developing leaders rapidly. To help leaders acquire the necessary abilities, the Army relies on a leader development system that compresses and accelerates development of professional expertise, maturity, and conceptual and team-building skills. Mentoring is a developmental tool that can effectively support many of these learning objectives.

7-66. It is not required for leaders to have the same occupational or educational background as those they coach or counsel. In comparison, mentors generally specialize in the same area as those they mentor. Mentors have likely experienced what their protégés are experiencing or are going to experience. Consequently, mentoring relationships tend to be occupation-specific, with the mentor having expertise in the particular area. Mentoring focuses primarily on developing a more experienced leader for the future.

7-67. *Mentorship* is the voluntary developmental relationship that exists between a person of greater experience and a person of lesser experience that is characterized by mutual trust and respect (AR 600-100). Mentorship is generally characterized by the following—

- Mentoring takes place when the mentor provides a less experienced leader with advice and counsel over time to help with professional and personal growth.
- The developing leader often initiates the relationship and seeks counsel from the mentor. The mentor takes the initiative to check on the well-being and development of that person.
- Mentorship affects personal development (maturity and interpersonal and communication skills) as well as professional development (technical, tactical, and career path knowledge).
- Mentorship helps the Army maintain a highly competent set of leaders.
- The strength of the mentoring relationship relies on mutual trust and respect. Protégés carefully consider assessment, feedback, and guidance; these become valuable for growth to occur.

7-68. Supportive mentoring occurs when a mentor does not outrank the person being mentored, but has extensive knowledge and experience. Contrary to common belief, mentoring relationships are not confined to the superior-subordinate relationship. They may occur between peers and often between senior NCOs and junior officers. This relationship can occur across many levels of rank. In many circumstances, this relationship extends past the time where one party has left the chain of command.

7-69. Individuals must be active participants in their developmental process. They must not wait for a mentor to choose them but have the responsibility to be proactive in their own development. Every Army officer, NCO, Soldier, and Civilian should identify personal strengths and areas for improvement. Each individual should then determine a developmental plan. Some strategies that may be used are—

Chapter 7

- Ask questions and pay attention to experts.
- Read and study.
- Watch those in leadership positions.
- Find educational opportunities (civilian, military, and correspondence).
- Seek and engage in new and varied opportunities.

7-70. Soldiers can increase their chances of mentorship by seeking performance feedback and by adopting an attitude of lifelong learning. These self-development actions enable mentoring opportunities. Soldiers who seek feedback to focus their development, coupled with dedicated, well-informed mentors, will embed the concepts of lifelong learning, self-development, and adaptability into the Army's culture.

7-71. While mentoring is generally associated with improving duty-related performance and growth, it may include a spiritual dimension. A chaplain or other spiritually trained individual may play a significant role in helping individuals cope with operational stress to find better professional balance and purpose.

Table 7-3. Counseling—Coaching—Mentoring Comparison

	Counseling	*Coaching*	*Mentoring*
Purpose	Review past or current performance to sustain and improve current or future performance.	Guide learning or improvement skills.	Provide guidance focused on professional or personal growth.
Source	Rater, chain of command.	Assigned coach or trainer with special knowledge.	Those with greater experience.
Interaction	As a formal or informal conversation between superior and subordinate.	During practice or performance between a coach/trainer and the individual, observation, guidance.	Conversation on a personal level.
How it works (what the counselor, coach or mentor does)	Identify the need. Prepare for the session. Conduct counseling to encourage subordinate's active participation. Set goals. Follow-up on progress.	From opportunities for demonstration of a skill, observe performance and provide guidance.	Apply the mentor's experience to guide the protégé.
Outcome	Formal (Individual Development Plan) or informal goals for sustainment and improvement.	Behaviors identified for improvement, higher performance level.	Personal commitment to career choices, intent to improve.
Requirement	Required – all subordinates are to be developed and counseled.	Required or voluntary.	Voluntary, mutual commitment.
Occurrence	Prescribed times IAW performance evaluation or upon event when rater determines a need.	Training or performance events.	Initiated by either party.

DEVELOPING ON THE JOB

7-72. The best development opportunities often occur on the job. Leaders who have an eye for developing others will encourage growth in current roles and positions. How a leader assigns tasks and duties can serve as a way to direct individual Soldiers or Army Civilians to extend their capabilities. The Army Civilian intern program is an excellent example of this type of training. Feedback from a leader during routine duty assignments can also direct subordinates to areas where they can focus their development. Some leaders constantly seek new ways to re-define duties or enrich a job to prepare subordinates for additional responsibilities in their current position or next assignment. Cross training on tasks provides dual benefits of building a more robust team and expanding the skill set of team members. Challenging subordinates with different job duties is a good way to keep them interested in routine work.

SUPPORTING LEADER DEVELOPMENT

7-73. Leader development represents a balanced commitment to education, training, and experience. It is a leader's responsibility to ensure subordinates receive the appropriate education, training, and experiences at the proper time for promotion as well as increasing their potential in current and future assignments.

7-74. Education is a programmed activity with the principal purpose of the development of one or more intellectual attributes. Education is more than just the professional military education associated with advancement to the next rank with the Officer, Noncommissioned Officer, and Civilian Education Systems. Education includes other opportunities to increase one's knowledge, skills, and attributes. Leaders ensure their subordinates attend appropriate educational opportunities.

7-75. Training is a programmed activity with the principal purpose of developing capabilities for competent and decisive action. Training is for Soldiers, leaders, and units to achieve tactical and technical competence that builds confidence and agility. Leaders ensure subordinates conduct training to accomplish missions and prepare for future responsibilities.

7-76. Experiences occur when the participant is subject to practical consequences of choices and actions. Experiences comprise knowledge and skills gained through involvement or exposure to an event. Experiences include deployments, assignments, jobs, training events, and educational opportunities. Leaders should offer and encourage broadening opportunities and professionally developing assignments to their subordinates.

TEAM CHARACTERISTICS AND STAGES

7-77. The national cause, mission purpose, and many other concerns may not be visible from the Soldier's perspective. Regardless of larger issues, Soldiers perform for others on the team or crew, for the Soldier on their right or left. It is a fundamental truth born of the Warrior Ethos: Soldiers get the job done because they do not want to fail each other. Similarly, Army Civilians are part of the installation and organizational team and want to be successful.

7-78. Developing close teams takes hard work, patience, and interpersonal skill on the part of the leader. It is a worthwhile investment because good teams complete missions on time with given resources and a minimum of wasted effort. In combat, cohesive teams are the most effective.

Characteristics of Teams

7-79. A team is any group that functions together to perform a mission or collective task. Teams that work well have the advantage of increasing motivation and accountability among members. The hallmarks of close teams include—
- Trusting each other and being able to predict what each will do.
- Working together to accomplish the mission.
- Executing tasks thoroughly and quickly.
- Meeting and exceeding the standard.
- Adapting to demanding challenges.
- Learning from their experiences and developing pride in their accomplishments.

7-80. The Army as a team includes many members who are not Soldiers. The contributions made by Army Civilians, contractors, and multinational workers in critical support missions during operations are often forgotten. In today's operational environment, many military objectives could not be achieved without the dedicated support of the Army's civilian team members.

7-81. Within a larger team, smaller teams may be at different stages of development. For instance, members of First Squad may be accustomed to working together. They trust one another and accomplish the mission, usually exceeding the standard without wasted effort. Second Squad in the same platoon just received three new Soldiers and a team leader from another company. As a team, Second Squad will take time to mature. Second Squad's new team members have to learn how things work. First, they have to feel like team members. Subsequently, they must learn the standards of their new unit and demonstrate competence before other members accept them. Finally, they must practice working together.

7-82. Competent leaders are sensitive to the characteristics of the team and its individual members. Teams develop differently and the boundaries between stages are not hard and fast. The results can help determine what to expect of the team and what improves its capabilities.

Stages of Team Building

7-83. Teams do not come together by accident. Leaders must guide them through three developmental stages: formation, enrichment, and sustainment.

Formation Stage

7-84. Army leaders often do not have a hand in selecting team members, but have the responsibility to ensure the team forms into a high performing unit. Teams work best when new members quickly feel a part of the team. The two critical steps of the formation stage—reception and orientation—are dramatically different in peace and combat. In combat, a good sponsorship process can literally make the difference between life and death for new arrivals and the entire team. In combat, Army leaders have countless things to worry about and the mental state of new arrivals might seem low on the list. If Soldiers cannot fight, the unit will suffer needless casualties and may ultimately fail to complete the mission.

7-85. Reception is the leader's welcome to new members of the organization. Time permitting, it should include a personal introduction. Orientation begins with meeting other team members, learning the layout and schedule of the workplace, and generally getting to know the environment. In combat, leaders may not have much time. In this case, new arrivals should receive sponsors. Sponsors help orient new members.

7-86. Leaders have an instrumental role in how a team works together, beginning with team formation. Leaders provide direction and reinforce the norms for how team members relate to one another and the standards of performance. Relational skills include everything from perceptiveness of each other's strengths, habits, and limits to tendencies in communicating and helping each other. The people skills internal to a team are important for how well the team performs technical skills. During team formation, leaders assess skills and expertise present on the team and determine procedures for optimal coordination.

Enrichment Stage

7-87. New team members gradually move from questioning everything to trusting themselves, their peers, and their leaders. Team members who trust each other are more willing to resolve differences of opinion and fact. Having trust in leaders allows members to suspend any doubts, to concentrate on duties and mission accomplishment. Leaders learn to trust by listening, following up on what they hear, establishing clear lines of authority, and enforcing standards. Leaders should understand signs of distrust during team building. Indicators of distrust include persistent defense of one's opinion, avoidance of conflict, ignoring the importance of team membership and goals, and suspicion about the motivation of others. Leaders can improve trust and build morale by getting to know team members, communicating truthfully with them, treating them fairly, and recognizing good work and teamwork. The most important thing is training. Training takes a group of individuals and molds them into a team while preparing them to accomplish missions. Training occurs during all three stages of team building, but is particularly important during enrichment. The team builds collective proficiency during this stage.

Sustainment Stage

7-88. During this stage, members identify with "their team." They own it, have pride in it, and want the team to succeed. At this stage, team members will do what is necessary without direction. Cohesion characterizes this stage of team building. Cohesion is a bond of relationships and motivational factors that make a team want to stay and work together. A cohesive team puts aside any interfering differences and chooses to work together. Every new mission gives the leader a chance to strengthen the bonds and challenge the team to reach new levels of accomplishment and confidence. The team's attitude about its capabilities elevates motivation and the desire to meet new challenges.

7-89. Teams can have ups and downs in the sustainment stage. Effective team leaders will watch for signs of complacency and intervene when it occurs by reinforcing good interaction practices and holding the team to standard. Changes for which the team is not prepared can be another challenge for the team leader. Shared experiences and regular training help teams address unexpected changes in situations. Empowering the team to improve coordination and SOPs can strengthen its ability to handle change.

7-90. Key responsibilities of the team leader in all stages of team building and teamwork include trust, cooperation, task commitment, accountability, and the work to be completed. When any of these erodes—trust is broken, conflict arises, commitments are disregarded, members are not accountable, or work goes undone—the leader must step in and get the team back on track.

Table 7-4. Summary of the competency *Develops others*

Leaders encourage and support others to grow as individuals and teams. They facilitate the achievement of organizational goals through helping others to develop. They prepare others to assume new positions elsewhere in the organization, making the organization more versatile and productive.	
Assesses developmental needs of others	• Determines strengths and weaknesses of subordinates under different conditions. • Evaluates subordinates in a fair and consistent manner. • Assesses tasks and subordinate motivation to consider methods of improving work assignments, when job enrichment would be useful, methods of cross-training on tasks and methods of accomplishing missions. • Designs ways to challenge subordinates to improve weaknesses and sustain strengths. • Encourages subordinates to improve processes.
Counsels, coaches and mentors	• Improves subordinate's understanding and proficiency. • Uses experience and knowledge to improve future performance. • Counsels, coaches and mentors subordinates, subordinate leaders, and others.
Facilitates ongoing development	• Maintains awareness of existing individual and organizational development programs and removes barriers to development. • Supports opportunities for self-development. • Arranges training opportunities to help subordinates improve self-awareness, confidence, and competence. • Encourages subordinates to pursue institutional learning opportunities. • Provide subordinates information about institutional training and career progression. • Maintains resources related to development.
Builds team or group skills and processes	• Presents challenging assignments for team or group interaction. • Provides resources and support for realistic, mission-oriented training. • Sustains and improves the relationships among team or group members. • Provides feedback on team processes.

STEWARDS THE PROFESSION

7-91. The Army requires focus on accomplishing the mission and improving the organization. The competencies dealing with positive environment, self-improvement, and developing others are the competencies related to stewardship. Stewardship is the group of strategies, policies, principles, and beliefs that pertain to the purposeful management and sustainment of the resources, expertise, and time-honored traditions and customs that make up the profession. Leaders serving as good stewards have concern for the lasting effects of their decisions about all of the resources they use and manage. Stewardship requires prioritization and sacrifice. All leaders will have choices that require contributing some capability or effective subordinate from their unit for the greater benefit of the Army. Stewardship is about the development and support of members of the Army team.

SUPPORTING PROFESSIONAL AND PERSONAL GROWTH

7-92. Developing multiskilled leaders is the goal of preparing self and subordinates to lead. The adaptable leader will more readily comprehend the challenges of a constantly evolving strategic environment, demanding not only warfighting skills, but also creativity and a degree of diplomacy combined with multicultural sensitivity. To achieve this balance, the Army creates positive learning environments at all levels to support its lifelong learning strategy.

7-93. Encouraging lifelong learning, the Army addresses the differences between operations today and in the future and continuously enhances leader development capabilities. Army leaders who look at their experiences and learn from them will find better ways of doing things. It takes openness and imagination to create an effective organizational learning environment. Leaders are not afraid to make mistakes. Instead, they learn from them. Leaders must remain confident in their own and their subordinates' ability to make learning a lifelong commitment. This attitude will allow growth into new responsibilities and adaptation to inevitable changes.

7-94. Leaders who have the interest of others and the organization in mind will fully support available developmental opportunities, nominate and encourage subordinates for those opportunities, help remove barriers to capitalize on opportunities, and reinforce the new knowledge and skills once they return.

IMPROVING THE ORGANIZATION FOR THE LONG-TERM

7-95. Leaders demonstrate stewardship when they act to improve the organization beyond their own tenure. Improving the organization for the long-term is deciding and taking action to manage people or resources when the benefits will not occur during a leader's tour of duty with an organization.

Table 7-5. Summary of the competency *Stewards the profession*

Leaders take care of the Army profession by applying a mindset that embodies cooperative planning and management of all resources, but especially providing for a strong Army team. Leaders actively engage in sustaining full military readiness and preventing the loss of effectiveness as far into the future as possible.	
Supports professional and personal growth	• Supports developmental opportunities for subordinates such as PME attendance, key developmental assignments in other organizations, and broadening assignments.
Improves the organization	• Makes decisions and takes action to improve the organization beyond their tenure.

Chapter 8
Achieves

GETS RESULTS

8-1. Leadership builds effective organizations. Effectiveness directly relates to the core leader competency of getting results. From the definition of leadership, achieving focuses on accomplishing the mission. Mission accomplishment co-exists with an extended perspective towards maintaining and building the organization's capabilities. Achieving begins in the short-term by setting objectives. In the long-term, achieving requires getting results in pursuit of those objectives. Getting results focuses on structuring what to do to produce consistent results.

8-2. Getting results embraces all actions to get the job done on time and to standard:
- Providing direction, guidance, and clear priorities involves guiding teams in what needs to be done and how.
- Monitoring performance to identify strengths and correct weaknesses in organizations, groups, and individuals allows for accomplishing missions consistently and ethically.

PROVIDING DIRECTION, GUIDANCE, AND PRIORITIES

8-3. As leaders operate in larger organizations, their purpose, direction, guidance, and priorities typically become forward-looking and wider in application. Direct level leaders usually operate with less time for formal planning than organizational and strategic level leaders. Although leaders use different techniques for guidance depending on the amounts of time and staff available, the basics are the same. The leader provides guidance so subordinates and others understand the goals and priorities.

8-4. Leaders match their teams or units to the work required. Standard operating procedures or tasks define most work. As new missions develop and priorities change, assignments will differ. In higher-level positions, commanders and directors have staff to help perform these assignment and prioritization functions. Higher-level organizations have procedures such as running estimates and the military decisionmaking process to define and synchronize planning activities (see ADRP 5-0).

8-5. Leaders should provide guidance from both near-term and long-term perspectives. Effective leaders make thoughtful trade-offs between providing too much or too little guidance. Near-term focus is based on critical actions that must be accomplished immediately. In contrast, by delegating, leaders prepare others to handle missions competently and are available for higher-level coordination.

8-6. When tasks are difficult, adaptive leaders identify and account for the capabilities of the team. Some tasks will be routine and require little clarification, while others will present new challenges for the team. When new tasks are undertaken, leaders are alert to group organization, capabilities, and commitment.

8-7. Leaders should provide frequent feedback as an embedded, natural part of the work. While it is important to have set periods for developmental performance counseling, it is important to provide feedback on a regular basis. Making feedback part of the normal performance of work is a technique leaders use to guide how duties are accomplished.

8-8. Often the most challenging aspect of a leader's job is to identify and clarify conflicts in followers' roles and responsibilities. Good communication techniques with backbriefs are useful for identifying conflicts. Leaders should resolve any role differences that may arise as they occur.

8-9. Good guidance depends on understanding how tasks are progressing, so the leader knows if and when to provide clarification. Most workers have a desire to demonstrate competence in their work, so leaders need to be careful that they do not reduce this drive.

Chapter 8

8-10. A leader's primary responsibility is to help organizations operate effectively. They must accomplish the mission, which begins with a well-conceived plan and thorough preparation. Planning is one of the four steps of the operations process. ADRP 5-0 discusses planning, preparation, execution, and assessment.

ADAPTING TO CHANGES

8-11. Competent and realistic leaders keep in mind that friction and uncertainty affect plans. The leader must be prepared to replace portions of the original plan with new ideas and initiatives. Leaders must have the confidence and resilience to fight through setbacks, staying focused on the mission and the intent two levels up. Leaders preserve freedom of action by adapting to changing situations. They should keep their people mission-focused, motivated, and able to react with agility to changes while influencing the team to accomplish the mission as envisioned in the plan.

8-12. Facing unanticipated obstacles requires adjustments. In increasingly busy times, leaders need to provide an environment in which subordinates can focus and accomplish critical tasks. Minimizing and preventing distractions allows subordinates to focus on mission accomplishment. Leaders must ensure additional taskings are within the capabilities of the organization. If not, the leader needs to seek relief by going to superiors and clarifying the additional workload impact. Experienced leaders anticipate cyclical workloads and schedule accordingly. Competent leaders will make good decisions about when to push or ease back and narrow focus on the one or two most important tasks if performance is in decline.

8-13. Leaders constantly monitor what is happening within the environment. With situational awareness, leaders recognize when the situation has changed or when the plan is not achieving the desired outcomes. If the situation changes significantly, leaders will consider options for proceeding, including the review of contingencies that were developed to address new circumstances. Leaders make on-the-spot adjustments during action to keep moving toward designated goals.

MANAGING RESOURCES

8-14. A main responsibility of leaders—whether officers, NCOs, or Army Civilians—is to accomplish the mission, which includes making the best use of available resources. Some Army leaders specialize in managing single categories of resources, such as ammunition, food, personnel, or finances, but all leaders have an interest in overseeing all categories of resources are provided and used wisely.

8-15. Managing resources consists of multiple steps that require different approaches and even different skills. In many cases, Army leaders need to acquire needed resources for themselves or others. Resources can take the form of money, materiel, personnel, or time. The acquisition process can be a relatively straightforward process of putting in a request through established support channels, contracting for support, or local national purchasing. Other times, a leader may need to be more creative and resourceful. In such cases, the effective use of influence tactics (see chapter 7) may be instrumental in successfully acquiring needed resources.

8-16. After acquiring resources, leaders are responsible for allocating them in a manner that recognizes different needs and priorities. A leader may have multiple requests for limited resources and will need to make decisions about the best distribution. Doing so in a way that recognizes and resolves potential ethical problems requires a firm grounding in the Army Values (see chapter 4). Ultimately, a leader must decide how to best allocate resources in ways to meet the mission. Leaders need to deal openly and honestly with their allocation decisions and be prepared to handle reactions from those who feel the leader handled their requests unfairly or ineffectively.

8-17. Leaders should evaluate if limited resources are used wisely and effectively. Do the resources advance the mission of the Army and the organization? Conversely, were resources squandered or used in ways that did not enhance the effectiveness of the individual, unit, or the Army as a whole? In cases of unwise resource use, a leader should follow this evaluation with appropriate counseling and actions for those accountable for the resources in question.

MONITORING PERFORMANCE

8-18. The ability to assess a situation accurately and reliably against desired outcomes, established values, and ethical standards is a critical tool for leaders to achieve consistent results and mission success. Assessment occurs continually during planning, preparation, and execution; it is not solely an after-the-fact evaluation. Accurate assessment requires instinct and intuition based on experience and learning. It demands a feel for the reliability and validity of information and its sources. Periodic assessment is necessary to determine organizational weaknesses and prevent mishaps. Accurately determining causes is essential to training management, developing subordinate leadership, and initiating quality improvements.

REINFORCING GOOD PERFORMANCE

8-19. To accomplish missions consistently, leaders need to maintain motivation within the team. One of the best ways to do this is to recognize and reward good performance. Leaders who recognize individual and team accomplishments shape positive motivation and actions for the future. Recognizing individuals and teams in front of superiors and others gives those contributors an increased sense of worth. This encourages Soldiers and Army Civilians to sustain and improve performance.

8-20. Leaders should not overlook giving credit to subordinates. Sharing credit has enormous payoffs in terms of building trust and motivation. A leader who understands how individuals feel about team accomplishments will have a better basis for motivating individuals based on their interests.

IMPROVING ORGANIZATIONAL PERFORMANCE

8-21. High performing units are learning organizations that take advantage of opportunities to improve performance. Leaders need to encourage a performance improvement mindset that allows for conformity but goes beyond meeting standards to strive for increased efficiencies and effectiveness. Several actions are characteristic of performance improvement:

- Ask incisive questions about how to perform tasks better.
- Anticipate the need for change and action.
- Analyze activities to determine how to achieve or affect desired end states.
- Identify ways to improve unit or organizational procedures.
- Consider how information and communication technologies can improve effectiveness.
- Model critical and creative thinking and encourage it from others.

8-22. Too often, leaders unknowingly discourage ideas and subordinates are less inclined to present new ideas. Leaders respond to subordinates' ideas with reactions about what is and is not desired. This can be perceived as closed-mindedness and under-appreciation of the subordinate's insight. "We've tried that before." "There's no budget for that." "You've misunderstood my request." "Don't rock the boat." These phrases can kill initiative and discourage others from thinking about changes to improve the organization. Leaders need to encourage a climate of reflection and encourage ideas for improvement. The concept of lifelong learning applies equally to the organization as well as to the individual.

COMPETENCIES APPLIED FOR SUCCESS

8-23. Army leaders pursue excellence whenever possible. They ensure that all members know the important roles they play every day. They look for everyday examples occurring under ordinary circumstances: how a Soldier digs a fighting position, prepares for guard duty, fixes a radio, or lays an artillery battery; or how an Army Civilian improves maintenance procedures, processes critical combat supplies, and supports the families of deploying servicemembers. Army leaders know each of these people contributes to the mission.

8-24. Competent leaders understand that excellence in leadership does not mean perfection. On the contrary, competent leaders allow subordinates room to learn from their mistakes as well as their successes. In an open and positive work climate, people excel to improve and accept risks to learn. It is the best way to improve the force and develop confident leaders. Competent and confident leaders tolerate honest mistakes that do not result from negligence. It involves trying, learning, trying again, and getting better each time. However, the best efforts and intentions do not negate an individual's responsibility for their own actions.

Table 8-1. Summary of the competency *Gets results*

A leader's ultimate purpose is to accomplish organizational results. A leader gets results by providing guidance and managing resources, as well as performing the other leader competencies. *Gets results* focuses on consistent and ethical task accomplishment through supervising, managing, monitoring, and controlling the work.	
Prioritizes, organizes and coordinates taskings for teams or other organizations structures/groups	• Ensures the course of action achieves the desired outcome through planning. • Organizes groups and teams to accomplish work. • Ensures all tasks can be executed in the time available and that tasks depending on other tasks are executed in the correct sequence. • Limits overspecification and micromanagement.
Identifies and accounts for capabilities and commitment to task	• Considers duty positions, capabilities, and developmental needs when assigning tasks. • Conducts initial assessments to assume a new task or a new position.
Designates, clarifies, and deconflicts roles	• Establishes and employs procedures for monitoring, coordinating, and regulating subordinate's actions and activities. • Mediates peer conflicts and disagreements.
Identifies, contends for, allocates and manages resources	• Tracks people and equipment. • Allocates adequate time for task completion. • Allocates time to prepare and conduct rehearsals. • Continually seeks improvement in operating efficiency, resource conservation, and fiscal responsibility. • Attracts, recognizes, and retains talent.
Removes work barriers	• Protects organization from unnecessary taskings and distractions. • Recognizes and resolves scheduling conflicts. • Overcomes obstacles preventing accomplishment of the mission.
Recognizes and rewards good performance	• Recognizes individual and team accomplishments; rewards appropriately. • Credits subordinates for good performance; builds on successes. • Explores reward systems and individual reward motivations.
Seeks, recognizes and takes advantage of opportunities to improve performance	• Asks incisive questions. • Anticipates needs for actions; envisions ways to improve. • Acts to improve the organization's collective performance. • Recommends best methods to accomplish tasks; uses information and technology to improve individual and group effectiveness. • Encourages staff to use creativity to solve problems.
Makes feedback part of work processes	• Gives and seeks accurate and timely feedback. • Uses feedback to modify duties, tasks, procedures, requirements, and goals. • Uses assessment techniques and evaluation tools (such as AARs) to identify lessons learned and facilitate consistent improvement. • Determines the appropriate setting and timing for feedback.
Executes plans to accomplish the mission	• Schedules activities to meet commitments in critical performance areas. • Notifies peers and subordinates in advance of required support. • Keeps track of task assignments and suspenses; attends to details. • Adjusts assignments, if necessary.
Identifies and adjusts to external influences on the mission and organization	• Gathers and analyzes relevant information about changing conditions. • Determines causes, effects, and contributing factors of problems. • Considers contingencies and their consequences. • Makes necessary, on-the-spot adjustments.

Chapter 9
Leadership in Practice

CHALLENGES OF THE OPERATIONAL ENVIRONMENT

9-1. Each day as a leader brings new challenges. Some of these challenges are predictable based on experiences. Some are unpredictable, surfacing because of a situation or place in time in which Soldiers find themselves. Leaders must be prepared to face the effects of stress, fear in combat, external influences from the media, the geopolitical climate, and changing technology.

9-2. Awareness, proper training, and open and frank discussion mitigate some of these factors. Army leaders must consider these external influences and plan accordingly. An effective leader recognizes the tools needed to adapt in changing situations.

EVOLVING THREATS

9-3. Agility and adaptability at all levels of Army organizations are important to address unanticipated situations. The Army must adapt to constantly evolving threats while taking advantage of the latest technological innovations and adjusting to societal changes. The uncertain nature of the threat will always have major impact on Army leadership. ADP 3-0 discusses evolving and hybrid threats.

MEDIA

9-4. Another influence on leadership is the media. The media can be both an asset and impediment. Embedded media can tell the story from the Soldier's perspective to an anxious nation at home. The media can provide real-time information, sometimes unfiltered and raw, which the enemy could exploit as a means to change the international political climate. Leaders must understand the speed and scrutiny of continuous news coverage and that the enemy does not bear the same responsibility for telling the truth.

9-5. The media not only report the situation, but also affect the situation. Leaders must train subordinate leaders and Soldiers to work with the media, understand the effects of pervasive media, and understand the long-term effects of stories and images. Commanders synchronize actions and messages to inform domestic audiences and influence selected foreign audiences (see ADRP 6-0 and FM 3-13).

JOINT AND MULTINATIONAL ENVIRONMENT

9-6. Soldiers find themselves serving with members of other Services and other countries' forces more often. Understanding the unique cultures and subcultures of these various groups can be essential to success in a volatile and changing world.

9-7. Within the Army, leaders should recognize the existence of subcultures such as law enforcement, special operations forces, and medical and branch-specific communities. Consequently, leaders involved in conducting operations need to understand how members of these specialized units train and work. Often, they approach missions from a different perspective and sometimes use unconventional methods to accomplish them. These functional subcultures can be useful as a means to exchange knowledge and provide corporate solutions when the Army needs answers from subject matter experts.

GEOPOLITICAL SITUATION

9-8. Though technology and economic ties interconnect the world, it remains very diverse in terms of religions, cultures, living conditions, education, and health. Within the political sphere, maintaining presence in foreign countries through a careful mix of diplomatic and military arrangements remains an important challenge. Leaders must be aware that the balance between diplomacy and military power is fragile. Army leaders must consistently consider the impact on local civilians, as well as on cultural and religious treasures, before committing forces.

9-9. Leaders can expect to operate in many different environments worldwide. While most Soldiers speak English as their first language, continued deployments and global interaction require an understanding of other languages and cultures. Leaders will need to become multilingual and study the cultures and histories of other regions of interest. Technology provides a vehicle for gaining geopolitical knowledge.

TECHNOLOGY

9-10. While the stresses of combat have been constant for centuries, another aspect of the human dimension has assumed increasing importance—the effect of rapid technological advances on organizations and people. Technological changes and the speed at which they occur force the Army and its leaders to adapt and respond.

9-11. Army leaders must stay abreast of technological advances and their applications, advantages, and requirements. Together with technical specialists, leaders can make technology work for the Soldier. Properly integrated technology can increase operational effectiveness, survivability, and lethality.

9-12. Technological challenges facing Army leaders include—
- Learning the strengths and vulnerabilities of different technologies that support the organization and its mission.
- Thinking through how the organization will operate with other less or more technologically complex organizations, such as operating with unified action partners.
- Considering the effect of technology on the time available to analyze problems, make a decision, and act. Events happen faster today and the stress encountered as an Army leader is correspondingly greater.
- Using technology to influence dispersed teams given the increasing availability and necessity to use reachback and split-based operations.

9-13. Technology can lead to operational issues. A growing reliance on GPS navigation technology since the Desert Storm era decreased emphasis on manual land navigation skills in training, rendering forces vulnerable if the technology fails. Leaders determined how to exploit GPS technology while guarding against its weaknesses through improved training. This included reintroducing essential land navigation training and detailed instructions on the maintenance and operation of GPS equipment.

9-14. Technology changes the leadership environment in many aspects, especially how much information is available for decisionmakers. Although advances allow the modern leader to handle large amounts of information more effectively than before, enhanced technology can still cause information overload. Leaders must be able to sift through provided information then analyze, synthesize, and forward only the important data up the chain of command. Senior leaders rely on subordinates to process information, isolating critical information to expedite decisions. Leaders owe their subordinates information gathering and reporting procedures that streamlines work for already stretched staffs and units.

9-15. Army leaders and staffs have always needed to determine mission-critical information, prioritize incoming reports, and process them quickly. The volume of information provided by current technology makes this ability even more critical. The answer lies in the agile and adaptable human mind. Sometimes a nontechnological approach can divert the flood of technological help into channels the leader and staff can manage. For example, understanding the commander's intent and commander's critical information requirements can free leaders from nonessential information overload. The Army concept of mission command is important in an environment of information overload. Mission command delegates most decisions to lower echelons to free higher echelons for critical decisions only they can make. Army leaders should continue to resist the lure of centralized decisionmaking even though they have more information available to them.

SYSTEMS

9-16. Army leaders require systems understanding and increased technical and tactical knowledge than before. Leaders must understand the fine line between a healthy questioning of new systems' capabilities and an unreasonable hostility that rejects the advantages technology offers. The adaptable leader remains aware of the capabilities and shortcomings of advanced technology and ensures subordinates do as well.

9-17. Leaders must consider systems in their organization—how they work together, how using one affects others, and how to get the best performance from the whole. They must think beyond their own organizations and consider how the actions of their organization influence other organizations and the team as a whole.

9-18. Technology changes battlefield dispersal and the speed of operations. Instant global communications are accelerating the pace of military actions. GPS and night vision capabilities mean the Army can fight at night and during periods of limited visibility—conditions that used to slow things down. Additionally, nonlinear and noncontiguous operations make it more difficult for commanders to determine critical points on the battlefield.

9-19. Modern technology has increased the complexity of skills the Army requires. Leaders must carefully manage low-density occupational specialties and fill critical positions with properly trained people who maintain proficiency in these perishable high-tech skills. Army leaders must balance leadership, personnel management, and training management to ensure their organizations have people with the appropriate specialty training and that the entire organization stays continuously trained, certified, and ready.

HEALTH OF THE COMMAND

9-20. The health threat faced by the deployed force is a combination of ongoing or potential enemy threats; adverse environmental, occupational, and geographic and meteorological conditions; endemic diseases; and employment of chemical, biological, radiological, and nuclear weapons. To counter the health threat, commanders and leaders must ensure that field hygiene and sanitation, preventive medicine measures, inspection of potable water and field feeding facilities, sleep discipline (including work and rest schedules), and personal protective measures are instituted and receive command emphasis. Leaders must ensure Soldiers practice these activities continuously during the force projection and postdeployment process.

9-21. Additionally, concussive injuries are associated with explosions or blasts and blows to the head during training activities or contact sports. Leaders and Soldiers at all echelons must be aware of this invisible injury and receive education and training to help decrease any stigma associated with seeking medical assistance. Leaders have a responsibility to ensure their Soldiers receive a medical evaluation following a concussive event, no matter how mild. Prompt medical attention maximizes recovery, decreases risk of a subsequent concussion while the brain heals, and ultimately preserves combat power.

COMBAT AND OPERATIONAL STRESS

9-22. Stress in response to threatening or uncertain situations occurs in all types of military operations as well as during training exercises, in garrison, and issues related to family and home life. Military experiences expose Soldiers to various combat and operational stresses throughout their careers. Combat and operational stress control does not take away the experiences faced while engaged in such operations, but provides mechanisms to mitigate reactions to those experiences so that Soldiers remain combat effective and maintain the quality of life to which they are entitled.

9-23. Leaders must understand stress and anticipate Soldiers' reactions. It takes mental discipline and resilience to overcome obstacles, Soldiers becoming wounded or dying, and the enemy attacking unexpectedly. Off-site leaders cannot discount the fear Soldiers may experience. A leader who does not share the same risks could easily fall into the trap of making a decision that could prove unworkable given the psychological state of the Soldiers. Army leaders with responsibility over a distributed team should ask for detailed input from the Soldiers or subordinate commanders who are closer to the action and can provide the most accurate information about the situation.

Chapter 9

9-24. When preparing for sustained operations, leaders must thoroughly condition their Soldiers to address combat and operational stress during all phases of force projection—mobilization, deployment, employment, sustainment, and redeployment. Positive action to reduce combat and operational stress helps Soldiers and Army Civilians cope with normal, everyday situations and enhance adaptive stress reactions.

9-25. When possible, Soldiers should have access to combat and operational stress control team/behavioral health personnel, medical personnel and chaplains to continue their physical and psychological recovery to ensure successful reintegration. Experts treating the psychologically wounded must work hand-in-hand with the unit chain of command to stress the importance of maintaining good order and discipline. Leaders must not tolerate aggressive or criminal behavior as compensation for negative operational experiences.

9-26. The Army has implemented a comprehensive recovery plan for all returning Soldiers to counter post-combat and operational stress. Sound leadership, unit cohesion, and close camaraderie are essential to assure expeditious psychological recovery from combat experiences.

OVERCOMING FEAR IN BATTLE

9-27. Leaders need to understand that danger and fear will always be a part of their job. Battling fear means recognizing fear and effectively dealing with it. Understanding the situation and acting with foresight and purpose overcomes fear. Army leaders must expect fear to take hold when setbacks occur, the unit fails to complete a mission, or there are casualties. Fear can paralyze a Soldier. Fear of the unknown can be terrifying. Soldiers who see their friends killed or wounded become aware of their own mortality.

9-28. Good preparation, planning, and rigorous training carry Soldiers through the challenges of operating under hazardous conditions. Realistic training developed around critical tasks and battle drills is a primary source for the resilience and confidence to succeed along with the ability to gut it out when things get tough. Leader competence, confidence, agility, courage, and resilience help units persevere and find workable solutions to tough problems. The Warrior Ethos and resilience mobilize the ability to forge success out of chaos to overcome fear, hunger, deprivation, and fatigue to accomplish the mission.

STRESS IN TRAINING AND OPERATIONS

9-29. Training to high standards, using scenarios that closely resemble the stresses and effects of the actual battlefield, is essential to success and survival in combat. A meaningful and productive mission with detailed constraints and limitations and high standards of performance induces a basic level of stress. Leaders must add unanticipated conditions to training to create a demanding learning environment.

STRESS OF CHANGE

9-30. To succeed in an environment of continuous change, leaders emphasize the constants of the Army Values, teamwork, and discipline while helping their subordinates anticipate change, adapt to change, and seek new ways to improve. Competent leadership implies managing change, adapting, and making change work for the team. Leaders determine what requires change. Often, it is better to build on what already exists to limit stress.

9-31. Stress is a major part of the leadership environment. Major sources of stress include an ever-changing geopolitical situation, combat and operational stress and related fears, the rapid pace of change, and the increasing complexity of technology. A leader's character and professional competence are important factors in mitigating stress for the organization and achieving mission accomplishment, despite environmental pressures and changes. When dealing with these factors, adaptability is essential to success.

TOOLS FOR ADAPTABILITY

9-32. The Army developed the Comprehensive Soldier Fitness Program to provide critical adaptation, resilience, and coping skills to Soldiers, Army Civilians and family members to handle transitions such as deploying to new geographical regions, career changes, and dealing with family and life situations. The program intends to maximize potential through improved performance and readiness.

9-33. Operational adaptability is the ability to shape conditions and respond effectively to changing threats and situations with appropriate, flexible, and timely actions. Leaders exhibit this quality through critical thinking, creative thinking, displaying comfort with ambiguity, willingness to accept prudent risk, and ability to adjust rapidly while continuously assessing the situation. Leaders possess a clear understanding of the commander's intent and apply initiative to defeat enemies, influence foreign populations, and control terrain. Leaders enable operationally adaptive units through flexibility, collaborative planning, and decentralized execution. Mission command fosters initiative and the ability to operate aggressively and independently within the commander's intent.

9-34. Adaptable leaders monitor the environment, derive the key characteristics of the situation, and are aware of what it will take to perform in the changed environment. Leaders must be particularly observant for evidence that the environment has changed in unexpected ways. They recognize that they face highly adaptive enemies and operate within dynamic, ever-changing environments. Sometimes the environment changes suddenly and unexpectedly from a calm, relatively safe operation to a close combat situation. Other times environments differ (from a combat deployment to a humanitarian one) and adaptation is required for mindsets and instincts to change.

9-35. Highly adaptable leaders are comfortable entering unfamiliar environments. They have the proper frame of mind for operating under mission orders in any organization. Successful mission command results from subordinate leaders at all echelons exercising disciplined initiative within the higher commander's intent. Adaptable leaders can quickly assess the situation and determine the skills needed to address it. If the skills they learned in the past are not sufficient for success in the new environment, adaptable leaders seek to apply new or modified skills and applicable competencies.

9-36. Adaptive leadership includes being an agent of change. This means helping other members of the organization, especially key leaders, recognize that an environment is changing and build consensus as change occurs. As consensus builds, adaptive leaders can influence the course of the organization. Depending on the immediacy of the problem, adaptive leaders may use several different methods for influencing their organization. These can range from crisis action meetings (when time is very short) to publishing white papers that convey the need for change (when more time is available).

9-37. Leaders lacking adaptability enter every situation in the same manner and often expect their experience in one job to carry them to the next. Consequently, they may use ill-fitting or outdated strategies. Failure to adapt may result in poor performance in the new environment or outright organizational failure. Determining when and how to adapt is important. Adaptation does not produce certainty that change will improve results. Sometimes, persistence on a given course of action may have merit over change.

9-38. Adaptable leaders are comfortable with ambiguity. They are flexible and innovative—ready to face the challenges at hand with the resources available. The adaptable leader is most likely a passionate learner, able to handle multiple demands, shifting priorities, and rapid change smoothly. Adaptable leaders see each change thrust upon them as an opportunity rather than a liability.

9-39. Adaptability has two key components:
- The ability to identify the essential elements critical for performance in each new situation.
- The ability to change practices or the unit by quickly capitalizing on strengths and minimizing weaknesses.

9-40. Like self-awareness, adaptability takes effort. To become adaptable, leaders must challenge previously held ideas and assumptions by seeking out novel and unfamiliar situations. Leaders who remain safely inside their comfort zone provided by their current level of education, training, and experience will never learn to recognize change or understand inevitable changes in their environment. Adaptability is encouraged by a collection of thought habits. These include open-mindedness, ability to consider multiple perspectives, not jumping to conclusions about what a situation is or what it means, willingness to take risks, and being resilient to setbacks. To become more adaptable, leaders should:

- Embrace opportunities to adapt. Leaders must go beyond what they are comfortable with and experience the unfamiliar through diverse and dynamic challenges. For example, the Army's best training uses thinking like an enemy (red teaming) to help leaders recognize and accept that no plan survives contact. This encourages adaptive thinking. Adaptive training involves variety, particularly in training that may have become routine.
- Lead across cultures. Leaders must actively seek out diverse relationships and situations to gain insight into people who think and act differently than most Soldiers or average United States citizens. Leaders can grow their capacity for adaptability by seizing such opportunities.
- Seek challenges. Leaders must seek out and engage in assignments that involve major changes in the operational environment. Leaders can be specialists, but their base of experience should still be broad. As the breadth of experience accumulates, so does the capacity to adapt. Leaders exposed to change and new challenges will learn the value of adaptation. They carry forward the skills to develop adaptable Soldiers, Army Civilians, units, and organizations.

9-41. While adaptability is an important tool, leaders at all levels must use their cognitive abilities to counteract the challenges of the operational environment through logical problem solving processes such as the military decisionmaking process and the Army Design Methodology. Concepts of the Army Design Methodology underpin the leader's role in promoting innovative, adaptive work and guiding planning, preparation, execution and assessment in operations. It requires agile, versatile leaders who foster continuous organizational learning while engaging in iterative collaboration and dialogue to enhance decisionmaking (see ADRP 5-0).

PART FOUR

Leading at Organizational and Strategic Levels

Part Four builds upon the leadership foundations, attributes, and competencies covered in earlier sections.

Army leaders consistently prepare themselves for greater responsibilities while mastering core leader competencies. By the time they become organizational and strategic leaders, they should be multiskilled leaders who can comfortably operate at all levels of leadership inside or outside the Army and apply their vast experiences and knowledge for success across the spectrum of operations. They oversee continuous transformation of the Army and respond to evolving operational environments. They mentor and develop the leadership of the future force.

Chapter 10

Organizational Leadership

LEADING

10-1. Whether they fight for key terrain or work to achieve readiness in training, organizational leaders must be able to translate complex concepts into understandable operational and tactical plans and decisive action. Organizational leaders develop the programs and plans and synchronize the appropriate systems allowing Soldiers in units to turn tactical and operational models into action.

10-2. Through leadership by example, a wide range of knowledge, and the application of leader competencies, organizational leaders build teams of teams with discipline, cohesion, trust, and proficiency. They focus their organizations down to the lowest level on the mission by disseminating a clear intent, sound operational concepts, and a systematic approach to execution.

10-3. Successful organizational leaders build on direct leader experiences, reflect the Army Values, and instill pride within organizations. Since they lead complex organizations throughout the operational Army and generating force, organizational leaders often apply elements of direct, organizational, and strategic leadership simultaneously. Modern organizational level leaders must carefully extend their influence beyond the chain of command by balancing their role as Soldier with being a diplomat in uniform.

LEADS OTHERS

10-4. Modern organizational leaders have developed a strong background in fundamentals as well as an appreciation for the geopolitical consequences of their application. From their experiences, they have grown the instincts, intuition, and knowledge that form the understanding of the interrelation of tactical and operational processes. Their refined tactical skills allow them to understand, integrate, and synchronize the activities of multiple systems, employing resources and systems across the range of military operations.

10-5. Given the increased size of their organizations, organizational leaders influence indirectly more often than directly. They rely heavily on developing subordinates and empowering them to execute missions and responsibilities. When appropriate, they use concepts of the Army Design Methodology to understand and visualize the effect on the organization and mission when making decisions. Soldiers and subordinate leaders, in turn, look to their organizational leaders to set achievable standards, to provide clear intent, and to provide the necessary resources.

10-6. Decisions and actions by organizational leaders have greater consequences for more people over a longer time than those of direct leaders. Since the connections between action and effect are sometimes more remote and difficult to see, organizational leaders spend more time than direct leaders coordinating, thinking, and reflecting about what they are doing and how they are doing it. Organizational leaders develop clear concepts for operations as well as policies and procedures to control and monitor execution.

EXTENDS INFLUENCE BEYOND THE CHAIN OF COMMAND

10-7. While organizational leaders primarily exert direct influence through their chain of command and staff, they extend influence beyond their chain of command and organization by other means. These include persuasion, empowerment, motivation, negotiation, conflict resolution, bargaining, advocacy, and diplomacy. They often apply various skills when serving as military negotiators, consensus builders, and operational diplomats. Chiefs of special directorates within and outside the Army also need these skills. As leaders, they affect the operational situation in their area of operations by extending influence through local leaders such as police chiefs, mayors, and tribal elders. Experiences show that the organizational leader, when effectively balancing the functions of combat leader and military diplomat, can set the stage for military, political, and social stability in assigned areas.

Leveraging Capabilities of Unified Action Partners

10-8. Organizational leaders and their staffs must understand joint doctrine as well as Army fundamentals and procedures. Additionally, corps or divisions may control forces of other nations. Therefore they, and even brigades and below, may have liaison officers from other nations. In some cases, United States staffs may have members of other nations permanently assigned, creating a multinational staff. Often, brigades have interagency representation embedded in their staffs or operating in their areas. Leaders impart influence by the way they conduct themselves—setting an impression of themselves, the Army, and the nation it serves.

10-9. Today's operations present Army leaders, particularly organizational leaders, with a nonlinear, dynamic environment. These varied conditions create an information-intense environment, challenging leaders to synchronize efforts beyond the traditional military chain. Today's mission complexities demand the full integration and cooperation of unified action partners to accomplish missions.

Negotiating, Building Consensus and Resolving Conflicts

10-10. Leaders often must use negotiation skills to obtain the cooperation and support necessary to accomplish a mission beyond the traditional chain of command. During complex operations, different unified action partners might operate under constraints of their national or organizational chains. This can result in important negotiations and conflict resolution versus a simpler process of issuing binding orders.

10-11. Successful negotiation, employing a joint problem-solving approach, involves building effective relationships, establishing two-way communication, understanding positions to clarify interests, creating possible solutions, using fair standards, and creating a good choice from firm, clear commitments and realistic alternatives. Good negotiators test their assumptions, measure success appropriately for the given situation, systematically prepare, make deliberate process-oriented decisions in conducting negotiations, and thoroughly review interactions.

10-12. The art of persuasion is an important method of extending influence. Working through controversy in a positive and open way helps overcome resistance to an idea or plan and build support. Proactively involving partners frees communications with them and places value on their opinions. Openness to discussing one's perceptions and a positive attitude toward a dissenting view often diffuses conflict, increases mutual trust, and saves time.

Leads by Example

10-13. Army operations have shown that organizations must be capable of adapting to rapidly changing situations. It is often the ability to make quality decisions quickly and execute them within the enemy's decision cycle that determines who succeeds in a sudden engagement.

10-14. The Army's organizational leaders play a critical part when it comes to maintaining focus on fighting the enemy and not the plan. They are at the forefront of adapting to changes in the operational environment and exploiting emerging opportunities by applying a combination of intuition, analytical problem solving, systems integration, and leadership by example—as close to the action as feasible.

10-15. Organizational leaders position themselves with the necessary means to maintain contact with critical elements and headquarters. Proximity to operations provides organizational commanders with the required awareness to apply quick creative thinking in collaboration with subordinate leaders. It facilitates adjustments for deficiencies in planning and shortens reaction time when applying sound tactical and operational solutions to changing realities. Operations require leaders who understand the context of the factors affecting the situation, act within that understanding, continually assess and adapt those actions based on the interactions and circumstances of the enemy and environment, consolidate tactical and operational opportunities into strategic aims and be able to effectively transition operations.

Communicates

Ensuring Shared Understanding

10-16. Organizational leaders know themselves, the mission, and the message. They owe it to their organization and subordinates to share as much information as possible. Teams appreciate an open, two-way exchange of information that reinforces sharing team values and signals constructive input.

10-17. Communicating openly and clearly with superiors is important for organizational leaders. Understanding the intent, priorities, and thought processes makes it easier to anticipate future planning and resource priorities. Understanding the direction of the higher headquarters reduces course corrections at the lower levels, thus minimizing friction and maintaining a stable organizational tempo and climate.

Using the Staff as a Communications Tool

10-18. Organizational leaders need to understand what is happening within their organization, developing laterally, and unfolding within the next two higher echelons. Networking between staffs gives organizational leaders a broader picture of the overall operational environment. Coordination allows leaders to constantly interact and share thoughts, ideas, and priorities through multiple channels, creating a more complete picture. With reliable information, staffs can productively turn policies, concepts, plans, and programs into achievable results and quality products.

10-19. By interacting with the next-higher staff, organizational leaders understand the superior's priorities and impending shifts. This helps set the conditions for their own requirements and changes. Constantly sensing, observing, talking, questioning, and actively listening helps organizational leaders better identify and solve potential problems or to avoid them. It allows them to anticipate decisions and put their organization in the best possible position in time and space to appropriately respond and execute.

Using Persuasion to Build Teams and Consensus

10-20. Persuasion is an important method of communication for organizational leaders. Well-developed skills of persuasion and openness to working through controversy positively help organizational leaders overcome resistance and build support. These characteristics are important in dealing with other organizational leaders, multinational partners, and in the socio-political arena. By reducing grounds for misunderstanding, persuasion reduces wasted time in overcoming unimportant issues. It ensures involvement of others, opens communication with them, and places value on their opinions—all critical team-building actions. Openness to discussing one's position and a positive attitude toward a dissenting view often defuses tension and saves time. By demonstrating these traits, organizational leaders provide an example that subordinates can use in self-development. In some circumstances, persuasion may be inappropriate. During operations, leaders must often make decisions quickly, requiring a more direct style when leading and deciding on courses of action.

DEVELOPING

10-21. Comparatively, organizational leaders take a long-term approach to developing the entire organization. They prepare their organizations for the next quarter, next year, or even five years from now. The responsibility to determine how the Army fights the next war lies with today's Army leaders, especially those at the organizational and strategic levels. Leaders at the organizational level rely more on indirect leadership methods, which can make leading, developing, and achieving more difficult.

CREATES A POSITIVE ENVIRONMENT

10-22. An organization's climate springs from its leader's attitudes, actions, and priorities engrained through choices, policies, and programs. Leaders in organizational leadership positions determine the organizational climate by assessing the organization from the bottom up. With a completed assessment, the leader can provide clear guidance and focus (purpose, direction, and motivation) to move the organization towards the desired end state.

10-23. A climate that promotes the Army Values and fosters the Warrior Ethos encourages learning, promotes creativity and performance, and establishes cohesion. The foundation for a positive environment is a healthy ethical climate, although that alone is insufficient. Characteristics of successful organizational climates include a clear, widely known purpose; well-trained and confident Soldiers; disciplined, cohesive teams; and trusted, competent leaders.

10-24. To create such a climate, organizational leaders recognize mistakes as opportunities to learn, create cohesive teams, and reward leaders of character and competence with increasing responsibilities. Organizational leaders value honest feedback and constantly use available means to maintain a feel for the organization. Special staff members who may be good sources for quality feedback include equal opportunity advisors, chaplains, medical officers, and legal advisors. Feedback methods may include town hall meetings, councils, social media, or surveys. An organizational leader can initiate command climate surveys or a Multi-source Assessment and Feedback event (see AR 350-1) to collect climate input while protecting the anonymity of individuals. The organizational-level leader ensures company commanders meet requirements for initial and annual climate surveys (see AR 600-20). These leaders should assess subordinate command climate results and supplemental indicators such as instances of misconduct.

10-25. Organizational-level leaders are stewards of the Army profession. They fulfill this function by placing a high priority upon investment in future leaders at all levels. Leader development is an investment required to maintain the Army as a profession and is a key source of combat power. The organizational leader sets conditions for a robust leader development system for a professional Army that supports national security objectives. Establishing priorities for adequate investments in Soldier and leader development remains a vexing challenge facing the Army and its leaders.

PREPARES SELF

10-26. Leadership begins at the top and so does developing. Organizational leaders keep a focus on where the organization needs to go and what leaders must be capable of accomplishing. As role models, they develop themselves and actively counsel their subordinate leaders in professional growth. Organizational leaders continue to seek broadening experiences to expand their knowledge, skills, and capabilities and encourage subordinates to seek additional broadening opportunities. At the organizational level, leaders ensure that systems and conditions are in place for objective feedback, counseling, and mentoring for all the organization's members.

10-27. Self-aware organizational leaders who know their organizations generally achieve high quality results. Confident and competent organizational leaders do not shy away from asking close subordinates to give them informal feedback. It is part of an open assessment and feedback effort. When they are part of official AARs, organizational leaders should invite subordinates to comment on how the leaders could have made things better. Errors by organizational leaders are spotted easily and often affect those they lead.

Consequently, admitting, analyzing, and learning from these errors add value to the training. For the Army's organizational leaders—just as leaders at other levels—reflecting, learning, and applying corrective actions in operations is critical for effectiveness.

10-28. While leader competencies stay the same across levels, moving from direct to the organizational level requires a shift in approach. The Army designs the Professional Military Education system and Civilian Education System to facilitate the transition in the scope and breadth of responsibilities. Leaders need to accustom themselves to rely on less direct means of direction, control, and monitoring.

10-29. The demands on leaders vary at different levels. What may occupy a great deal of a leader's time at a lower level (for example, face-to-face supervision of Soldiers) may involve less time at higher levels. Certain technical skills vital to a direct leader may be of little importance to a strategic leader who must spend time on strategic, system-wide issues. Therefore, leaders emphasize some skills less as the focus of leadership changes.

DEVELOPS OTHERS

10-30. An important organizational leader responsibility is to create an environment that enables and supports organization members to learn from their experiences and those of others. Operational leaders know they bear responsibility for training the leadership of tomorrow's Army—clearly an act of stewardship. They rely on an environment that uses learning as well as self-development through various procedures such as multisource assessment and feedback. To strengthen learning, organizational leaders can make numerous avenues available for lifelong learning: assignment-oriented training, simulations, learning centers, and virtual training.

10-31. Effective organizational leaders develop leaders at all levels within the organization. Organizational leaders determine the potential of others. This takes awareness of others and flexibility to build on strengths and address weaknesses. Developing others at this level is challenging; the organizational leader has to balance the criticality of the job and who would do the best job with the developmental needs of all subordinates.

10-32. Another consideration for organizational leaders is how and what individuals need to learn. Learning by making mistakes may be acceptable for some leaders, but others need to experience more successes than failures to develop self-confidence and initiative. Commanders lead, coach, and mentor subordinate leaders.

Building Team Skills and Processes

10-33. Organizational leaders recognize that the Army is a team of teams. As such, it is comprised of numerous functional organizations. These organizations perform necessary tasks and missions that in unison produce the effort of all Army components. Strategic leaders influence organizational leaders. Organizational leaders, in turn, influence subordinate leaders to achieve organizational goals.

10-34. Generally, organizational leaders rely on others to follow and execute their intent and guidance as well as to communicate effectively that intent and guidance to their subordinates. Turning a battlefield vision or training goal into reality takes the combined efforts of many teams inside and outside of the organization. Organizational leaders build solid, effective teams by developing and training them.

10-35. The Army transformed from a division-based force to a modular brigade-based force. This allowed for a modular force task-organized to the needs of the mission while creating options to use forces less than full divisions. However, this modular construct creates a challenge for commanders trying to build trust and confidence within subordinate organizations. These organizations are task-organized to meet mission requirements and often not habitually associated with a higher headquarters. Often they have not trained with the higher headquarters that employs them. Collaboration and dialogue with subordinate organizations create the shared understanding required for successful operations. Commanders gain insight into the needs of subordinate leaders while sharing their own clear vision and commander's intent.

10-36. By circulating among subordinate units, commanders can assess subordinates' understanding of intent, their preparation, and execution, and can compel successful mission command. Commanders get to know new units in the task organization and personally motivate Soldiers by their presence. Commanders work with subordinate units to create shared understanding in each critical situation. Together they identify the options of greatest value and manage high-risk actions. Commanders act with other leaders across the chain of command to create the context for fostering organizational and team capabilities.

10-37. Well-trained subordinates who work hard and fight tenaciously sense they are part of a first-rate team. Collective confidence comes from succeeding under challenging and stressful conditions. Sense of belonging derives from experiencing technical and tactical proficiency—first as individuals and later collectively. That proficiency expresses itself in the confidence team members have in their peers and their leaders and the trust all have in each other. Ultimately, cohesive teams combine into a network—a team of teams. Effective organizations work in synchronized fashion to complete tasks and missions.

Encouraging Initiative and Acceptance of Responsibility

10-38. Since missions for larger organizations are more complex and involve concurrent efforts, leaders at higher levels must encourage subordinate initiative. Effective organizational leaders must delegate authority and support their subordinates' decisions while holding them accountable for their actions.

10-39. Successful delegation of authority involves convincing subordinates that they are empowered and have the freedom to act independently. Empowered subordinates understand that they bear more than the responsibility to get the job done. They have the authority to operate as they see fit, within the limits of the commander's intent, missions, task organization, and available resources. This helps them lead their people with determination.

10-40. Since delegation is a critical factor for success at the organizational level of leadership, leaders must know the character of their subordinates. Organizational leaders must know the resident talent within the organization and prepare subordinates to assume critical roles when necessary. To empower the diverse elements within a larger organization, organizational leaders must exploit the value of a creative staff composed of competent and trustworthy subordinates.

Choosing Talented Staff Leaders

10-41. A high-performing staff begins with putting the right people in the right positions. Organizational leaders make time to evaluate the staff and develop them to full capability with focused training. They avoid micromanaging the staff while trusting and empowering them to think creatively and provide truthful answers and feasible options.

10-42. One of the most important decisions for a commander is to select the right chief of staff or deputy. By definition, the chief of staff or deputy is the principal assistant for directing, coordinating, supervising, and training the staff except in areas the commander reserves. This leader has the respect of the team and can take charge of the staff, focus it, inspire it, and move it to achieve results in the absence of a commander. Although staff sections work as equals, it requires good chief of staff leadership to make them function as a cohesive team.

10-43. Inquisitive leaders who conduct regular assessments of themselves and their organizations hold their organizations to the highest standards. Open-minded reflection and corrective action in training is critical for effective performance in crisis. The continuous assessment process helps organizational leaders to translate critical training lessons into decisive operations.

ACHIEVING

10-44. To get consistent results, organizational leaders have to be competent in planning, preparing, executing, and assessing. They must provide clear focus with their intent so subordinates accomplish the mission, regardless of the original plan.

PROVIDING DIRECTION, GUIDANCE, AND CLEAR PRIORITIES IN A TIMELY MANNER

10-45. Organizational leaders are more likely than direct leaders to provide guidance and make decisions with incomplete information. Part of the organizational leaders' analysis must determine which decisions to make themselves or push to lower levels. While determining the right course of action, they consider possible second- and third-order effects and project into the future—months or even years. Organizational leaders must consider the timing of their decisions. In many cases, organizational leaders may have to exercise patience and not make immediate decisions.

ACCOMPLISHING MISSIONS CONSISTENTLY

10-46. During operations, organizational leaders integrate and synchronize available resources. They assign missions and empower their subordinates to execute within the given intent. The core strength for successfully executing the larger operational requirement centers on the leader's vision and the team's confidence and professionalism.

10-47. While a single leader in isolation can make good decisions, the organizational leader needs a creative staff to make quality decisions in an environment where operations dominate a 24/7 cycle. In the complex operational environments faced today, organizational leaders must be able to rely on a creative and trustworthy staff to help acquire and filter huge amounts of information, monitor vital resources, synchronize systems, and assess operational progress and success.

10-48. Today's organizational leaders process a tremendous amount of information. Analysis and synthesis are essential to effective decisionmaking and program development. Analysis breaks a problem into its component parts. Synthesis assembles complex and disorganized data into a solution.

10-49. Good information management filters relevant information to enable organizational leaders and staffs to exercise effective mission command. Information management uses procedures and information systems to collect, process, store, display, and disseminate information.

10-50. Organizational leaders analyze systems and results to improve the organization and its processes. Performance indicators and standards for systems enable analysis. Once organizational leaders complete an assessment and identify problems, they can develop appropriate solutions to address the problems.

MASTERING RESOURCES AND SYSTEMS

10-51. Organizational leaders must be masters of resourcing. Resources—including time, equipment, facilities, budgets, and people—are required to achieve organizational goals. Organizational leaders aggressively manage and prioritize the resources at their disposal to ensure optimal readiness of the organization. A leader's job is more difficult when unanticipated events shift priorities.

10-52. Organizational leaders are stewards of their people's time and energy, as well as their own. They do not waste resources but skillfully evaluate objectives, anticipate resource requirements, and efficiently allocate what is available. They balance available resources with organizational requirements and distribute them in a way that best achieves organizational goals.

10-53. For example, in the early phases of an operation, airfields and supply routes may be austere or nonexistent. Innovative logisticians coordinate available airlift, time-phasing cargo destined for forward operating bases. What takes priority: ammunition, food, water, fuel, personnel replacements, or mail? A good organizational leader will base prioritization decisions on multiple information sources: Soldiers' assessments, input from supporting units, personal situation assessments, and the commander's intent.

10-54. Because of the more indirect nature of their influence, organizational leaders continuously assess interrelated systems and design longer-term plans to accomplish missions. They must sharpen their abilities to assess and balance their environments, organization, and people. Organizational leaders determine the cause and effect of shortcomings and translate these new understandings into workable plans and programs. They then allow subordinate leaders latitude to execute and get the job done.

10-55. Leaders who reach the organizational level should have a comprehensive systems perspective. This allows them to balance doctrine, organization, training, materiel, leadership and education, personnel, and facilities. Together with the Army Values and the Warrior Ethos, these systems provide the framework for influencing people and organizations at all levels. They are the foundation for conducting a wide variety of operations and continually improving the organization and the force.

Understanding and Synchronizing Systems for Combat Power

10-56. Leaders apply a systems perspective to shape and employ their organizations. The ability to understand and effectively employ systems is critical to achieving organizational goals, objectives, and tasks. Organizational leadership, combined with effective information and systems management, can effectively generate combat power.

10-57. Organizational leaders must be masters of tactical and operational synchronization. They must arrange activities in time, space, and purpose to mass maximum relative combat power or organizational effort at a decisive point and time. Combat power consists of the six warfighting functions (mission command, movement and maneuver, intelligence, fires, sustainment and protection), information, and leadership. Commanders and leaders apply leadership across, and multiply the effects of, the six elements of combat power. Through synchronization, organizational leaders focus warfighting functions to mass the effects of combat power at the chosen place and time to overwhelm an enemy or to dominate a situation.

10-58. Organizational leaders further synchronize by applying the complementary and reinforcing effects of joint military and nonmilitary assets to overwhelm opponents at one or more decisive points. Effective synchronization requires leaders to pull together technical, interpersonal, and conceptual abilities and apply them to warfighting goals, objectives, and tasks.

Assessing to Ensure Mission Success and Organizational Improvement

10-59. Assessing situations reliably—and looking at the state of the organizations and their component elements—is critical for organizational leaders to achieve consistent results and mission success. Accurate assessment requires their instincts and intuitions based on the reliability of information and their sources. Quality organizational assessment can determine weaknesses and force focused improvements.

10-60. In addition to designing effective assessment systems, organizational leaders set achievable and measurable assessment standards. To get it right, organizational leaders ask—
- What is the standard?
- Does the standard make sense to all concerned?
- Did we meet it?
- What system measures it?
- Who is responsible for the system?
- How do we reinforce or correct our findings?

10-61. Because their decisions can have wide-ranging effects, leaders must be sensitive to how their actions affect the organization's climate. The ability to discern and predict second- and third-order effects helps organizational leaders assess the health of the organizational climate and provide constructive feedback to subordinates.

10-62. Attempting to predict second- and third-order effects may result in identifying resource requirements and changes to organizations and procedures. For instance, when the Army Chief of Staff approves a new military occupational specialty code for the Army, the consequences are wide-ranging. Second-order effects may mean specialized schooling, a revised promotion system for different career patterns, and requirements for more doctrinal and training material to support new specialties. Third-order effects may include resource needs for training material and additional instructor positions at the appropriate training centers and schools. Leaders are responsible for anticipating the consequences of any action. Thorough planning and staff analysis can help, but anticipation requires imagination, vision, and an appreciation of other people, talents, and organizations.

Chapter 11
Strategic Leadership

OVERVIEW OF STRATEGIC LEADERSHIP

11-1. This chapter covers strategic leadership and puts the role of the strategic leader in perspective for those who support strategic leaders. Strategic leadership is the process used to affect the achievement of a desirable and clearly understood vision by influencing the organizational culture, allocating resources, directing through policy and directive, and building consensus.

11-2. Strategic leaders serve inside or outside the Army and must thoroughly understand political-military relationships. Army strategic leaders have responsibilities that extend beyond the Army to the national government, its leaders, and ultimately, to the American people. Those serving in strategic leadership positions may lead complex organizations comprised of members of the Army, other United States armed services and those of other nations, members of federal agencies, and non-governmental entities. Strategic leaders, regardless of their position, apply professional expertise and remain true to the Army Values and Warrior Ethos. This is the basis for their legitimacy and contributes to leader effectiveness.

11-3. When taking the oath of office, leaders swear to uphold the Constitution. This oath subordinates the military leader to the laws of the nation and its elected and appointed leaders, creating a distinct civil-military relationship. A critical element of this relationship is the trust that civilian leaders have in their military leaders to represent the military and provide professional military advice. To be effective, this relationship requires candor and authority to execute the decisions of the civilian leaders. These decisions provide the strategic direction and framework in which strategic military leaders operate. Strategic leaders need to understand organizational, national, and world politics. They operate in intricate networks of overlapping and sometimes competing constituencies.

11-4. To maintain focus, strategic leaders survey the environment to understand the context for their roles. Strategic leaders must think in multiple timelines to anticipate change and be agile and adaptive to manage resultant changes. In addition to accepting harsher consequences for their actions, strategic leaders extend influence in an environment where they interact with other high-level leaders and influential figures over whom they have minimal formal authority or no authority at all.

11-5. Strategic leaders represent a finely balanced combination of high-level thinkers, accomplished warfighters, and geopolitical military experts. Strategic leaders simultaneously sustain what is necessary in the current environment, envision the future, and convey that vision to a wide audience. They often personally spearhead change. America's complex national security environment requires an in-depth knowledge of the diplomatic, informational, military, and economic instruments of national power. Strategic leaders understand the interrelationships among these instruments and use them to achieve strategic ends.

11-6. Strategic leaders are keenly aware of the complexities of the national and international security environment. Their actions affect acquisitions, budget constraints, Reserve issues, civilian programs, research, contracting, congressional hearings, and inter-service cooperation. Strategic leaders process information from these areas while assessing alternatives. They formulate practical decisions and garner support. Highly developed interpersonal abilities and intergroup relations are essential to building consensus with civilian and military policy makers on national and international levels.

11-7. Strategic leaders operate with the same general attributes and competencies as direct and organizational leaders. The situations and environments create differences in how attributes and competencies apply. In general, strategic leaders accommodate—
- Greater complexity under high uncertainty.
- Broader scope with longer time spans.

- Greater risks and stakes.
- Higher level interests, goals, and priorities at the national level.

11-8. While direct and organizational leaders have a more near- and mid-term focus, strategic leaders must concentrate on the future. They spend much of their time looking toward long-term goals and positioning for long-term success even as they contend with mid-term and immediate issues.

11-9. To create powerful organizations and institutions capable of adapting, strategic leaders and their staffs develop networks of knowledgeable individuals who can positively shape their own organizations. Through continuous assessments, strategic leaders seek to understand the personal strengths and weaknesses of the main players on a particular issue. Strategic leaders adeptly read other people while disciplining their own actions and reactions. Strategic leaders influence external events by providing quality leadership, timely and relevant information, and access to the right people and agencies.

LEADING

11-10. When leading at the highest levels of the Army, the DOD, and the national security establishment, Army strategic leaders spearhead changes and, at the same time, must balance risks. They balance current operational risks against future institutional or operational risks. To mitigate future institutional risks, these leaders are responsible for providing leadership to the men and women who serve in their organizations and developing their successors to meet the challenges of the future.

LEADS OTHERS

11-11. Strategic leaders influence both the organization and the external environment. Like direct and organizational leaders, strategic leaders lead by example and exert indirect leadership by communicating, inspiring, and motivating. Strategic leaders make decisions for the right balance of delegation, empowerment, and control. Empowerment enables strategic leaders to accomplish all that needs to occur. They work with others to create a shared understanding of history, current state, and goals for the organization. A truly effective strategic leader understands the organization at multiple levels, transcending from an inside perspective to how outsiders see it. Strategic leaders transcend experiential biases. Envisioning is a key function of strategic leaders. Leaders determine a vision by applying judgment to the environment. In visioning as well as execution, strategic leaders have to apply thoughtful analysis.

11-12. Strategic leaders develop the wisdom and reference framework to identify information relevant to the situation. They use their interpersonal abilities to develop a network of knowledgeable people in those organizations. They encourage staff members to develop similar networks. Through these formal and informal networks, strategic leaders actively seek information relevant to their organizations as well as subject matter experts who can help. Using their networks, strategic leaders can call on the nation's best minds and information sources because they may face situations where nothing less will suffice.

Providing Vision, Motivation, and Inspiration

11-13. When providing vision, direction, giving guidance, and setting priorities, strategic leaders must judge realistically what the future may hold. They incorporate new ideas, new technologies, and new capabilities. From a mixture of ideas, facts, conjecture, and personal experience, they create an image of what their organizations need to be and where it must go to get desired results.

11-14. Strategic leaders seek to keep their vision consistent with the external environment, alliance goals, and national strategy. The strategic leader's vision provides the ultimate sense of purpose, direction, and motivation. It is the starting point for developing goals and plans, a yardstick for measuring accomplishment, and a check on organizational values. A strategic leader's vision for the organization may have a time horizon of years or even decades.

11-15. The ability to provide clear vision is vital to the strategic leader, but forming a vision is pointless until the leader shares it with a broad audience, gains widespread support, and uses it as a compass to guide the organization. For the vision to provide purpose, direction, and motivation, the strategic leader must personally commit to it, gain commitment from the organization as a whole, and persistently pursue the goals and objectives that will spread the vision throughout the organization.

11-16. Strategic leaders identify trends, opportunities, and threats that could affect the Army's future and move vigorously to mobilize the talent that will help create strategic vision. Strategic leaders are open to ideas from many sources, not just their own organizations. The Army's values-based culture affirms the importance of high standards, leader development, and lifelong learning initiatives.

EXTENDS INFLUENCE

11-17. Whether by nuance or overt presentation, strategic leaders represent the Army and influence other organizations and agencies by communicating what the Army is doing and where it is going. Their audience is the Army itself, the nation, and the rest of the world. Strategic leaders must be proactive in creating relationships. Extending influence requires a shift from direct leadership influence to greater reliance on indirect methods. Often the influence focuses on increasing engagement with multiple parties or organizations and creating the conditions to maximize unity of effort. Strategic leaders convey ideas to the American people who can then make informed decisions about how to support their military with the essential resources of money and people. Strategic leaders rely on writing and public speaking to reinforce their central messages.

11-18. Strategic leaders use focused messages to extend influence and to gain public support during crisis. An example of extending influence beyond the Army's sphere was Operation Desert Shield. During the deployment phase, strategic leaders decided to invite local reporters to the theater of operations to focus reporting on mobilized reserve component units from local communities. The reporting focus had several positive effects. It conveyed the Army's deployment story to the citizens of hometown America, which resulted in a flood of mail from countless citizens to their deployed Soldiers. The most significant effect was soon felt by all Soldiers—a renewed pride in themselves and the Army.

Negotiating Within and Beyond National Boundaries

11-19. Strategic leaders must often rely on negotiation skills to obtain the cooperation and support necessary to accomplish a mission. The North Atlantic Treaty Organization (NATO) provides many good examples. When NATO sent national contingents as part of the implementation force to Bosnia in response to the Dayton Peace Accords of 1995, all contingents had national operational limitations imposed on them. All contingent commanders maintained direct lines to their national governments to clarify situations immediately that may have exceeded those limits. Based on these political and cultural boundaries, NATO strategic leaders had to negotiate plans and actions that ordinarily would have required issuing simple orders. In the spirit of cooperation, commanders had to interpret all requirements to the satisfaction of one or more foreign governments.

11-20. Recent experiences have shown that successful negotiating requires a wide range of interpersonal skills. To resolve conflicting views, strategic leaders visualize several possible end states while maintaining a clear idea of the best end state from the national command's perspective. Strategic leaders must use tact to justify standing firm on nonnegotiable points while still communicating respect for other participants.

11-21. A successful negotiator must be particularly skilled in active listening. Other essential personal characteristics include good judgment and mental agility. Successful negotiating involves communicating a clear position on the issues while conveying a willingness to bargain on negotiable portions. Negotiators must be able to diagnose unspoken agendas and detach themselves from the negotiation process. This requires recognizing what is acceptable to all concerned parties and working towards a common goal.

11-22. To reach acceptable consensus, strategic leaders often circulate proposals early so that further negotiations can focus on critical issues and solutions. Strategic leaders' commitment to selfless service enables them to subordinate the need for personal recognition for good ideas to finding positive solutions that produce the greatest good for their organization, the Army, and the nation.

Building Strategic Consensus

11-23. Outside Army boundaries, strategic leaders have a role as integrator, alliance builder, negotiator, and arbitrator. Strategic leaders are skilled at reaching consensus and building coalitions. They may apply these skills to tasks—such as designing combatant commands, joint task forces, and policy working-groups—or determine the direction of a major command or the Army as an institution. Strategic leaders routinely bring designated people together for missions lasting from a few months to years. Using peer leadership rather than strict positional authority, strategic leaders carefully monitor progress toward a visualized end state. They focus on the health of the relationships necessary to achieve it. Interpersonal contact sets the tone for professional relations: strategic leaders must be tactful.

11-24. General Dwight D. Eisenhower's creation of Supreme Headquarters Allied Expeditionary Force (SHAEF) during World War II is an inspiring example of coalition building and sustaining fragile relationships. General Eisenhower exercised his authority through an integrated command and staff structure that respected the contributions of all nations involved. To underscore the united team spirit, sections within SHAEF had chiefs of one nationality and deputies of another.

11-25. Across the Atlantic Ocean, General George C. Marshall, the Army Chief of Staff, had to seek strategic consensus with demanding peers such as Admiral Ernest J. King, Commander in Chief, U.S. Fleet and Chief of Naval Operations. General Marshall expended great personal energy ensuring that inter-Service feuding at the top did not dilute the nation's effort. Admiral King, a forceful leader with strong and often differing views, responded in kind. Because of their ability to find consensus, President Franklin D. Roosevelt had few issues of major consequence to resolve once he issued a decision and guidance.

LEADS BY EXAMPLE

11-26. Strategic leaders are the ultimate representatives of the organization and its cause and purpose. Not only do they represent the organization but as the top leaders for the Nation's military, they serve as champions, diplomats, and ambassadors for the country. Due to their elevated level of responsibilities and visibility, strategic leaders are held to higher expectations and receive increased scrutiny. They must exude positivism and confidence. With greater visibility and opportunities, strategic leaders use multiple outlets to convey strategic messages and set desired conditions to advance national security interests. Their responsibilities involve spanning the boundaries among the Army and other Services, other militaries, coalitions, Congress, business forums, and the national and international presses.

11-27. Due to the greater consequences and longer horizons of their decisionmaking, timing and attention to detail are vital. A strategic leader's decision at a critical moment can rapidly alter the course of an entire campaign or affect the execution of budgets several years into the future. Strategic leaders have to set the example for time management. Effective leaders at the strategic level not only make timely decisions but also sense at what level of detail to engage and what to delegate. Strategic leaders seek counsel from established networks in a timely manner and invest sufficient time to prepare for decisions. Likewise, poor focus and poor time management can have enormous cascading effects.

Leading and Inspiring Change

11-28. To fulfill its mission, the Army must be able to address inevitable change. The Army's strategic leadership recognizes that as an institution, the Army is in a nearly constant state of flux: processing and integrating new people, missions, technologies, equipment, and information. The challenge for strategic leaders is to create grounded future-oriented change. Strategic leaders lead change by—

- Identifying the force capabilities necessary to accomplish the National Defense Strategy.
- Assigning strategic and operational missions, including priorities for allocating resources.
- Preparing plans for using military forces.
- Creating, resourcing, and sustaining organizational systems, including force modernization programs, requisite personnel and equipment resources, and essential mission command systems.
- Developing and improving doctrine as well as the training methods supporting it.
- Planning for the second- and third-order effects of change.
- Maintaining an effective leader development program and other human resource initiatives.

11-29. Strategic leaders are proactive toward change. They anticipate change even as they shield their organizations from unimportant and bothersome distracters. Generally, strategic leaders know that change requires influence grounded in commitment rather than forced compliance. Leaders must reinforce commitment consistently throughout the multiple levels of the organization. While all levels of leaders lead change, strategic level leaders make the most-sweeping changes and ones that focus on the most distant time horizon. Strategic leaders guide their organizations through eight distinct steps if their initiatives for change are to make lasting progress. The critical steps of the leading change process are—

- Demonstrate a sense of urgency by showing both the benefits and necessity for change.
- Form guiding coalitions to work change from concept through implementation.
- With the guiding coalitions, develop a vision of the future and strategy for making it a reality.
- Clearly communicate the future vision to be embraced by all members.
- Empower subordinates at all levels to pursue widespread, parallel efforts.
- Plan for short-term successes to validate key programs and keep the vision credible.
- Consolidate the successful programs to produce further change.
- Ensure that the change is culturally preserved.

Displaying Confidence in Adverse Conditions—Dealing with Uncertainty and Ambiguity

11-30. Planning and foresight cannot predict or influence all future events; therefore, strategic leaders prepare intellectually for a range of threats and scenarios. Strategic leaders work carefully to shape the future with the means available through the diplomatic, informational, military, and economic instruments of national power, as well as their character, competence, and confidence.

11-31. Strategic leaders best address complexity by embracing it. This means they expand their frame of reference to fit a situation rather than reducing a situation to fit their preconceptions. Because of their sense of duty, competence, intellectual capacity, and wise judgment, they tolerate ambiguity, as they will never have all the information they want. Instead, strategic leaders carefully analyze events and decide when to make a decision, realizing that they must innovate and accept some risk.

11-32. In addition to demonstrating the agility required to handle competing demands, strategic leaders understand complex cause-and-effect relationships and anticipate the second- and third-order effects of their decisions throughout the organization. Some second- and third-order effects are desirable and leaders can purposely pursue actions to achieve them. While the highly volatile nature of the strategic environment may tempt some strategic leaders to concentrate mainly on the short term, they cannot allow the crisis of the moment to absorb them. They must remain focused on their responsibility to shape an organization or policies that will perform successfully over the next ten to twenty years.

COMMUNICATES

11-33. Words are as powerful as weapons at the strategic level. In their interaction with others, strategic leaders need to have a sharp sense of organizational and personal dynamics. Communication at the strategic level encompasses a wide array of staffs and functional and operational components interacting with each other as well as external agencies. One prominent difference between strategic leaders and leaders at other levels is the greater emphasis on symbolic communication. Strategic leaders' words, decisions, and actions have meaning beyond their immediate consequences.

11-34. Candor and integrity must always be the hallmark of a strategic leader to earn general trust. They must carefully use their authority to identify messages and to convey them to the right target audiences. Knowing when to speak and to whom can be just as important as what is said. Strategic leaders generally send messages of a broader scope that support traditions, the Army Values, or a particular program. The message represents priorities and direction. Strategic leaders become experts in the art of persuasion.

11-35. To achieve the desired effect, strategic leaders commit to a few powerful and consistent messages that they repeat in different settings. They devise and follow a communications plan outlining how to address each target group. When preparing to address an audience, they determine its composition and agenda beforehand so they know how best to reach its members. They carefully assess the message impact in the categories of medium, frequency, specific words, and the general context. It is essential to ensure the message is going to the right groups with the desired effect.

11-36. Strategic leaders use dialogue to persuade individuals or groups. Dialogue takes the forms of advocacy and inquiry. Advocacy seeks to advance a position while inquiry looks to find out about another's position or perspective. Dialogue that blends the two has value for leaders who must address issues more complex than personal experience. To advocate a view, leaders make reasoning explicit, invite others to consider the view, encourage others to provide different views, and explore how views differ. When inquiring into another's view, leaders should voice their assumptions and seek to identify what support exists for other views. Open dialogue can help overcome reluctance to consider different points of view.

DEVELOPING

11-37. Strategic leaders make investments with a long-term focus. Most importantly, strategic leaders set the conditions for long-term success by developing subordinates who can take the institution to its next level of capability. This effort calls for initiative to experiment and innovate. Developing the institution, its organizations, and people involves an ongoing balance of operating today and building for tomorrow and, in general, being good stewards of the resources the nation entrusts to its care.

CREATES A POSITIVE ENVIRONMENT TO PREPARE FOR THE FUTURE

11-38. Strategic leaders shape the culture of the Army and define the azimuth for cultural change and organizational climate change. Strategic leaders, as well as leaders at all levels, are responsible for creating a positive environment in which to work and where individuals can thrive and be most productive. As an outcome, strategic leaders want groups to align towards common purpose.

11-39. The nation expects military professionals as individuals and the Army as an institution to learn from the experience of others and apply that learning to understand the present and prepare for the future. Such learning requires both individual and institutional commitments. Strategic leaders, by personal example and critical resourcing decisions, sustain the culture and policies that encourage both the individual and the Army to learn and evolve.

11-40. Strategic leaders ensure the Army Values and the Warrior Ethos remain fundamental to the Army's culture. A solid, values-based culture defines the boundaries of acceptable behavior and determines how to approach problems, make judgments, determine right from wrong, and establish proper priorities.

11-41. A healthy culture is a powerful motivational tool. Strategic leaders use culture to guide and inspire large and diverse organizations. They employ culture to support vision, accomplish the mission, and improve the organization. A cohesive culture molds the organization's morale, reinforcing an ethical climate solidly resting on the Army Values.

11-42. Strategic leaders promote learning by underwriting systems for studying the force and future environments. They resource a structure that constantly reflects on how the nation fights and what success requires. It requires constantly assessing the culture and deliberately encouraging creativity and learning. Strategic leaders work to ensure that evolving forces have optimal capability over time. They prepare plans to integrate new equipment and concepts into the force as soon as components are available The integration of systems or their separate components often occurs during especially designed exercises to gain early feedback. Strategic leaders commission forward-looking projects because the Army is dedicated to learning about operations in new environments and against evolving threats.

11-43. Strategic leaders are at the forefront of making the Army a lifelong learning organization, embracing the entire Army—Regular Army, Reserve Components, and Army Civilians. Modern strategic leaders must use evolving information technology and distributed learning, thus turning many institutions into classrooms without walls. The overarching goal is to provide the right education and training and to incorporate the best ideas rapidly into doctrine that ultimately improve and refine operational readiness.

PREPARES SELF WITH STRATEGIC ORIENTATION

11-44. Strategic leaders develop throughout their career and when they arrive at the strategic level, they benefit greatly by having accurate self-knowledge. An honest understanding of self is important to be able to draw on strengths and compensate for weaknesses. Neither General Marshall nor General Eisenhower had led troops in combat before assuming strategic leadership positions in World War II, but both were instrumental in preparing and leading the United States and its allies to victory through their leadership. Eisenhower especially felt disadvantaged by his lack of experience. Both future strategic leaders compensated with professional education between the wars, gaining a strategic appreciation of their environment and the future that was far better than those with extensive combat experience.

11-45. Self-aware Army leaders build a personal frame of reference from schooling, experience, self-study, and assessment while reflecting on current events, history, and geography. Strategic leaders create a comprehensive frame of reference that encompasses their entire organization and places it in the strategic environment. Strategic leaders are unafraid to rethink past experiences to learn from them. They are comfortable with abstractions common to operational and strategic environments. A well-developed frame of reference gives strategic leaders a thorough knowledge of organizational subsystems. Aware of the relationships among systems, strategic leaders foresee the possible effects of one system as it could affect the actions in others. That vision helps them anticipate and prevent potential problems.

11-46. Strategic leaders look at events for patterns to determine when to intervene or act. A strategic leader's broad frame of reference helps identify the information most relevant to a strategic situation and find the heart of a matter without distraction. Cognizant strategic leaders with comprehensive frames of reference and the wisdom that comes from experience and mental agility are equipped to assess and address events with complex causes. They envision creative and innovative solutions.

Expanding Knowledge in Cultural and Geopolitical Areas—Mastering Strategic Art

11-47. Strategic leaders require broad technical skills and mastery of strategic art. Broadly defined, strategic art is the skillful formulation, coordination, and application of ends, ways, and means to promote and defend the national interest. Masters of the strategic art integrate the three roles performed by the complete strategist: strategic leader, strategic practitioner, and strategic theorist.

11-48. Using their understanding of the systems within their own organizations, strategic leaders work through the complexity and uncertainty of the operational environment and translate abstract concepts into concrete actions. Proficiency in the science of leadership theory, programs, schedules, and systems helps organizational leaders succeed. For strategic leaders, the intangible qualities of leadership draw on their long and varied experience to produce a rare art.

11-49. By reconciling political and economic constraints with the Army's needs, strategic leaders navigate to move the force forward using a combination of strategy and budget processes. They spend a great deal of time obtaining and allocating resources and determining conceptual directions, especially those judged critical for future strategic positioning and others necessary to prevent readiness shortfalls. They oversee the Army's responsibilities under Title 10 of the United States Code.

11-50. Strategic leaders focus not so much on internal processes, but how the organization fits into DOD and the international arena. They ask broad questions, such as—
- What are the relationships among external organizations?
- What are the political and social systems in which the organization and the Army must operate?

11-51. Because of the complex reporting and coordinating relationships, strategic leaders must fully understand their roles, the boundaries of these roles, and the expectations of other departments and agencies. Understanding those interdependencies outside the Army helps strategic leaders do the right thing for the programs, systems, and people within the Army as well as for the nation.

Self-Awareness and Recognition of Impact on Others—Drawing on Conceptual Abilities

11-52. Strategic leaders, more so than direct and organizational leaders, draw on their self-awareness and conceptual abilities to comprehend and manage their complex environmental concerns. Their environmental challenges include national security, theater strategies, operating in the strategic and theater contexts, and helping vast, complex organizations evolve. The variety and scope of strategic leaders' concerns demand the application of more sophisticated concepts and wisdom beyond pure knowledge.

DEVELOPS LEADERS

11-53. Strategic leaders, as all leaders, have the responsibility to take an active role in developing direct subordinates. Strategic leaders are the top-level stewards of the Army, caring for and managing the people, physical, and financial resources entrusted to them. Strategic leaders share the benefit of their perspective and experience (mentoring). Strategic leaders become enablers as they underwrite the learning, efforts, projects, and ideas of rising leaders. Through developing others, strategic leaders help build a team of leaders prepared to fill critical positions in the future.

Counseling, Coaching, and Mentoring

11-54. More than a matter of following formats and structured sessions, mentoring by strategic leaders means giving the right people an intellectual boost so that they make the leap to successfully operating and creatively thinking at the highest levels. Strategic leaders influence their subordinates' self-development. Leaders advise them on what to study, where to focus attention, whom to study as examples, and how to proceed in their career. Leaders speak to audiences at service schools about what happens at their level and share their perspectives with those who have not yet reached the highest levels of Army leadership. Today's subordinates will become the next generation of strategic leaders.

Building Team Skills and Processes

11-55. Given the rapid transfer speed for all types of information, today's strategic leaders often have less time to assess situations, make plans, prepare an appropriate response, and execute for success. A world strategic environment in constant flux has increased the importance of building agile, honest, and competent staffs and command teams. Strategic leaders mold staffs and organizational teams able to package concise, unbiased information and build networks across organizational lines. Strategic leaders make wide-ranging and interrelated decisions so they must be able to rely on imaginative staff and subordinate leaders who comprehend the environment, foresee consequences of many courses of action, and identify key information.

11-56. Because they must be able to compensate for their own weaknesses, strategic leaders cannot afford to have staffs that blindly agree with everything they say. Strategic leaders encourage staffs to participate in open dialogue with them, discuss alternative points of view, and explore all facts, assumptions, and implications. Such dialogue, that includes inquiry and advocacy, enables strategic leaders to assess all aspects of an issue and helps clarify their vision, intent, and guidance. As strategic leaders build and use effective staffs, they continually seek honest and competent people of diverse backgrounds.

Assessing Developmental Needs and Fostering Job Development

11-57. Strategic leaders set priorities by committing money to select programs and projects or investing additional time and resources to actions. Ultimately, the Soldiers and Army Civilians who develop those ideas become trusted assets themselves. Strategic leaders can choose wisely the ideas that bridge the gap between today and tomorrow and skillfully determine how best to resource critical ideas and people.

11-58. Living with time and budget constraints, strategic leaders must make difficult decisions about how much institutional development suffices. They can calculate how much time it will take to develop the Army's leaders and nourish ideas for the future. They balance today's operational requirements against tomorrow's force structure and leadership needs. Their goal is to steward the profession by developing a core of Army leaders with the relevant competencies. Broadening assignments such as training with industry, advanced civil schooling, and foreign area officer education complement the training and education available in Army schools and contribute to shaping the people who will shape the Army's future. They skillfully complement this effort with resources offered by other Services or the public sector.

11-59. After the Vietnam War, the Army's leadership acknowledged that investing in officer development was so critically important that newly developed courses revitalized professional education. Establishing the Training and Doctrine Command revived Army doctrine as a central intellectual pillar. The Goldwater-Nichols DOD Reorganization Act of 1986 provided similar attention and increased emphasis on professional joint education and doctrine. The Army Learning Concept reinforces the necessity of development. Strategic leaders bring a vast wealth of experience to their positions, but rely on their training and education to embrace decisionmaking at this level.

ACHIEVING

11-60. Strategic leaders organize and integrate their efforts to prepare for and achieve the goals of the Army, joint forces, the nation, and organizations with which they collaborate. Their ability to get results is a function of how well they integrate their performance on all the leader competencies. The National Security Strategy, National Defense Strategy, and National Military Strategy guide strategic leaders as they develop their visions. Strategic leaders must define for their diverse organizations what success means. They monitor progress and results by drawing on personal observations, organized review and analysis, strategic management plans, and informal discussions with Soldiers and Army Civilians.

STRATEGIC PLANNING AND EXECUTION

11-61. Strategic-level plans must balance competing demands across the DOD. The fundamental requirements for strategic-level planning are the same as planning at the direct and organizational levels. At all levels, leaders establish realistic priorities and communicate decisions. What adds complexity at the strategic level is the sheer number of players and resource factors that can affect the organization.

11-62. The shift from Cold War to regional conflicts within a decade demonstrates that the conduct of war continuously changes. Strategic leaders must therefore seek current information about the shifting strategic environment to determine what sort of force to prepare. Questions strategic leaders must consider are—
- Where is the next threat?
- Will we have allies or contend alone?
- What will our national and military goals be?
- What will the exit strategy be?

11-63. Strategic leaders must be able to address the technological, leadership, and ethical considerations associated with conducting missions on the battlefield and typified by operations in Iraq and Afghanistan after the collapse of the original power structure. Strategic leaders will find themselves more than ever at the center of the tension between traditional warfare and the newer kinds of multiparty conflict emerging outside the industrialized world.

Allocating the Right Resources

11-64. Because lives are precious and materiel is scarce, strategic leaders must make tough decisions about priorities. Strategic Army priorities focus on projecting landpower. When planning for tomorrow, strategic leaders consistently call on their understanding and knowledge of the budgetary process to determine which technologies will provide the capability commensurate with the cost. Visionary Army leaders of the 1970s and 1980s realized that superior night-fighting systems and greater standoff ranges would expose fewer Soldiers to danger, yet kill more of the enemy. Those leaders committed the necessary resources to developing and procuring these and other superior systems. During Operation Iraqi Freedom, the senior Army leaders received the necessary resources to develop technology and materiel solutions to detect and reduce the improvised explosive device threat.

Capitalizing on Unified Action Partner Assets

11-65. Strategic leaders oversee the relationship between their organizations as part of the nation's total defense force and the national policy apparatus. Among their duties, strategic leaders—
- Provide military counsel in national policy forums.
- Interpret national policy guidelines and directions.
- Plan for and maintain the military capability required to implement national policy.
- Present the organization's resource requirements.
- Develop strategies to support national objectives.
- Bridge the gap between political decisions made as part of national strategy and the individuals and organizations that must carry out those decisions.

11-66. Just as direct and organizational leaders consider sister units and support agencies, strategic leaders consider and work with other Services and government agencies. Most of the Army's four-star billets are joint or multinational. Lieutenant generals hold similar positions on the Joint Staff, with the DOD, or in combatant commands. While other strategic leaders are assigned to nominally single service organizations (such as Forces Command, Training and Doctrine Command, and Army Materiel Command), they frequently work outside Army channels. In addition, many Army Civilian strategic leaders hold positions that require a well-rounded joint perspective.

Operating and Succeeding in a Multicultural Context

11-67. Creating a hybrid culture that bridges the gap between partners in multinational operations is often critical for success in the international environment. Strategic leaders take time to learn about their partners' cultures including political, social, and economic aspects. Cultural sensitivity and geopolitical awareness are critical tools for getting things done beyond the traditional chain of command. When the Army's immediate needs conflict with the objectives of other agencies, strategic leaders should work to reconcile the differences. Continued disagreement can impair the Army's ability to serve the nation. Consequently, strategic leaders must devise Army courses of action that reflect national policy objectives and consider the interests of other organizations and agencies.

Capitalizing on Technology

11-68. Superior United States technology has given strategic leaders advantages in force projection, mission command, and the generation of overwhelming combat power. Technology use has increased the tempo of operations, the speed of maneuver, the precision of firepower, and the pace at which critical information is processed. Well-managed information and technology enhance communication and situational understanding. Part of using emerging technology includes envisioning desired future capabilities that a particular technology could exploit. Another aspect is rethinking the shape and composition of organizations to take advantage of new processes previously not available.

ACCOMPLISHES MISSIONS CONSISTENTLY AND ETHICALLY

11-69. To put strategic vision, concepts, and plans into reality, strategic leaders must employ reliable feedback systems to monitor progress and adherence to values and ethics. They have to assess many environmental elements to determine the success of policies, operations, and vision. Like leaders at other levels, they must assess themselves, their leadership, strengths, and weaknesses. Other assessment efforts involve understanding the will and opinions of the American people, expressed partly through law, policy, leaders, and the media.

11-70. To gain a complete picture, strategic leaders cast a wide net to assess their own organizations. They develop performance indicators to signal how well they are communicating and how well established systems and processes are balancing the imperatives of doctrine, organization, training, materiel, leadership and education, personnel, and facilities. Assessment starts early in each operation and continues through conclusion. They may include monitoring such diverse areas as resource use, development of subordinates, efficiency, effects of stress and fatigue, morale, ethical considerations, and mission accomplishment.

11-71. Strategic leaders routinely address diversity, complexity, ambiguity, rapid change, and alignment of policies. They are responsible for developing well-reasoned positions and provide advice to the nation's highest leaders. Strategic leaders seek to determine what is important now and what will be important in the future. Their experience, wisdom, and conceptual abilities contribute to solid insight and sound judgment across many simultaneous challenges. Strategic leaders need an acute sense of timing—knowing when to accept prudent risk and proceed vigorously or when to proceed incrementally, testing the waters as they go. Their insight on issues is strong and they can skillfully sort relevant from irrelevant connections.

Glossary

The glossary lists acronyms and terms with Army or joint definitions. The proponent manual for other terms is listed in parentheses after the definition

SECTION I – ACRONYMS AND ABBREVIATIONS

AAR	after action review
ADP	Army doctrine publication
ADRP	Army doctrine reference publication
AR	Army regulation
DOD	Department of Defense
FM	field manual
JP	joint publication
MSAF	Multi-Source Assessment and Feedback
NATO	North Atlantic Treaty Organization
NCO	noncommissioned officer
SHAEF	Supreme Headquarters Allied Expeditionary Force
TC	training circular
TTP	tactics, techniques, and procedures

SECTION II – TERMS

command

The authority that a commander in the armed forces lawfully exercises over subordinates by virtue of rank or assignment. Command includes the authority and responsibility for effectively using available resources and for planning the employment of, organizing, directing, coordinating, and controlling military forces for the accomplishment of assigned missions. It also includes responsibility for health, welfare, morale, and discipline of assigned personnel. (JP 1-02)

leader development

Leader development is a deliberate, continuous, sequential, and progressive process grounded in the Army Values. It grows Soldiers and Army Civilians into competent, confident leaders capable of directing teams and organizations. (AR 350-1)

leadership

The process of influencing people by providing purpose, direction, and motivation to accomplish the mission and improve the organization. (ADP 6-22)

mentorship

The voluntary developmental relationship that exists between a person of greater experience and a person of lesser experience that is characterized by mutual trust and respect. (AR 600-100)

mission command

The exercise of authority and direction by the commander using mission orders to enable disciplined initiative within the commander's intent to empower agile and adaptive leaders in the conduct of decisive action. (ADP 6-0)

This page intentionally left blank.

References

REQUIRED PUBLICATIONS

These documents must be available to intended users of this publication.

JP 1-02. *Department of Defense Dictionary of Military and Associated Terms*. 8 November 2010 (As amended through 15 April 2012).

RELATED PUBLICATIONS

These sources contain relevant supplemental information.

JOINT AND DEPARTMENT OF DEFENSE PUBLICATIONS

DOD directives are available online: <http://www.dtic.mil/whs/directives>

Joint publications are available online: <http://www.dtic.mil/doctrine/new_pubs/jointpub.htm>

DODI 1430.16. *Growing Civilian Leaders*. 19 November 2009.

JP 3-0. *Joint Operations*. 11 August 2011.

ARMY PUBLICATIONS

Army publications are available online: <http://armypubs.army.mil/index.html>

ADP 3-0. *Unified Land Operations*. 10 October 2011.

ADP 6-0. *Mission Command*. 17 May 2012.

ADP 6-22. *Army Leadership*. 1 August 2012.

ADRP 5-0. *The Operations Process*. 17 May 2012.

ADRP 6-0. *Mission Command*. 17 May 2012.

AR 350-1. *Army Training and Leader Development*. 4 August 2011.

AR 600-20. *Army Command Policy*. 4 August 2011.

AR 600-100. *Army Leadership*. 8 March 2007.

FM 3-13. *Information Operations: Doctrine, Tactics, Techniques, and Procedures*. 28 November 2003.

FM 27-10. *The Law of Land Warfare*. 18 July 1956.

TC 1-05. *Religious Support Handbook for the Unit Ministry Team*. 10 May 2005.

WEB SITES

Army 360 Multi-Source Assessment and Feedback (MSAF) Program: <https://msaf.army.mil>

Comprehensive Soldier Fitness Program: <http://www.army.mil/csf/index.html>

OTHER PUBLICATIONS

Fisher, Roger, and William Ury. *Getting to Yes: Negotiating Agreement Without Giving In*. New York: Penguin Books, 1991.

Hughes, Jonathan, and Jeff Weiss. *Making partnerships work: A relationship management handbook*. Boston, MA: Vantage Partners, 2001.

Hughes, Jonathan, Jeff Weiss, Stuart Kliman, and David Chapnick. "Negotiation Systems and Strategies." *International Contract Manual*. Boston, MA: Brighton Landing West, 2008.

Kotter, John P. *Leading Change*. Cambridge, MA: Harvard Business School Press, 1996.

Yukl, Gary. *Leadership in Organizations*. 8th ed. Boston, MA: Pearson, Education, Inc., 2012.

Yukl, Gary, Carolyn Chavez, and Charles F. Seifert. "Assessing the Construct Validity and Utility of Two New Influence Tactics." *Journal of Organizational Behavior*, 26 (2005): 1-21.

Yukl, Gary, and J. Bruce Tracey. "Consequences of Influence Tactics Used With Subordinates, Peers, and the Boss." *Journal of Applied Psychology*, 77, (1992): 525-535.

PRESCRIBED FORMS
None.

REFERENCED FORMS
DA Form 2028. *Recommended Changes to Publications and Blank Forms.*

Index

Entries are by paragraph number unless specified otherwise.

A-B

achieving (gets results), 8-1–8-24, table 8-1
active listening, 6-77–6-78
adaptability, 7-42, 9-3, 9-31, 9-32–9-41
    changes, 8-11–8-13
ambiguity, 11-30–11-32
Army Civilian Creed, figure 3-2
Army Civilians, 2-17–2-21,
Army Leadership Requirements Model, 1-27–1-28, figure 1-1
Army Values, 3-3–3-16
    duty, 3-7
    honor, 3-11–3-12
    integrity, 3-13–3-14
    loyalty, 3-5–3-6
    personal courage, 3-15
    respect, 3-8–3-9
    selfless service, 3-10
attributes, 1-30
    Army Values, 3-3–3-16
    confidence, 4-10
    discipline, 3-24–3-25
    empathy, 3-17–3-20
    expertise, 5-19
    fitness, 4-5–4-9
    innovation, 5-9–5-10
    interpersonal tact, 5-11
    mental agility, 5-3–5-5
    military and professional bearing, 4-4
    resilience, 4-11–4-13
    sound judgment, 5-6–5-8
    Warrior Ethos/service ethos, 3-21–3-23
balance, 5-17
balancing mission and welfare, 6-42–6-47
building cohesion and trust, 7-26–7-28
builds trust, 6-48–6-52, table 6-2
    outside lines of authority, 6-57–6-60

C

character, 3-1–3-2, table 3-1
    Army Values, 3-3–3-16
    and beliefs, 3-30–3-32
    development, 3-26–3-29
    discipline, 3-24–3-25
    empathy, 3-17–3-20
    and ethics, 3-33–3-36
    ethical orders, 3-42–3-45
    ethical reasoning, 3-37–3-41
    Service Ethos, 3-21
    Warrior Ethos, 3-21–3-23, figure 3-1
civilian-military linkage, 1-12–1-14
coaching, 7-62–7-64
collective leadership. *See* leadership.
combat and operational stress, 9-22–9-26
commitment, 6-4
communicates, 6-76–6-86, 10-16–10-20, 11-33–11-36, table 6-5
competencies, builds trust, 6-48–6-52, table 6-2
    communicates, 6-76–6-86, 10-16–10-20, 11-33–11-36, table 6-5
    creates a positive environment/fosters esprit de corps, 7-5–7-31, 10-22–10-25, 11-38–11-43, table 7-1
    develops others, 7-49–7-90, 10-3–10-32, table 7-4
    extends influence beyond the chain of command, 6-54–6-65, 10-7, 11-17–11-18, table 6-3
    gets results, 8-1–8-24, table 8-1
    leads by example, 6-66–6-75, 10-13–10-15, 11-26–11-27, table 6-4
    leads others, 6-1–6-47, 10-4–10-6, 11-11–11-12, table 6-1
    prepares self, 7-32–7-48, 10-26–10-29, 11-44–11-46, table 7-2
    stewards the profession, 7-91–7-95, table 7-5
compliance, 6-2–6-3
confidence, 4-10
counseling, 7-60–7-61
create shared understanding, 6-79–6-86
creates a positive environment/fosters esprit de corps, 7-5–7-31, 10-22–10-25, 11-38–11-43, table 7-1
creative thinking, 5-4, 5-9
critical thinking, 5-4–5-5
cultural and geopolitical knowledge, 5-26–5-29

D-E-F-G-H

demonstrate care for people, 7-31
demonstrate competence, 6-73–6-75
develops others, 7-49–7-90, 10-3–10-32, table 7-4
direct level leadership. *See* leadership.
discipline, 3-24–3-25
displaying character, 6-66–6-72
diversity, recognizing, 5-12
duty, 3-7
emotional factors, 5-15
empathy, 3-17–3-20
empowering subordinates, 1-25
encouraging initiative, 7-29–7-30
esprit de corps, 7-8–7-9
expertise, 5-19
extends influence beyond the chain of command, 6-53–6-65, 10-7, 11-17–11-18, table 6-3
fear, 9-27–9-28
fitness, 4-5–4-9
formal leadership. *See* leadership.
gets results, 8-1–8-24, table 8-1
honor, 3-11–3-12

I-J-K

individual development plan, 7-58
influence, application of, 6-15–6-17
    apprising, 6-12
    collaboration, 6-10
    exchange, defined, 6-8
    inspirational appeals, 6-13
    legitimating, 6-7
    participation, 6-14
    personal appeals, 6-9
    pressure, 6-6
    rational persuasion, 6-11
    understanding sphere, means and limits, 6-61–6-63

informal leadership. *See* leadership.

innovation, 5-9–5-10

integrity, 3-13–3-14

intellect, basics, 5-1–5-2, table 5-1
   mental agility, 5-3–5-5
   sound judgment, 5-6–5-8
   innovation, 5-9–5-10
   interpersonal tact, 5-11–5-18
   expertise, 5-19–5-29

interpersonal tact, 5-11

joint knowledge, 5-25

L

leader, attributes of, 1-30, table 3-1, table 4-1, table 5-1
   competencies of, 1-3–1-35, table 6-1, table 6-2, table 6-3, table 6-4, table 6-5, table 7-1, table 7-2, table 7-4, table 7-5, table 8-1
   responsibilities, 3-7, 3-16, 3-27, 3-40, 5-24, 6-4, 6-31, 6-47, 6-71, 7-1, 7-7, 7-13, 7-23, 7-29, 7-53, 7-73, 7-84, 7-90, 8-8, 8-10, 8-14, 9-21, 10-21, 10-30, 11-26, 11-32, 11-53
   role models, 1-18, 2-1, 2-10, 2-13, 10-26

leadership, and command authority, 1-15–1-18
   collective, 2-40
   defined, 1-1
   direct level, 2-28–2-30
   formal, 1-21
   informal, 1-22–1-24
   organizational level, 2-31–2-34, 10-1–10-62
   strategic level, 2-35–2-39, 11-1–11-71

leadership and command authority. *See* leadership.

leads by example, 6-66–6-75, 10-13–10-15, 11-26–11-27, table 6-4

leads others, 6-1–6-47, 10-4–10-6, 11-11–11-12, table 6-1

loyalty, 3-5–3-6

M-N-O

managing resources, 8-14–8-17

mental agility, 5-3–5-5

mentoring, 7-65–7-70

military and professional bearing, 4-4

mission command, 1-19

monitoring performance, 8-18
   improving organizational performance, 8-21–8-22
   reinforcing good performance, 8-19–8-20

negotiating, 6-64–6-65

noncommissioned officers, 2-12–2-16

officers, 2-6–2-11

operational environment, challenges of, 9-1–9-21

organizational level leadership. *See* leadership.

P-Q-R

personal courage, 3-15

positive environment, creates, 7-5–7-7
   setting conditions for, 7-10–7-25

prepares self, 7-32–7-48, 10-26–10-29, 11-44–11-46, table 7-2
   developing self-awareness, 7-42–7-48
   expanding knowledge, 7-39–7-41

presence, basics, 4-1–4-3, table 4-1
   confidence, 4-10
   fitness, 4-5–4-9
   military and professional bearing, 4-4
   resilience, 4-11–4-13

providing purpose and motivation, 6-22–6-31

resilience, 4-11–4-13

resistance, 6-18–6-21

resolving conflicts, 6-35–6-36

respect, 3-8–3-9

S-T-U-V

self-awareness, 7-42–7-48

self-control, 5-14

self-development, 1-31, 3-25, 7-32–7-38, 7-51, 7-69, 10-30, 11-54

selfless service, 3-10

Service Ethos, 3-21

Soldier's Creed, figure 3-1

sound judgment, 5-6–5-8

stability, 5-18

standards, enforcing, 6-37–6-41

stewards the profession, 7-91–7-95, table 7-5

strategic leadership. *See* leadership.

stress, change, 9-30–9-31
   in training and operations, 9-29

supporting leader development, 7-73–7-76

tactical knowledge, 5-20–5-21

teams, characteristics of, 7-79–7-82
   stages of, 7-83–7-90

technical knowledge, 5-22–5-24

unified action partners, 2-22–2-23

WXYZ

Warrior Ethos, 3-21–3-23

ADRP 6-22
1 August 2012

By Order of the Secretary of the Army:

RAYMOND T. ODIERNO
General, United States Army
Chief of Staff

Official:

JOYCE E. MORROW
Administrative Assistant to the
Secretary of the Army
1220107

DISTRIBUTION:

Active Army, Army National Guard, and United States Army Reserve: To be distributed in accordance with the initial distribution number (IDN) 110180, requirements for ADRP 6-22.

This page intentionally left blank.

ATP 6-22.1

The Counseling Process

July 2014

DISTRIBUTION RESTRICTION. Approved for public release; distribution unlimited.

Headquarters, Department of the Army

This page intentionally left blank.

ATP 6-22.1(FM 6-22)

Army Techniques Publication
No. 6-22.1

Headquarters
Department of the Army
Washington, DC, 1 July 2014

The Counseling Process

Contents

		Page
	PREFACE	ii
	INTRODUCTION	iii
Chapter 1	COUNSELING	1-1
	Types of Developmental Counseling	1-1
Chapter 2	COUSELING FUNDAMENTALS	2-1
	The Leader as Counselor	2-1
	The Qualities of the Counselor	2-1
	Counseling Skills	2-1
	Counseling Practices	2-3
	Accepting Limitations	2-3
	Addressing Resistance	2-3
	The Four-Stage Counseling Process	2-4
	Summary – The Counseling Process at a Glance	2-10
	GLOSSARY	Glossary-1
	REFERENCES	References-1
	INDEX	Index-1

Figures

Figure 2-1. Example of a counseling outline 2-6
Figure 2-2. Example counseling session 2-9

Tables

Table 2-1. Counseling approach summary 2-7
Table 2-2. A summary of counseling 2-10

Distribution Restriction: Approved for public release; distribution unlimited.

*This publication supersedes Appendix B, "Counseling," except paragraph B-2, of FM 6-22, dated 12 October 2006.

Preface

Army Techniques Publication (ATP) 6-22.1 provides doctrinal guidance for all leaders, military and civilian, responsible for planning, preparing, executing, and assessing counseling actions. Trainers and educators throughout the Army will also use this publication.

Commanders, staffs, and subordinates ensure their decisions and actions comply with applicable U.S., international, and, in some cases, host-nation laws and regulations. Commanders at all levels ensure their Soldiers operate in accordance with the law of war and the rules of engagement. (See Field Manual [FM] 27-10.)

ATP 6-22.1 applies to the Active Army, Army National Guard/Army National Guard of the United States, and United States Army Reserve unless otherwise stated. For specifics in addressing Army Civilian counseling requirements, leaders should contact the servicing civilian personnel office.

The proponent of ATP 6-22.1 is Headquarters, U.S. Army Training and Doctrine Command. The preparing agency is the Center for Army Leadership, Mission Command Center of Excellence, United States Army Combined Arms Center. Send comments and recommendations on DA Form 2028 (Recommended Changes to Publications and Blank Forms) to Center for Army Leadership ATTN: ATZL-MCV-R (ATP 6-22.1), 290 Stimson Avenue, Fort Leavenworth, KS 66027-1293 or electronically to usarmy.leavenworth.tradoc.mbx.6-22@mail.mil.

Introduction

ATP 6-22.1 provides a doctrinal framework for counseling subordinates. ATP 6-22.1 consists of two chapters:
- Chapter 1 addresses the types of developmental counseling: event, performance, and professional growth.
- Chapter 2 addresses counseling fundamentals supporting effective counseling:
  - Counselor qualities.
  - Counseling skills.
  - Counseling practices.
  - Accepting limitations.
  - Addressing resistance.
  - The four-stage counseling process.
  - Counseling approaches and techniques.

Based on current doctrinal changes, counseling is no longer a formally defined doctrinal term.

This page intentionally left blank.

Chapter 1
Counseling

Counseling is the process used by leaders to review with a subordinate the subordinate's demonstrated performance and potential. Counseling, one of the most important leadership and professional development responsibilities, enables Army leaders to help Soldiers and Army Civilians become more capable, resilient, satisfied, and better prepared for current and future responsibilities. Counseling is required of leaders and occurs at prescribed times. The related developmental processes of coaching and mentoring are done voluntarily. The Army's future and the legacy of today's Army leaders rests on the shoulders of those they help prepare for greater responsibility.

TYPES OF DEVELOPMENTAL COUNSELING

1-1. Regular developmental counseling is the Army's most important tool for developing future leaders at every level. Counseling responsibilities are inherent in leadership. Leaders at all levels must understand the counseling process. More importantly, Army leaders must understand that effective counseling helps achieve desired goals and effects, manages expectations, and improves the organization. Leaders should emphasize routine counseling to reinforce positive behavior and superior performance. Regular counseling provides leaders with opportunities to:
- Demonstrate genuine interest in subordinates.
- Help subordinates understand their role in accomplishing the unit's mission.
- Acknowledge and reinforce exceptional work or dedication.
- Evaluate subordinates' potential for development.
- Provide subordinates with assistance or resources to address issues or further strengths.
- Empower subordinates to identify and solve issues on their own so they are more self-reliant.
- Identify issues before they become significant problems.
- Identify and pre-empt causes of sub-standard performance.

1-2. Developmental counseling is categorized by the purpose of the session. Understanding the purpose and types of counseling enables the leader to adapt the counseling session to the individual subordinate's needs in order to achieve desired outcomes and manage expectations. Counseling is not a one-size-fits-all endeavor; it is a shared effort between the leader and subordinate.

1-3. The three major categories of developmental counseling are:
- Event counseling.
- Performance counseling.
- Professional growth counseling.

1-4. While these categories can help organize and focus counseling sessions, they should not be viewed as separate or exhaustive. For example, a counseling session that focuses on resolving an issue may also address improving duty performance. A session focused on performance often includes a discussion on opportunities for professional growth. Regardless of the purpose or topic of the counseling session, leaders should follow a basic format for preparation, execution, and follow-up. DA Form 4856 (Developmental Counseling Form) provides a useful framework to prepare for counseling. It helps organize the relevant issues to discuss during counseling sessions.

Chapter 1

EVENT COUNSELING

1-5. Event-oriented counseling involves a specific event or situation. It may precede events such as participating in promotion boards, attending training courses, and preparing for deployment or redeployment. It also addresses events such as noteworthy duty performance, an issue with performance or mission accomplishment, or a personal issue. Examples of event-oriented counseling include, but are not limited to:
- Specific instances of superior or substandard performance.
- Reception and integration counseling.
- Crisis counseling.
- Referral counseling.
- Promotion counseling.
- Transition counseling.
- Adverse separation counseling.

Specific Instances of Superior or Substandard Performance

1-6. Often counseling is tied to specific instances of superior or substandard duty performance. The leader uses the counseling session to convey to the subordinate whether or not the performance met the standard and what the subordinate did right or wrong. Successful counseling for specific performance occurs as close to the event as possible. Leaders should counsel subordinates for exceptional as well as substandard duty performance.

1-7. Leaders should always counsel subordinates who do not meet the standard. If performance is unsatisfactory because of a lack of knowledge or ability, leader and subordinate can develop a plan for improvement. Corrective training helps ensure that the subordinate knows and consistently achieves the standard. When counseling a subordinate for specific performance, leaders take the following actions:
- Explain the purpose of the counseling—what was expected and how the subordinate exceeded or failed to meet the standard.
- Remain neutral.
- Address and explain the specific behavior or action—do not address the subordinate's character.
- Explain the effect of the behavior, action, or performance on the rest of the organization.
- Actively listen to the subordinate's responses (see Chapter 2).
- If failing to meet the standard, teach the subordinate how to meet the standard and recognize patterns of behavior that may keep the subordinate from meeting the standard.
- Be prepared to conduct personal counseling, since a failure to meet the standard may be the result of an unresolved personal issue.
- Explain to the subordinate how developing an individual development plan will improve performance and identify specific responsibilities in implementing the plan. Continue to assess and follow up on the subordinate's progress. Adjust the plan as necessary.

Reception and Integration Counseling

1-8. Army leaders should counsel all new team members when they join the organization. Reception and integration counseling serves two important purposes:
- It identifies and helps alleviate any issues or concerns that new members may have, including any issues resulting from the new duty assignment.
- It familiarizes new team members with organizational standards, roles, and assignments.

1-9. Reception and integration counseling should include but is not limited to the following areas:
- Organizational history, structure, and mission.
- Organizational standards (such as discipline, maintenance, training, and fitness).
- Organizational policies.
- Chain of command familiarization.

- NCO support channel familiarization.
- Key leader contact information.
- Soldier programs within the organization, such as Soldier of the Month/Quarter/Year and educational and training opportunities.
- Security and safety issues.
- On- and off-duty conduct.
- Off-limits and danger areas.
- Personnel procedures.
- Initial and special clothing issue.
- On- and off-post recreational, educational, cultural, and historical opportunities.
- Support activities functions and locations.
- Foreign nation or host nation orientation, as applicable.
- Other items of interest as determined by the leader or organization.

Crisis Counseling

1-10. Crisis counseling focuses on the subordinate's immediate short-term needs and assists a Soldier or employee through a period of shock after receiving negative news, such as the notification of the death of a loved one. Leaders may assist by listening and providing appropriate assistance. Assistance may include coordinating for external agency support, such as obtaining emergency funding for transportation or putting them in contact with a chaplain.

Referral Counseling

1-11. Referral counseling occurs when issues are beyond the capability or expertise of a subordinate's leaders. Referral counseling helps subordinates work through personal situations that may affect performance. It may or may not follow crisis counseling. Referral counseling aims at preventing a challenge or issue from becoming unmanageable for the subordinate. Army leaders assist by identifying issues in time and referring the subordinate to the appropriate outside resources, such as Army Community Services, a chaplain, or an alcohol and drug counselor.

Promotion Counseling

1-12. Army leaders must conduct promotion counseling for all specialists, corporals, and sergeants who are eligible for advancement without waivers (see AR 600-8-19). Army regulations require that Soldiers within this category receive initial (event-oriented) counseling when they attain full promotion eligibility and then periodic (performance/professional growth) counseling thereafter. Soldiers not recommended for promotion must be counseled as to why they were not recommended and should address these shortcomings and plans of action to overcome the identified shortcomings.

Transition Counseling

1-13. Transition counseling assists Soldiers who are demobilizing, separating, or retiring from active duty. Transition counseling prepares subordinates for employment, education, and other post-service opportunities and benefits. Transition requires planning throughout the individual's service starting with identifying military and long-term goals at the first unit of assignment. Leaders and subordinates should review and revise these goals as necessary during subsequent professional development counseling sessions.

1-14. Leaders will assist subordinates with transition activities in concert with the servicing Army Career and Alumni Program (ACAP) office and other transition assistance resources (see AR 600-8).

Chapter 1

Adverse Separation Counseling

1-15. Adverse separation counseling may involve informing the Soldier of the administrative actions available to the commander in the event substandard performance continues and of the consequences associated with those administrative actions (see AR 635-200).

1-16. Developmental counseling may not apply when an individual has engaged in serious acts of misconduct. In those situations, leaders should refer the matter to the commander and the servicing staff judge advocate. When rehabilitative efforts fail, counseling with a view toward separation is required. It is an administrative prerequisite to many administrative discharges. It is advisable to involve the chain of command as soon as it is determined that adverse separation counseling might be required. A unit first sergeant or the commander should inform the Soldier of such proceedings based on the notification requirements outlined in AR 635-200.

PERFORMANCE COUNSELING

1-17. Performance counseling is the review of a subordinate's duty performance during a specified period. The leader and the subordinate jointly establish performance objectives and clear standards for the next counseling period. The counseling focuses on the subordinate's strengths, areas to improve, and potential. Effective counseling includes providing specific examples of strengths and areas needing improvement and providing guidance on how subordinates can improve their performance. Performance counseling is required under the officer, noncommissioned officer, and Army Civilian evaluation reporting systems (see AR 623-3 or AR 690-400 for specifics).

1-18. During performance counseling, leaders conduct a review of a subordinate's duty performance over a certain period. Simultaneously, leader and subordinate jointly establish performance objectives and standards for the next period.

1-19. Counseling at the beginning of and during the evaluation period ensures the subordinate's personal involvement in the evaluation process. Performance counseling communicates standards and is an opportunity for leaders to establish and clarify the expected values, attributes, and competencies. Army leaders ensure that performance objectives and standards focus on the organization's objectives and the individual's professional development. They should also echo the objectives on their leader's support form as a team member's performance contributes to mission accomplishment.

PROFESSIONAL GROWTH COUNSELING

1-20. Professional growth counseling includes planning for the accomplishment of individual and professional goals. During the counseling, leader and subordinate conduct a review to identify and discuss the subordinate's strengths and weaknesses and to create an individual development plan that builds upon those strengths and compensates for (or eliminates) shortcomings. Leaders can assist subordinates in prioritizing development efforts based upon those perceived strengths and weaknesses.

1-21. As part of professional growth counseling, the leader and subordinate may choose to develop a pathway to success with short- and long-term goals and objectives. The discussion includes opportunities for civilian or military schooling, future duty assignments, special programs, available training support resources, reenlistment options, and promotion opportunities and considerations. Documentation of this discussion results in an individual development plan. Each individual development plan will vary as every person's needs and interests are different.

Chapter 2
Counseling Fundamentals

THE LEADER AS COUNSELOR

2-1. To be effective, counseling must be a shared effort. Leaders assist their subordinates in identifying strengths and weaknesses and creating plans of action. Once an individual development plan is agreed upon, leaders support their Soldiers and Army Civilians throughout implementation and continued assessment. To achieve success, subordinates must be forthright in their commitment to improve and candid in their own assessments and goal setting.

2-2. Army leaders evaluate Army Civilian job performance using procedures prescribed under civilian personnel policies. Use of DA Form 4856 is appropriate to counsel Army Civilians on professional growth and career goals. The servicing civilian personnel office should be consulted when using a DA Form 4856 to counsel an Army Civilian concerning misconduct or poor performance.

2-3. Army leaders conduct counseling to help subordinates become better team members, maintain or improve performance, and prepare for the future. While it is not easy to address every possible counseling situation, leader self-awareness and an adaptable counseling style focusing on key characteristics will enhance personal effectiveness as a counselor. These key characteristics include:
- Purpose: Clearly define the purpose of the counseling.
- Flexibility: Adapt the counseling approach to each subordinate, situation, and relationship.
- Respect: View subordinates as unique, complex individuals with distinct values, beliefs, and attitudes.
- Communication: Establish open, two-way communication with subordinates using verbal and nonverbal actions (such as body language or gestures). Effective counselors listen more than they speak.
- Support: Encourage subordinates through direction, guidance, and supportive actions.

THE QUALITIES OF THE COUNSELOR

2-4. Army leaders must demonstrate certain qualities to be effective counselors. These qualities include respect for subordinates, self-awareness, cultural awareness, empathy, and credibility.

2-5. One challenging aspect of counseling is selecting the proper approach to a specific situation. To counsel effectively, the technique used must fit the situation, leader capabilities, and subordinate expectations. Sometimes, leaders may only need to give information or listen, while in other situations a subordinate's improvement may call for a brief word of praise. Difficult circumstances may require structured counseling followed by definite actions, such as referrals to outside agencies.

2-6. Self-aware Army leaders consistently develop and improve their own counseling abilities. They do so by studying human behavior, understanding the kinds of problems that affect their subordinates, and developing their interpersonal skills. The techniques needed to provide effective counseling vary from person to person and session to session. However, general skills that leaders will need in almost every situation include active listening, responding, and appropriate questioning.

COUNSELING SKILLS

2-7. Military leaders are trained to analyze missions, identify required tasks, and take appropriate actions. Some of these skills apply to counseling as leaders use problem-solving and decisionmaking skills to identify and apply the proper counseling techniques to specific counseling situations.

Chapter 2

2-8. To be effective, counselors must have these basic counseling skills:
- Active listening.
- Responding.
- Appropriate questioning.

ACTIVE LISTENING

2-9. Active listening implies listening thoughtfully and deliberately to capture the nuances of the subordinate's language. Stay alert for common themes. A subordinate's opening and closing statements as well as recurring references may indicate personal priorities. Inconsistencies and gaps may indicate an avoidance of the real issue. Certain inconsistencies may suggest additional questions by the counselor.

2-10. Active listening communicates that the leader values the subordinate and enables reception of the subordinate's message. To capture and understand the message fully, leaders listen to what is said and observe the subordinate's mannerisms. Key elements of active listening include:
- Eye contact. Maintaining eye contact without staring helps show sincere interest. Occasional breaks of eye contact are normal and acceptable, while excessive breaks, paper shuffling, clock-watching, and repeated mobile telephone checks may indicate a lack of interest or concern.
- Body posture. Being relaxed and comfortable will help put the subordinate at ease. However, an overly relaxed position or slouching may be interpreted as a lack of interest.
- Head nods. Occasional nodding indicates attention and encourages the subordinate to continue.
- Facial expressions. Keep facial expressions natural and relaxed to signal a sincere interest.
- Verbal expressions. Refrain from talking too much and avoid interrupting. Let the subordinate do the talking, while keeping the discussion on the counseling subject.
- Check for understanding. Paraphrase or summarize points back to the subordinate for confirmation; for example, "What I heard was…".

2-11. Leaders pay attention to the subordinate's gestures to understand the complete message. By watching a subordinate's actions, leaders identify the emotions behind the words. Not all actions are proof of feelings but they should be considered. Nonverbal indicators of leader and subordinate attitude include:
- Interest, friendliness, and openness. Be aware that counselor actions must be context and situation specific. For example, leaning toward the subordinate may be considered as expressing interest or being aggressive—the counselor must be able to understand how the subordinate will interpret this action.
- Self-confidence. Standing tall, leaning back with hands behind the head, and maintaining steady eye contact.
- Anxiety. Sitting on the edge of the chair with arms uncrossed and hands open.
- Boredom. Drumming on the table, doodling, clicking a ballpoint pen, or resting the head in the palm of the hand.
- Defensiveness. Pushing deeply into a chair, glaring, or making sarcastic comments as well as crossing or folding arms in front of the chest.
- Frustration. Rubbing eyes, pulling on an ear, taking short breaths, wringing the hands, or frequently changing total body position.

2-12. Leaders consider each indicator carefully. Although each may reveal something about the subordinate, do not judge too quickly. When unsure, leaders look for reinforcing indicators or check the subordinate to understand the behavior, determine what underlies it, and allow the subordinate to understand the conditions that led to the behavior and to take responsibility.

RESPONDING

2-13. A leader responds verbally and nonverbally to show understanding of the subordinate. Verbal responses consist of summarizing, interpreting, and clarifying the subordinate's message. Nonverbal responses include eye contact and occasional gestures such as a head nod. A counselor's responses should encourage the subordinate to continue.

APPROPRIATE QUESTIONING

2-14. Although focused questioning is an important skill, counselors should use it with caution. During professional growth counseling, leaders should ask open-ended questions to obtain information or to get the subordinate to think deeper about a particular situation. Questions should evoke more than a yes or no answer and not lead toward a specific answer or conclusion. Well-posed questions deepen understanding, encourage further discussion, and create a constructive experience. Too many questions can aggravate the power differential between a leader and a subordinate and place the subordinate in a passive mode. The subordinate may also react to excessive questioning, especially if it resembles an interrogation, as an intrusion of privacy and become defensive.

COUNSELING PRACTICES

2-15. Dominating the session by talking too much, giving unnecessary or inappropriate advice, not truly listening, and projecting biases and prejudices all interfere with effective counseling. Competent leaders avoid rash judgments, stereotyping, losing emotional control, inflexible counseling methods, or improper follow-up. Leaders should be open to new ideas and thoughts.

2-16. Leaders conduct effective counseling sessions and improve their counseling skills when they follow these general guidelines:
- Determine the subordinate's role in the situation and what has been done to resolve the issue.
- Focus attention on the subordinate. Listen to what is said and how it is said to understand what the subordinate says and feels.
- Encourage the subordinate to take the initiative and speak aloud.
- Remain objective; avoid confirming a subordinate's prejudices.
- Display empathy when discussing the issue. Be receptive to the subordinate's emotions without feeling responsible.
- Ask open-ended questions for relevant information; avoid interrogating the subordinate.
- Listen more and talk less; avoid interrupting.
- Keep personal experiences out of the counseling session.
- Draw conclusions based on all available information, not just the subordinate's statement.
- Enable the subordinate to help himself or herself.
- Know what information to keep confidential and what to present to the chain of command, if necessary.

ACCEPTING LIMITATIONS

2-17. Army leaders cannot help everyone in every situation. Army leaders should recognize their personal limitations and seek outside assistance when required. When necessary, leaders refer a subordinate to an agency more qualified to help.

2-18. Although it is generally in an individual's best interest to begin by seeking help from his or her first-line leaders, leaders should respect an individual's preference to contact outside support agencies.

ADDRESSING RESISTANCE

2-19. Resistance in counseling may stem from either the leader or subordinate and may occur in several ways. Identifying and understanding the possible forms of resistance is essential. A leader may be reluctant to counsel subordinates because the leader has not been counseled, has had no effective role modeling for what is involved in the process, or does not understand how to conduct counseling. Additionally, leaders may feel there is no time to do counseling, counseling will not be a constructive use of time, or counseling will violate a regulation or policy. They may associate counseling with only negative issues such as dispensing punishment or correcting poor performance. Further, leaders may not want to confront a subordinate. Other typical reasons for leader reluctance involve a lack of respect for the subordinate, believing the subordinate lacks potential, or encountering constant issues with the subordinate.

2-20. Subordinate resistance often occurs as a reaction to the purpose or message of the counseling session. They may be embarrassed, misunderstand the intention of the counseling session, or disagree with the leader's assessment of the situation. Subordinates may not want to change, may blame the leader for the issue or behavior at hand, may dislike being held accountable, or may defy being disciplined. In some cases, the subordinate may not respect or trust the leader.

2-21. Leaders may preempt potential subordinate resistance by opening the counseling session with a discussion of the purpose of the session, expectations of the session, and how they relate to the subordinate's short- and long-term goals. Through regular periodic counseling, leaders should understand and be aware of the subordinate's goals. For the session to be effective, leaders must focus on the issue and adapt the counseling to the subordinate's needs and understanding.

2-22. Once a leader understands that counseling subordinates is a significant leader responsibility in developing subordinates' potential, leader reluctance to counsel can be overcome through preparation and improving counseling skills. Leaders successfully overcome subordinate resistance by applying positive counseling practices. After the leader identifies the source of a subordinate's resistance, then the counseling process can be adapted to accommodate and overcome the resistance.

2-23. To overcome resistance in counseling, leaders can employ several techniques to redirect the subordinate:
- Reconfirm the counseling session purpose—be specific and keep focused on the details (such as conditions, triggers, and outcomes) of the situation; refrain from any personal attacks on the subordinate.
- Keep the discussion professional and balanced in tone—do not argue or place blame on any party.
- Discuss the suspected resistance openly with the subordinate and respect his or her response.
- Slow the tempo of the session—rely on pertinent open-ended questions to give the subordinate the appropriate time and ability to reveal information and be an active participant in the counseling session.
- Focus on one specific behavior, its effect, and the consequences to minimize overwhelming the subordinate. It may be necessary to divide the session into multiple meetings to address each area adequately. Further, the leader should prioritize these discussions based on the needs of the individual and unit.

THE FOUR-STAGE COUNSELING PROCESS

2-24. Effective Army leaders use a four-stage counseling process:
- Identify the need for counseling.
- Prepare for counseling.
- Conduct the counseling session.
- Follow-up.

STAGE 1: IDENTIFY THE NEED FOR COUNSELING

2-25. The success of counseling depends on the preparatory steps that the counselor takes before the counseling session (formal or informal) occurs. The counselor must develop a clear purpose, have an assessment of the situation, and an idea of possible outcomes that are desired. However, counseling is an interactive and dynamic process where assessments and follow-on actions come from a trusted exchange between the counselor and individual receiving counseling. The counselor must consider desired outcomes during preparation or before conducting a counseling session. Counseling requires the leader to be informed and prepared for contingencies that may arise during the counseling session.

2-26. Army and organizational policies may direct the timing or focused elements of a counseling session, such as performance counseling associated with an evaluation or professional growth counseling. Leaders may conduct developmental counseling whenever the need arises for focused, two-way open communication aimed at a subordinate's development. Developing subordinates consists of observing the subordinate's performance, comparing it to established standards, and providing feedback through counseling. For event counseling, the leader must confirm or seek new information and remain open to new assessments of the event and related goals or corrections.

STAGE 2: PREPARE FOR COUNSELING

2-27. Successful counseling requires preparation in the following areas:
- Select a suitable place.
- Schedule the time.
- Notify the subordinate well in advance.
- Outline the components of the counseling session.
- Organize information and draft a plan of action.
- Plan the counseling strategy.
- Establish the right atmosphere.

Select a Suitable Place

2-28. Conduct the counseling session in an environment that minimizes interruptions and is free from distracting sights and sounds. The location should allow for privacy as the counseling session may cover personal issues not intended for public knowledge. In addition, the selected location needs to provide the right atmosphere appropriate for the counseling session.

Schedule the Time

2-29. When possible, leaders should formally counsel a subordinate during the duty day. Counseling after duty hours may be rushed or perceived as unfavorable. Select a time free from competition with other activities. Leaders should consider that important events occurring after the session could distract a subordinate from concentrating on the counseling session. The scheduled time for counseling should also be appropriate for the complexity of the issue at hand. Generally, counseling sessions should last less than an hour.

Notify the Subordinate Well in Advance

2-30. Counseling is a subordinate-centered, two-person effort for which the subordinate must have adequate time to prepare. The person being counseled should know why, where, and when the counseling takes place. Counseling tied to a specific event should happen as closely to the event occurrence as possible. For performance or professional development counseling, subordinates may need a week or more to prepare or review specific documents and resources, including evaluation support forms or counseling records.

Outline the Components of the Counseling Session

2-31. Using the available information, leaders determine the focus and specific topics for the counseling session. Leaders should identify what prompted the counseling requirement, aims our outcomes, and their role as counselor. In addition, leaders should identify possible comments and questions to keep the counseling session subordinate-centered and guide the subordinate through the session's stages. As subordinates may be unpredictable during counseling, a written outline can help keep the session on track and enhances the chances for success (see figure 2-1 on page 2-6).

> **Counseling Outline**
>
> **Type of counseling**: Initial NCOER counseling for SFC Taylor, a recently promoted new arrival to the unit.
>
> **Place and time**: The platoon office, Tuesday at 1500.
>
> **Time to notify the subordinate**: Notify SFC Taylor one week in advance of the counseling session.
>
> **Subordinate preparation**: Instruct SFC Taylor to develop a list of goals and objectives to complete over the next 90 to 180 days. Review the values, attributes, and competencies of ADRP 6-22.
>
> **Counselor preparation**:
> Review the NCO Counseling Checklist/Record.
> Update duty description; fill out the rating chain and duty description on a working copy of the NCOER.
> Review each of the values and responsibilities in NCOER Part IV and the values, attributes, and competencies in ADRP 6-22. Review how each applies to SFC Taylor's duties.
> Review the actions necessary for a success or excellence rating in each area.
> Make notes on relevant parts of the NCOER to assist in counseling.
>
> **Role as a counselor**: Help SFC Taylor to understand the expectations and standards associated with the platoon sergeant position. Assist SFC Taylor in developing the values, attributes, and competencies that enable him to achieve his performance objectives consistent with those of the platoon and company. Resolve any aspects of the job that SFC Taylor does not clearly understand.
>
> **Session outline**: Complete an outline following the counseling session components based on the draft duty description on the NCOER. This should happen two to three days prior to the actual counseling session.

Figure 2-1. Example of a counseling outline

Organize Information and Draft a Plan of Action

2-32. The counselor should review all pertinent information, including the purpose of the counseling, facts, and observations about the person to be counseled, identification of possible issues, and main points of discussion with possible questions to pose to the subordinate. In addition, as part of organizing information, the counselor should assess the situation and consider the subordinate's performance and any prior issues. The counselor can outline a possible plan of action with clear obtainable goals as a basis for the final plan development between counselor and the Soldier or Army Civilian.

Plan the Counseling Strategy

2-33. Leaders plan each counseling session, tailoring the counseling session to the individual and situation. Part of the planning process includes identifying the counseling approach, assessing the individual's situation and reputation, and identifying any anticipated resistance.

2-34. An effective leader approaches each subordinate as an individual. Different people and different situations require different counseling approaches—counseling is not a one-size-fits-all endeavor. Army leaders may employ three major approaches to counseling: nondirective, directive, or combined.

2-35. The Army leader can select from several techniques when counseling subordinates. These techniques may cause subordinates to change behavior and improve their performance. Counseling techniques leaders may explore during the nondirective or combined approaches include:
- Suggesting alternatives. Discuss alternative actions the subordinate may take. Leader and subordinate together decide which course of action is most appropriate.
- Recommending. Recommend one course of action but leave the decision to accept it to the subordinate.

- Persuading. Persuade the subordinate that a given course of action is best, but leave the final decision to the subordinate. Successful persuasion depends on the leader's credibility, the subordinate's willingness to listen, and mutual trust.
- Advising. Advise the subordinate that a given course of action is best. This is the strongest form of influence not involving command.

2-36. Techniques to use during the directive approach to counseling include:
- Corrective training. Teach and assist the subordinate in attaining and maintaining the required standard. A subordinate completes corrective training once consistently meeting standards.
- Commanding. Order the subordinate to take a given course of action in clear, precise words. The subordinate will face consequences for failing to execute.

2-37. While these approaches differ in specific techniques, the major difference between the approaches is the degree to which the subordinate participates and interacts during a counseling session. Table 2-1 identifies the advantages and disadvantages of each approach.

Table 2-1. Counseling approach summary

	Advantages	*Disadvantages*
Nondirective	Encourages maturity. Encourages open communication. Develops personal responsibility.	More time-consuming. Requires greatest counselor skills.
Combined	Moderately quick. Encourages maturity. Encourages open communication. Allows counselors to use their experience.	May take too much time for some situations.
Directive	Quickest method. Good for those needing clear, concise direction. Allows counselors to use their experience.	Does not encourage subordinates to be part of the solution. Treats symptoms, not issues. Tends to discourage subordinates from talking freely. Solution is the counselor's, not the subordinate's.

Establish the Right Atmosphere

2-38. The right atmosphere promotes open, two-way communication between a leader and subordinate. To establish a more relaxed atmosphere, leaders may offer the subordinate a seat or a cup of coffee. If appropriate, choose to sit in a chair next to or facing the subordinate since a desk can serve as a barrier.

2-39. Some situations require formal settings. During counseling to correct substandard performance, leaders seated behind a desk may direct the subordinate to remain standing. This reinforces the leader's role and authority and underscores the severity of the situation.

STAGE 3: CONDUCT THE COUNSELING SESSION

2-40. Army leaders use a balanced mix of formal and informal counseling and learn to take advantage of daily events to provide Soldiers and Army Civilians with feedback. Figure 2-2 on page 2-9 portrays an example of a formal counseling session. Even during informal counseling, leaders should address the four basic components of a counseling session:
- Open the session.
- Discuss the issues.
- Develop a plan of action.
- Record and close the session.

Chapter 2

Open the Session

2-41. In opening, the leader makes the purpose clear and establishes a subordinate-centered setting as appropriate for the situation. The counselor establishes an atmosphere of shared purpose by inviting the subordinate to speak and acknowledge the purpose. An appropriate purpose statement might be "SFC Taylor, the purpose of this counseling is to discuss your duty performance over the past month and to create a plan to enhance performance and attain performance goals." If applicable, start the counseling session by reviewing the status of the current plan of action.

Discuss the Issues

2-42. The leader and counseled individual should attempt to develop a mutual and clear understanding of the counseling issues. Use active listening and invite the subordinate to do most of the talking—encourage the subordinate to participate fully in the session. Leaders respond and ask questions without dominating the conversation but help the subordinate better understand the subject of the counseling session, such as duty performance, a situation and its effects, or potential areas for growth. Leaders must be open to adjusting their understanding of the situation based on the subordinate's input.

2-43. To reduce the perception of bias or early judgment, both leader and subordinate should provide examples or cite specific observations. When the issue is substandard performance, the leader must be clear what did not meet the standard. During the discussion, the leader must clearly establish what the subordinate must do to meet the standard. It is very important that the leader frames the issue at hand as substandard performance and prevents the subordinate from labeling the issue as unreasonable. An exception would occur if the leader considers the current standard as negotiable or is willing to alter the conditions under which the subordinate can meet the standard.

Develop a Plan of Action

2-44. A plan of action identifies a method and pathway for achieving a desired result, limited to one or two realistic goals tied to work or life events with milestones that allow for monitoring progress. Before developing the plan of action, the leader must assess whether the counseled subordinate understands the purpose and any related issues. The plan of action must be appropriate and specific, showing the subordinate how to modify or maintain specific behaviors to reach goals set during the counseling session. For example: "PFC Miller, next week you'll attend the map reading class with 1st Platoon. After class, SGT Dixon will coach you through the land navigation course and help you develop your compass skills. After observing you going through the course with SGT Dixon, I will meet with you again to determine if you need additional training."

Record and Close the Session

2-45. Although requirements to record counseling sessions vary, a leader always benefits from documenting the main points of a counseling session, even informal ones. Documentation serves as a ready reference for the agreed-upon plan of action and helps the leader track the subordinate's accomplishments, personal preferences, or issues. A good record of counseling enables the leader to make proper recommendations for professional development, promotions, and evaluations. DA Form 4856 is designed to help Army leaders conduct and record counseling sessions. Leaders must decide when counseling, additional training, rehabilitation, reassignment, or other developmental options have been exhausted.

2-46. Army regulations require specific written records of counseling for certain personnel actions, such as barring a Soldier from reenlisting, processing an administrative separation or placing a Soldier in the overweight program. When a Soldier faces involuntary separation, the leader must maintain accurate counseling records. Documentation of substandard actions often conveys a strong message to subordinates that a further slip in performance or discipline could require more severe action or punishment.

2-47. Leaders should close the session by asking the counseled subordinate to summarize key points and expectations based on the proposed plan of action. Leaders should establish any necessary follow-up measures with the subordinate to support the successful implementation of the plan of action. Follow-up measures may include providing the subordinate with specific resources and time, periodic assessments of the plan and additional referrals. If possible, schedule future meetings before dismissing the subordinate.

Example of a Counseling Session

Prepare for the Session
- Identify the purpose and type of counseling, reflect on the situation, and consider appropriate ways to address the session.

Open the Session
- To establish a relaxed environment for open exchange, explain that discussing and understanding the importance of the Army Values, leader attributes and competencies makes it easier to develop and incorporate them for success into an individual leadership style.

- State the purpose of the initial counseling: what SFC Taylor must do to be a successful platoon sergeant. Agree on the duty description and specific performance requirements. Discuss related values, competencies, and standards for success. Explain subsequent counseling will address developmental needs and how well performance objectives are met. Urge SFC Taylor to identify developmental needs during the next quarter.

- Ensure that SFC Taylor knows the rating chain. Resolve any questions about the duty position and associated responsibilities. Discuss the close relationship that must exist between a platoon leader and a platoon sergeant including the importance of honest, two-way communication.

Discuss the Issues
- Jointly review the draft duty description including all associated responsibilities such as maintenance, training, and Soldier welfare. Relate the responsibilities to leader competencies, attributes, and values noted in ADRP 6-22. Revise the duty description, if needed. Highlight areas of special emphasis and additional duties.

- Explain that character, presence, and intellect are the basis for competent leadership; developing the desired leader attributes requires that Army leaders adopt them through self-awareness and lifelong learning. Emphasize that the plan of action to accomplish major performance objectives must include the appropriate values, attributes, and competencies.

Assist in Developing a Plan of Action (During the Counseling Session)
- Ask SFC Taylor to identify tasks to accomplish the performance objectives. Describe each by using the values, responsibilities, and competencies found in ADRP 6-22. Discuss specific examples of success and excellence in each area. Ask for suggestions to make the goals objective, specific, and measurable.

- Ensure that SFC Taylor has at least one example of a success or excellence statement for each area. Discuss SFC Taylor's promotion goals and ask what he considers as strengths and weaknesses. Obtain the last two master sergeant selection board results and compare stated goals and objectives.

Close the Session
- Verify SFC Taylor understands the duty description, performance objectives, and expectation to assist in your development as a platoon leader.

- Stress the importance of teamwork and two-way communication.

- Remind SFC Taylor to perform a self-assessment during the next quarter.

- Set a tentative date during the next quarter for the follow-up counseling.

Figure 2-2. Example of a counseling session

Stage 4: Follow-up

Leader Responsibilities

2-48. The counseling process does not end with the initial counseling session. It continues throughout the implementation of the plan of action consistent with the observed results. Sometimes the initial plan of action will require modification to meet the desired outcomes. Leaders must consistently support their subordinates in implementing the plan of action by teaching, coaching, mentoring, or providing additional time, referrals and other appropriate resources. Additional measures may include more focused follow-up counseling, informing the chain of command, or taking more severe corrective measures if appropriate.

Assess the Plan of Action

2-49. During assessment, the leader and the subordinate jointly determine if the desired results happened. They should determine the date for their initial assessment during the initial counseling session. The plan of action assessment provides useful information for future follow-up counseling sessions.

SUMMARY – THE COUNSELING PROCESS AT A GLANCE

2-50. Use Table 2-2 as a quick reference whenever counseling Soldiers or Army Civilian team members.

Table 2-2. A summary of counseling

| Leaders must demonstrate these qualities to counsel effectively:
• Respect for subordinates.
• Self and cultural awareness.
• Credibility.
• Empathy.
Leaders must employ these counseling skills appropriately:
• Active listening.
• Responding.
• Appropriate questioning.
Effective leaders avoid common counseling mistakes. Leaders should avoid:
• Personal bias.
• Rash judgments.
• Stereotyping.
• Losing emotional control.
• Inflexible counseling methods.
• Improper follow-up. | The Counseling Process
Identify the need for counseling.
Prepare for counseling:
• Select a suitable place.
• Schedule the time.
• Notify the subordinate well in advance.
• Organize information.
• Identify possible outcomes.
• Outline the components of the counseling session.
• Plan counseling strategy.
• Establish right atmosphere.
Conduct the counseling session:
• Open the session.
• Discuss the issue.
• Develop a plan of action (to include the leader's responsibilities).
• Record and close the session.
Follow-up:
• Support plan of action implementation.
• Assess the plan of action. |

Glossary

ACRONYMS AND ABBREVIATIONS

ACAP	Army Career and Alumni Program
ADRP	Army doctrine reference publication
AR	Army regulation
ATP	Army techniques publication
DA	Department of the Army
FM	field manual
NCO	noncommissioned officer
NCOER	noncommissioned officer evaluation report
PFC	private first class
SFC	sergeant first class
SGT	sergeant
U.S.	United States

This page intentionally left blank.

References

REQUIRED PUBLICATIONS
These documents must be available to intended users of this publication.
Joint publications are available online at http://www.dtic.mil/doctrine/new_pubs/jointpub.htm.

ADRP 1-02. *Terms and Military Symbols*. 24 September 2013.

JP 1-02. *Defense Dictionary of Military and Associated Terms*. 08 November 2010.

RELATED PUBLICATIONS
These sources contain relevant supplemental information.
Most Army publications are available online at http://www.apd.army.mil.

ADRP 6-22. *Army Leadership*. 1 August 2012.

AR 600-8. *Military Personnel Management*. 1 October 1989.

AR 600-8-19. *Enlisted Promotions and Reductions*. 30 April 2010.

AR 623-3. *Evaluation Reporting System*. 5 June 2012.

AR 635-200. *Active Duty Enlisted Administrative Separations*. 6 June 2005.

AR 690-400. *Chapter 4302 Total Army Performance Evaluation System*. 16 October 1998.

FM 27-10. *The Law of Land Warfare*. 18 July 1956.

PRESCRIBED FORMS
Unless otherwise indicated, DA Forms are available on the Army Publishing Directorate web site (www.apd.army.mil).

DA Form 4856. *Developmental Counseling Form*.

REFERENCED FORMS
Unless otherwise indicated, DA Forms are available on the Army Publishing Directorate web site (www.apd.army.mil).

DA Form 2028. *Recommended Changes to Publications and Blank Forms*.

RECOMMENDED FORMS
Unless otherwise indicated, DA Forms are available on the Army Publishing Directorate web site (www.apd.army.mil).

DA Form 67–9. *Officer Evaluation Report*.

DA Form 67–9–1. *Officer Evaluation Report Support Form*.

DA Form 67–9–1A. *Developmental Support Form*.

DA Form 1059. *Service School Academic Evaluation Report*.

DA Form 1059–1. *Civilian Institution Academic Evaluation Report*.

DA Form 2166–8. *NCO Evaluation Report*.

DA Form 2166–8–1. *NCOER Counseling and Support Form*.

DA Form 7222. *Senior System Civilian Evaluation Report*.

DA Form 7222-1. *Civilian Evaluation Report Support Form*.

DA Form 7223. *Base System Civilian Evaluation Report*.

DA Form 7223-1. *Base System Civilian Performance Counseling Checklist /Record*.

RECOMMENDED READINGS

AR 635-8. *Separation Processing and Documents*. 10 February 2014.

RECOMMENDED WEB SITES

All URLs were accessed on 14 March 2014.

Army 360 Multi-Source Assessment and Feedback (MSAF) Program. Available at https://msaf.army.mil.

Army Career & Alumni Program (ACAP). Available at https://www.acap.army.mil.

Army Career Tracker (ACT). Available at https://actnow.army.mil.

Army G1 Mentorship Program. Available at http://www.armyg1.army.mil/hr/mentorship.

Army Suicide Prevention Program. Available at http://www.armyg1.army.mil/hr/suicide.

Comprehensive Soldier Fitness Program. Available at http://www.army.mil/csf/index.html.

Military OneSource. Available at www.militaryonesource.mil.

Resilience Training. Available at https://www.resilience.army.mil.

U. S. Army Combat Readiness/Safety Center. Available at https://safety.army.mil/Default.aspx.

ATP 6-22.1
1 July 2014

By order of the Secretary of the Army:

RAYMOND T. ODIERNO
General, United States Army
Chief of Staff

Official:

GERALD B. O'KEEFE
Administrative Assistant to the
Secretary of the Army
1411105

DISTRIBUTION:

Active Army, Army National Guard, and United States Army Reserve: Distributed in electronic media only (EMO).

This page intentionally left blank.

Army Doctrine Reference Publication
No. 7-0

ADRP 7-0

Headquarters
Department of the Army
Washington, DC, 23 August 2012

Training Units and Developing Leaders

Contents

		Page
	PREFACE	iii
	INTRODUCTION	v
Chapter 1	THE ROLE OF TRAINING AND LEADER DEVELOPMENT	1-1
	Training and Leader Development	1-1
	Training	1-1
	Leader Development	1-2
	The Role of the Commander	1-3
Chapter 2	PRINCIPLES OF UNIT TRAINING AND LEADER DEVELOPMENT	2-1
	Principles of Unit Training	2-1
	Principles of Leader Development	2-3
Chapter 3	UNIT TRAINING MANAGEMENT	3-1
	The Operations Process in Unit Training and Leader Development	3-1
	Plan	3-2
	Prepare	3-9
	Execute	3-11
	Assess	3-11
	GLOSSARY	Glossary-1
	REFERENCES	References-1
	INDEX	Index-1

Distribution Restriction: Approved for public release; distribution is unlimited.

Figures

Introductory figure. Unit training and leader development underlying logic iv
Figure 1-1. The Army's leader development model 1-2
Figure 3-1. The operations process 3-2
Figure 3-2. Development of the unit training plan 3-3

Tables

Table 2-1. The Army principles of unit training 2-1
Table 2-2. The Army's principles of leader development 2-4

Preface

Army Doctrine Reference Publication (ADRP) 7-0, *Training Units and Developing Leaders*, augments fundamental principles discussed in Army Doctrine Publication (ADP) 7-0, *Training Units and Developing Leaders*. Both ADP 7-0 and ADRP 7-0 support the doctrine established in ADP 3-0 and ADRP 3-0. Army units will face a complex operational environment shaped by a wide range of threats, allies, and populations. Rapid advances in communications, weapons, transportation, information technologies, and space-based capabilities make it a challenge to just stay even with the pace of change. Because Army units face a wide mix of challenges—from strategic to tactical—they must develop leaders to conduct unified land operations anywhere in the world in any operation across the conflict continuum. Army training prepares units and leaders to be successful through challenging, realistic, and relevant unit training and leader development at home station, at the combat training centers, and in the schoolhouses.

ADRP 7-0 applies to all Army leaders, including Army civilians in leadership positions.

ADP 7-0 supports the implementation of North Atlantic Treaty Organization (known as NATO) standardization agreements for training.

ADRP 7-0 applies to the Active Army, the Army National Guard (ARNG)/Army National Guard of the United States (ARNGUS), and the United States Army Reserve (USAR) unless otherwise stated.

Terms for which ADRP 7-0 is the proponent (the authority) are indicated with an asterisk in the glossary. Definitions for which ADRP 7-0 is the proponent are printed in boldface in the text.

The proponent of ADRP 7-0 is the United States Army Combined Arms Center (CAC). The preparing agencies are the Combined Arms Doctrine Directorate (CADD) and the Training Management Directorate (TMD) within CAC–Training (CAC-T). Both CADD and CAC–T are subordinate to the United States Army Combined Arms Center. Send written comments and recommendations on Department of the Army (DA) Form 2028 (Recommended Changes to Publications and Blank Forms) to Commanding General, U.S. Army Combined Arms Center, Fort Leavenworth, ATTN: ATZL-MCK-D (ADRP 7-0), 300 McPherson Avenue, Fort Leavenworth, KS 66027-2337; by email to mailto:usarmy.leavenworth.mccoe.mbx.cadd-org-mailbox@mail.mil; or submit an electronic DA Form 2028.

Introductory figure. Unit training and leader development underlying logic

Introduction

Army Doctrine Reference Publication (ADRP) 7-0, *Training Units and Developing Leaders*, expands on the foundations and tenets found in Army Doctrine Publication (ADP) 7-0. The most significant change from the 2011 edition of Field Manual (FM) 7-0 is the inclusion of the operations process as the accepted model for planning not only operations, but also unit training and leader development. The ADRP rescinds the idea that a separate and distinct training management process exists from the operations process for training and leader development. Such earlier concepts as long-range planning and short-range planning are now based on the military decisionmaking process and troop leading procedures as defined by ADRP 5-0 and Army Tactics, Techniques, and Procedures (ATTP) 5-0.1. Both ADP 7-0 and ADRP 7-0 support the idea that training a unit is not fundamentally different from preparing a unit for an operation. Learning the concepts, ideas, and terminology of the operations process as units train will make the transition from training to operations a more seamless effort for both leaders and their units.

ADRP 7-0 contains three chapters:

Chapter 1 introduces the Army's concepts of training and leader development and the role of the commander in these. This chapter also specifies the role of the commander in training and leader development through the activities of understand, visualize, describe, direct, lead and assess.

Chapter 2 re-establishes and re-affirms the principles of unit training and principles of leader development from the 2011 edition of FM 7-0.

Chapter 3—
- Discusses the operations process in unit training and leader development. It introduces unit training management (UTM) concepts and discusses planning, preparing, executing, and assessing training.
- Describes how UTM details the over-arching Army training management process.
- Adopts the operations planning processes as the same processes used for planning unit training.
- Redefines the battalion- and company-level mission-essential task lists (METLs) as representing the tasks that support the unit's designed capabilities.
- Specifies mission-essential tasks at battalion and company levels.
- Replaces the unit long-range plan with the unit training plan.
- Rescinds the concept of short-range planning.
- Establishes operation orders, warning orders, and fragmentary orders as the formats used for communicating unit training plans and training events.
- Modifies the term *after action review*.

Based on current doctrinal changes, the following terms for which ADRP 7-0 is proponent have been modified for purposes of this manual: *after action review* and *mission-essential task*. The term *training domain* is no longer formally defined but retained based on common English usage. The glossary contains acronyms and defined terms.

This page intentionally left blank.

Chapter 1

The Role of Training and Leader Development

This chapter discusses the Army's fundamental role of training units and developing leaders. It explains the differences between individual and collective training. It then discusses the importance of leader development and the primary role of the commander in training.

TRAINING AND LEADER DEVELOPMENT

1-1. The Army provides combatant commanders with trained and ready units, leaders, and individuals. Army expeditionary forces are prepared to conduct unified land operations in support of unified action. The Army does this by conducting tough, realistic, standards-based, performance-oriented training. Units train all the time—while deployed, at home station, and at combat training centers. Unit commanders lead and assess training to ensure it is mission focused and done to standard.

1-2. Effective training and leader development form the cornerstone of operational success. Through training, units, leaders, and Soldiers achieve the tactical and technical competence that builds confidence and adaptability. Army forces train using training doctrine that sustains their expeditionary and campaign capabilities. Focused training and leader development prepares units, leaders, Soldiers, and civilians to deploy, fight, and win. The Army trains units, Soldiers, and civilians daily in individual and collective tasks under challenging and realistic conditions. Training continues in deployed units to sustain skills and adapt to changes in operational environments.

1-3. Army training includes a system of techniques and standards that allow units and Soldiers to determine, acquire, and practice necessary skills. Candid assessments, after action reviews, and applied lessons learned and best practices produce versatile units, quality Soldiers, and Army civilians ready for all aspects of an operational environment.

1-4. Training is becoming more complex. Doing business as the Army has in the past is not an option. During the Cold War, the Army trained to a largely identified potential adversary using well-researched tactics. During the overseas contingency operations, the Army trained to a known adversary using largely emergent counterinsurgency tactics. The nature, scope, breadth, and depth of future conflict require that commanders train to produce adaptation and flexibility in forces and are decisively engaged in training management. Effective commanders use the same principles of mission command found in ADP 6-0 to build learning organizations and empower subordinates to develop and conduct training at the lowest possible echelons.

TRAINING

1-5. Training and educating Soldiers and Army civilians begin the day they enter the Army. They continue learning until the day they retire or separate. Army forces conduct training at the individual level and collectively by units using the three training domains. (See ADP 7-0 for the training domains.)

INDIVIDUAL TRAINING

1-6. The foundation of a unit's readiness ties directly to the proficiencies of its individual Soldiers and Army civilians to perform specified tasks related to an assigned duty position and skill level. Training and education prepare individuals to perform assigned tasks to standard, accomplish their mission and duties, and survive on the battlefield. Training on individual tasks occurs in both institutional and unit training. Units continue individual training to improve and sustain individual task proficiency while training on collective tasks.

COLLECTIVE TRAINING

1-7. Unit collective training reinforces foundations established in the institutional training domain and introduces additional skills needed to support the unit's mission and readiness posture. Collective training requires interactions among individuals or organizations to perform tasks that contribute to the unit's training objectives and mission-essential task proficiency. Unit training occurs in the operational training domain at home station, maneuver combat training centers, and mobilization training centers. Units also train during joint training exercises and while operationally deployed. Unit training develops and sustains an organization's readiness by achieving and sustaining proficiency in mission-essential tasks. Installations ensure units have access to the training enablers needed to develop that mission readiness.

LEADER DEVELOPMENT

1-8. Leader development is a continuous and progressive process, spanning a leader's entire career. Leader development comprises training, education, and experience gained in schools, while assigned to organizations, and through the individual's own program of self-development. The Army capstone concept—a description that describes future armed conflict and how the Army will conduct future joint land operations—drives leader development. With limited time in the schoolhouse, the majority of leader development occurs in operational assignments and through self-development. The Army leader development model (see figure 1-1) illustrates how the Army develops competent and confident military and Army civilian leaders through these three mutually supporting training domains.

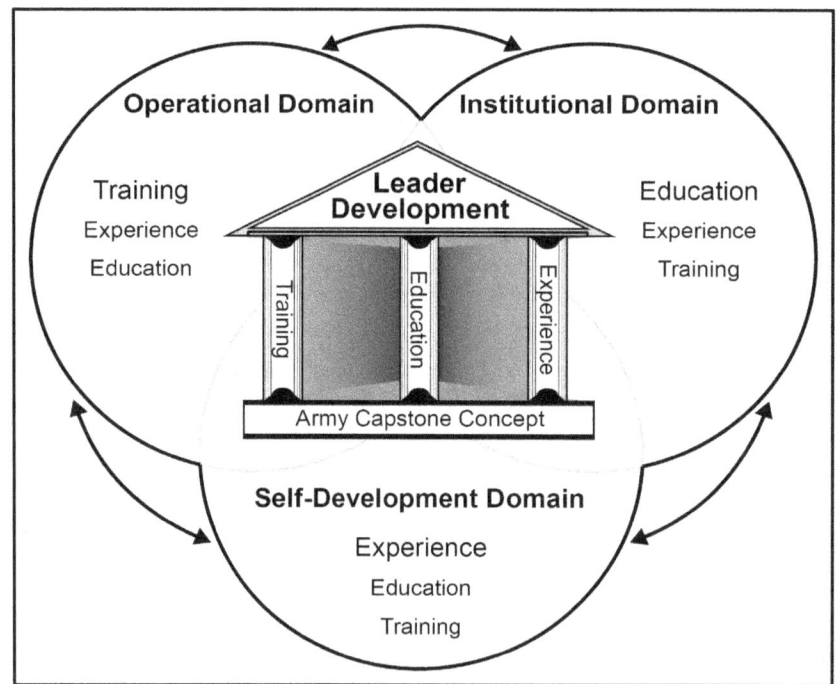

Figure 1-1. The Army's leader development model

1-9. Commanders and other leaders in the operating and generating forces build on the knowledge, skills, abilities, and behaviors their subordinate leaders gained in schools. They train and educate their subordinate leaders—and their emerging leaders—providing an environment of learning. They approach this responsibility with the same intensity that they use in training their units. They provide challenging assignments to further individual growth and learning. They help subordinates recognize their individual strengths and weaknesses, encouraging and supporting individual self-development programs.

THE ROLE OF THE COMMANDER

1-10. Commanders exercise mission command to give subordinates latitude in determining how to train their units to achieve the desired end state. Per the principle of "train as you will fight" (discussed in paragraphs 2-6 and 2-7), commanders and other leaders exercise mission command in training as well as in operations. They provide the commander's intent to subordinates, who determine how to achieve that commander's intent. Leaders encourage initiative and innovation in their subordinates by allowing them to determine the most effective ways to achieve the standards and meet training objectives. Commanders ensure their subordinate leaders have the necessary skills and knowledge to manage training and achieve desired levels of readiness. Commanders conduct training through the activities of understanding, visualizing, describing, directing, leading, and assessing.

UNDERSTAND

1-11. Commanders plan and execute unit training and leader development as they do in the operations process. A commander understands the higher commander's intent and its repercussions as the intent drives the collective tasks the unit must be able to perform. Understanding also means the commander must be knowledgeable of the environment in which the unit will eventually operate to better replicate it in training.

VISUALIZE

1-12. Commanders visualize both the end state of the training and the events that they will use to achieve that end state. Beginning with an understanding of the key collective tasks the unit must train, the current state of readiness, and the guidance from the higher commander, the commander creates a mental picture of the series of training events that will progressively lead the unit to the desired level of task proficiency.

DESCRIBE

1-13. After commanders visualize the plan, they describe it to their staffs and subordinates. Describing the plan facilitates a shared understanding of the tasks the unit will train to proficiency, the operational environment the unit will replicate, and the operational approach the unit will train to proficiency. This description takes the form of a unit training plan.

DIRECT

1-14. Commanders and other leaders oversee and adjust the unit training plan's execution. As the unit training plan is executed, commanders make decisions and provide guidance to ensure the training end state is achieved. Commanders direct training by—
- Personally observing the training.
- Participating in unit training meetings.
- Adjusting the plan and resources as required.

LEAD

1-15. Commanders lead by example and by their personal presence throughout the training. Their example and presence influence the training by providing purpose, direction, and motivation for the unit and subordinates. Since commanders are the unit's subject matter experts for training, they read and understand operations, training, and leader development doctrine. Commanders also familiarize themselves with training enablers such as the Army Training Network (ATN), the Digital Training Management System (DTMS), Combined Arms Training Strategies (CATS), and relevant training support and training development capabilities.

ASSESS

1-16. As the unit trains, the commander continually assesses not just the mission-essential task list and key collective tasks the unit must perform, but also the unit and its subordinate leaders as they train.

Chapter 1

Assessment not only considers task, unit, and leader proficiencies, but also reviews the relevance, realism, and quality of the training.

1-17. Leaders understand the unit's mission and the commander's intent. This understanding allows the unit to focus on training the few collective tasks that will best prepare it and its leaders to accomplish a mission or adapt to the requirements of a contingency mission. As units conduct training, commanders and subordinate leaders assess unit and leader proficiencies on individual and collective tasks.

1-18. Per the principle of "train as you will fight" (paragraphs 2-6 and 2-7), commanders and other leaders exercise mission command in training as well as in operations. They provide their commander's intent to subordinates, who determine how to achieve that commander's intent. Leaders encourage initiative and innovation in their subordinates by allowing them to determine the most effective ways to achieve the standards and meet training objectives.

Chapter 2
Principles of Unit Training and Leader Development

This chapter discusses the principles of unit training and the principles of leader development.

PRINCIPLES OF UNIT TRAINING

2-1. The principles of unit training in table 2-1 describe leader responsibilities and how effective leaders conduct training.

Table 2-1. The Army principles of unit training

- Commanders and other leaders are responsible for training.
- Noncommissioned officers train individuals, crews, and small teams.
- Train to standard.
- Train as you will fight.
- Train while operating.
- Train fundamentals first.
- Train to develop adaptability.
- Understand the operational environment.
- Train to sustain.
- Train to maintain.
- Conduct multiechelon and concurrent training.

COMMANDERS AND OTHER LEADERS ARE RESPONSIBLE FOR TRAINING

2-2. Unit commanders are responsible for training. They ensure their units are capable of accomplishing their missions. While commanders are the unit's overall training manager, subordinate leaders have responsibility for the proficiency of their respective organizations and subordinates. For example, a battalion S-3 oversees the training and resulting readiness of a section, but the battalion commander oversees the training and readiness of the battalion as a whole.

NONCOMMISSIONED OFFICERS TRAIN INDIVIDUALS, CREWS, AND SMALL TEAMS

2-3. Noncommissioned officers (NCOs) are the primary trainers of enlisted Soldiers, crews, and small teams. NCOs take broad guidance from their leaders; identify the necessary tasks, standards, and resources; and then plan, prepare, execute, and assess training. They ensure their Soldiers demonstrate proficiency in their individual military occupational specialty (commonly known as MOS) skills, warrior tasks, and battle drills. NCOs instill in Soldiers discipline, resiliency, the Warrior Ethos, and Army Values. In their assessment, NCOs provide feedback on task proficiency and the quality of the training.

2-4. NCOs help officers train units. NCOs develop and conduct training for their subordinates, coaching other NCOs, advising senior leaders, and helping develop junior officers. Leaders allot sufficient time and resources, and empower NCOs to plan, prepare, execute, and assess training with their Soldiers based on the NCO's analysis of identified strengths and weaknesses. Training management is an essential part of a unit's leader development program. Sergeant's time training (known as STT) is a common approach to NCO-led training events. NCOs conduct sergeant's time training to standard, not time.

Chapter 2

TRAIN TO STANDARD

2-5. Each individual and collective task has standards of performance. A standard is the accepted proficiency level required to accomplish a task. Mastery, the ability to perform the task instinctively, regardless of the conditions, is the desired level of proficiency. Units master tasks by limiting the number of tasks to train to the few key tasks required to accomplish the mission—assigned or contingency. Leaders know and enforce standards to ensure their organization meets mission requirements. When no standard exists, the commander establishes one and the next higher commander approves it.

TRAIN AS YOU WILL FIGHT

2-6. "Train as you will fight" means training under an expected operational environment for the mission. It also means adjusting the levels of intensity and complexity to improve unit and leader adaptability. Training conditions must enable leaders and Soldiers to assess challenges and employ critical thinking to develop sound, creative solutions rapidly.

2-7. Operations require leaders who understand the cultures in which they will operate. The cultures are not just foreign cultures; they include such non-Army cultures as those in other Services and government agencies. Individuals, units, and their leaders develop cultural understanding through education and frequent training with military and nonmilitary partners to avoid actions and perceptions that can undermine relationships and missions. Leaders develop proficiency in both cultural norms and language and, when possible, train with their partners before participating in operations. Commanders and other leaders replicate cultural settings as much as possible during training, using role players or actual partners.

TRAIN WHILE OPERATING

2-8. Units conduct training even when the unit is engaged in operations. As units operate, they learn from formal and informal after action reviews—during and after operations. Leaders continuously evaluate observations, insights, and lessons on planning, preparing, and execution. They also incorporate corrective action into training before the unit conducts the next operation. An after action review is a facilitated self-analysis of an organization's performance, with the objective of improving future performance (see paragraph 3-73). It addresses what went well and how to sustain it, and what went wrong and how to improve it. Usually, training during operations is more decentralized than during training at home station.

TRAIN FUNDAMENTALS FIRST

2-9. Fundamentals typically cover basic soldiering, the warrior tasks, battle drills, marksmanship, fitness, and military occupational specialty skills. Company-level units and below establish this fundamental by focusing training on individual and small-unit skills. Units proficient in fundamentals tend to integrate more easily into higher level, more complex collective tasks.

TRAIN TO DEVELOP ADAPTABILITY

2-10. Effective leaders understand that change is inevitable in any operational environment. The time to adjust to that change can be short. Leaders focus training on those tasks most essential to mission accomplishment. They also understand that Soldiers and leaders must be ready to perform tasks successfully for which they have not trained. By mastering the few key tasks under varying, challenging, and complex conditions, Soldiers and their leaders become confident that they can adapt to any new mission.

UNDERSTAND THE OPERATIONAL ENVIRONMENT

2-11. As commanders plan training, they must understand their expected operational environment. Once they understand these environments, they replicate the conditions as closely as possible in training. They often use the operational variables (known as PMESII-PT), mission variables (known as METT-TC), and tools found on the Army Training Network (ATN), such as scenarios, to create a training environment. Commanders conduct an analysis based on an actual operational environment if deploying, or an operational environment established in training guidance if not deploying, to determine the conditions required to train realistically.

TRAIN TO SUSTAIN

2-12. Units train to improve and enhance their capabilities and individual resiliency and endurance. Commanders and other leaders first design training to sustain unit proficiency. Then they build the capability of individuals to sustain themselves mentally and physically during long operations. Leaders incorporate comprehensive fitness programs into unit training and leader development.

TRAIN TO MAINTAIN

2-13. Commanders allocate time in training for units to maintain themselves and their equipment to standard. Maintaining is training. Maintenance training has clear, focused, and measurable objectives. Regular, routine maintenance training tends to instill discipline in individuals. Well-disciplined individuals properly care for themselves and their equipment. Organizations tend to perform maintenance during operations to the standards they practice in training.

2-14. Leaders instill in their subordinates an appreciation of the importance of personal and equipment maintenance through their presence, personal example, and involvement in maintenance training. Maintenance training is an essential aspect of leader development that involves the entire unit chain of command.

2-15. Soldiers learn stewardship of Army resources during training. Leaders and subordinates are responsible for protecting resources, including people, time, individual and organizational equipment, installation property, training areas, ranges, facilities, and funds. Good stewardship avoids costly and unnecessary expenditures for replacements and helps ensure that people and equipment are available and ready to deploy.

CONDUCT MULTIECHELON AND CONCURRENT TRAINING

2-16. **Multiechelon training is a training technique that allows for the simultaneous training of more than one echelon on different or complementary tasks.** It optimizes the use of time and resources to train more than one echelon simultaneously. Commanders ensure subordinate units have the opportunity to train their essential tasks during the higher unit's training event while still supporting the higher echelon's training objectives. Planning for these events requires detailed synchronization and coordination at each echelon. For example, an artillery battery commander supporting an infantry battalion during a non-firing exercise might conduct howitzer section training while the fire direction center maintains communications with fire support officers moving with the infantry.

2-17. During a training event, units may execute concurrent training on tasks not directly related to the training event to make the most efficient use of available training time. For example, while Soldiers are waiting their turn on the firing line at a marksmanship range, their leaders can train them on important tasks needing improvement, often using proficient Soldiers to train their peers.

PRINCIPLES OF LEADER DEVELOPMENT

2-18. Every Army leader is responsible for the professional development of their subordinate military and civilian leaders. Leaders execute this significant responsibility by assigning their subordinates to developmental positions and through training, education, coaching, and, in special cases, mentoring. Leader development is an investment, since good leaders will develop not only good training but also other good leaders.

2-19. Table 2-2 lists the Army's principles of leader development. Paragraphs 2-20 through 2-28 discuss these principles.

Table 2-2. The Army's principles of leader development

- Lead by example.
- Develop subordinate leaders.
- Create a learning environment for subordinate leaders.
- Train leaders in the art and science of mission command.
- Train to develop adaptive leaders.
- Train leaders to think critically and creatively.
- Train your leaders to know their subordinates and their families.

LEAD BY EXAMPLE

2-20. Everything a leader does and says is scrutinized, analyzed, and often imitated. What leaders do and say influences the behaviors, attitudes, and performance of their subordinates. Good leaders understand they are role models for others and demonstrate the desired leader attributes and core leader competencies found in ADP 6-22.

DEVELOP SUBORDINATE LEADERS

2-21. Leaders have the responsibility to develop subordinate leaders. All leaders need to understand if they are meeting standards. Leaders observe and assess subordinates. Much like an after action review, they facilitate discussions to help subordinates self-discover strengths and weaknesses and ways subordinate leaders can sustain and improve their performance, skills, knowledge, abilities, and behaviors. Leaders provide challenges in training to enhance their subordinates' capabilities and performance, allowing subordinates to rise to the level of expectations. Leaders ensure their subordinates attend professional military education at the right time in their careers, obtain functional training as needed, and ensure they get help and support if needed. They counsel all subordinates face-to-face, recognize high performers, and take remedial and disciplinary action as required.

CREATE A LEARNING ENVIRONMENT FOR SUBORDINATE LEADERS

2-22. Leader growth occurs when subordinates are provided opportunities to overcome obstacles and make difficult decisions. Learning comes from experiencing both success and failure. An environment that allows subordinate leaders to make honest—as opposed to repeated or careless—mistakes without prejudice is essential to leader development and personal growth.

2-23. Self-assessments and candid after action reviews are important in facilitating leader development. Good leaders know standards and expectations and are completely honest with themselves on how well they meet those standards and expectations. Successful leaders willingly accept constructive criticism and learn from their peers and subordinates as well as their leaders.

TRAIN IN THE ART AND SCIENCE OF MISSION COMMAND

2-24. Commanders train in the art of command and train their staffs in the science of control. Effective leaders conduct operations while exercising mission command (ADRP 3-0 and ADRP 6-0 address mission command). Exercising mission command to manage training not only improves mission command proficiency, but also encourages risk-taking, initiative, and creativity in subordinates.

TRAIN TO DEVELOP ADAPTIVE LEADERS

2-25. The Army continues to succeed under the most challenging conditions because Soldiers and Army civilians have learned to adapt to new tasks. Units and individuals cannot train on every task under every possible condition. They must excel at a few tasks and then adapt to new tasks. They improve their ability to adapt through exposure to—and the intuition gained from—multiple, complex, and unexpected situations in challenging, unfamiliar, and uncomfortable conditions. While individuals may not have trained on a specific task under specific conditions, they should have performed the task enough times under multiple conditions to confidently adapt to a new mission or environment. Change is inevitable. Agile

Principles of Unit Training and Leader Development

leaders expect change, develop plans to mitigate the effects of change, and look for indicators of change so that they can ease effects of change.

TRAIN LEADERS TO THINK CRITICALLY AND CREATIVELY

2-26. The Army develops leaders able to solve difficult, complex problems. Effective leaders comfortably make decisions with only partial information. Critical and creative thinkers—
- Are open-minded and consider alternative, sometimes nonconformist, solutions and the second- and third-order effects of those solutions.
- Collaborate with others for help in analyzing and war-gaming solutions.
- Make timely, informed decisions.
- Are adept at honestly assessing their own strengths and weaknesses and determining ways to sustain strengths and overcome weaknesses.

TRAIN YOUR LEADERS TO KNOW THEIR SUBORDINATES AND THEIR FAMILIES

2-27. All successful leaders know their subordinates at least two levels down—their strengths, weaknesses, and capabilities. Effective leaders maximize subordinates' strengths and help them overcome weaknesses. Similarly, an effective leader provides advice, counsel, and support as subordinate leaders develop their own subordinates. Leaders keep the relationship professional—fraternization with subordinates is unacceptable.

2-28. Family well-being is essential to unit and individual readiness. The Army trains leaders to know and help not only the subordinates, but also their families. Training and education ensure subordinate leaders recognize the importance of families and are adept at helping individuals solve family issues and sustain sound relationships.

This page intentionally left blank.

Chapter 3
Unit Training Management

This chapter discusses how the Army manages unit training using the operations process. It explains the planning, preparation, execution, and assessment of training. Unit training management on the Army Training Network provides the how-to details of performing the training management concepts described in this chapter.

THE OPERATIONS PROCESS IN UNIT TRAINING AND LEADER DEVELOPMENT

3-1. The operations process in unit training and leader development uses unit training management (UTM) to detail the Army training management processes. UTM is delivered in several ways for Soldiers to use. The primary portal to UTM is through the Army Training Network (ATN). This password-protected Web site enables users to view UTM modules, tutorials, and examples. UTM mirrors the Army's method to plan and operate rather than the artificialities of a distinct and separate training management process.

3-2. The Army's operations process provides a common framework for guiding commanders as they lead and manage unit training and leader development. Effective unit training results from a sound analysis of the unit's mission and its ability to accomplish that mission. The higher unit's mission, the unit mission-essential task list (METL), and higher commander's guidance drive the commander's selection of collective tasks on which the unit trains to accomplish mission success.

3-3. Commanders and other leaders plan to develop their subordinate leaders—through training, education, and experience—in the three training domains (institutional, operational, and self-development). Leaders use the operations process to integrate leader development into a unit training plan.

3-4. The commander is central to determining the few tasks on which the unit must train. Commanders, with the assistance of unit leadership, follow the operations process. Figure 3-1 illustrates the Army operations process (see ADRP 3-0) of plan, prepare, execute, and assess. Commanders first plan for training. They identify the collective tasks on which to train, identify, and sequence training events; identify resources required; and provide the guidance necessary to achieve mission readiness. While commanders plan, they exercise mission command to enable their subordinates to determine how they will achieve their training objectives. Thorough preparation ensures that training conditions reflect the expected mission and that commanders have the resources and enablers necessary to train. Commanders then execute the training. Lastly, they assess the training. Assessments help commanders determine if units need to retrain tasks and if the training plan requires modification.

Chapter 3

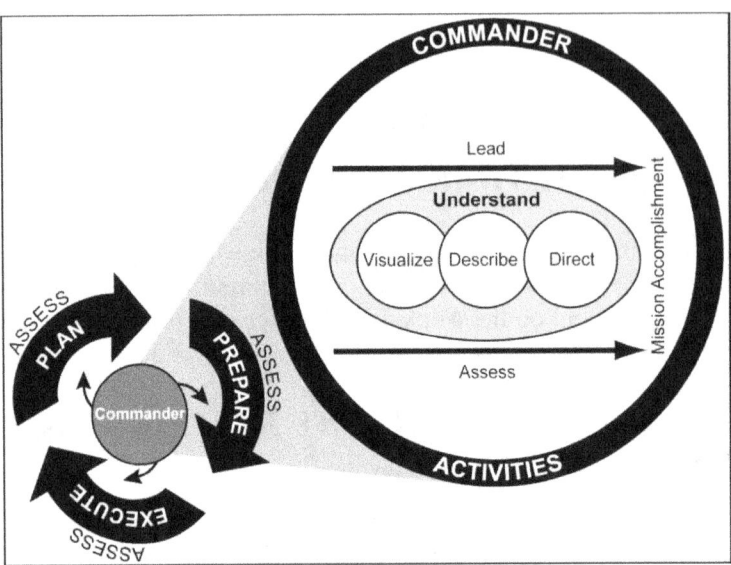

Figure 3-1. The operations process

3-5. A *mission-essential task* represents a task a unit could perform based on its design, equipment, manning, and table of organization and equipment/table of distribution and allowances mission. A *mission-essential task list* is a compilation of mission-essential tasks. For brigade and higher units, headquarters, the Department of the Army standardizes METLs for like-type units. The standardized METL represents the tasks of decisive action that a unit could perform based on its table of organization and equipment or table of distribution and allowance. A unit given a non-standard mission (such as an artillery unit given a transportation unit mission) will not change its standardized METL; instead, it will determine the additional transportation unit tasks it must train for the mission. When reporting its readiness to headquarters, Department of the Army, the commander rates only the mission-essential tasks (METs) in the standardized METL. A unit does not have the resources to train on every MET; therefore, units sometimes only partially train or not train on some METs.

3-6. At the battalion and company levels, the higher commander collaborates with the subordinate commander on the latter's METL. A MET at battalion and company levels can be a universal joint task list (known as the UJTL) task, an Army tactical task from the Army universal task list (known as the AUTL), a Combined Arms Training Strategies (CATS) task selection, a task group from the brigade or higher unit Department of the Army standardized METL, or a major collective task. The higher commander approves the subordinate unit's METL. Subordinate unit METLs align with, nest with, and support their next higher unit's METL. Subordinate unit METLs usually do not change since they are based on the higher unit's METL and the unit's designed mission. Based on the unit's METL and the higher commander's guidance, the unit trains on the supporting collective tasks most important to the success of the mission and gives the unit the most flexibility to adapt to new missions.

3-7. Because training time and other essential resources are often limited, units cannot train all the METL tasks to proficiency at once. Based on the unit mission and higher commander's guidance, commanders use the unit METL as a primary source to select the few, most important supporting collective tasks to train.

PLAN

3-8. Planning for unit training begins with the commander determining the unit mission, reviewing the unit's METL, and determining the tasks that the unit must perform to support the higher unit's mission. Figure 3-2 describes the development of a unit training plan. (Paragraph 3-30 discusses unit training plan.)

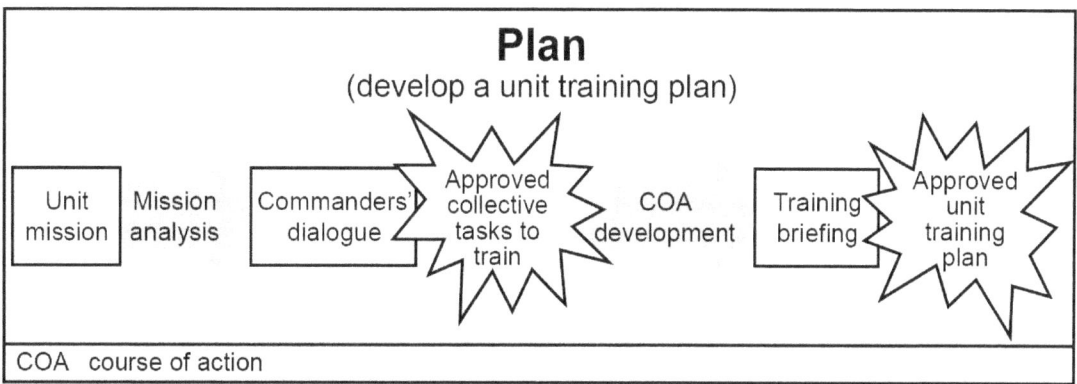

Figure 3-2. Development of the unit training plan

3-9. At battalion level and higher (units with a coordinating staff), commanders follow the steps of the military decisionmaking process (MDMP) to plan unit training. ADRP 5-0 discusses the MDMP in detail. Some steps of the MDMP for operations translate differently for training and are addressed beginning in paragraph 3-11. Company level and below (units without a coordinating staff) use troop leading procedures. (Paragraph 3-33 discusses troop leading procedures.)

THE MILITARY DECISIONMAKING PROCESS FOR DEVELOPING A UNIT TRAINING PLAN

3-10. The steps of MDMP are as follows:
- Step 1 – Receipt of Mission
- Step 2 – Mission Analysis
- Step 3 – Course of Action Development
- Step 4 – Course of Action Analysis (War Game)
- Step 5 – Course of Action Comparison
- Step 6 – Course of Action Approval
- Step 7 – Orders Production

Receipt of Mission

3-11. When the commander receives a mission from the higher commander, the commander begins the process of determining and analyzing the tasks the unit must be able to perform in support of the new mission. The commander determines how the unit will train for proficiency in those tasks. To ensure parallel planning throughout the command, the commander sends a warning order to subordinate units to begin their planning processes.

Mission Analysis

3-12. The commander begins mission analysis with the unit's re-stated mission, the higher commander's guidance, and the unit METL. Commanders conduct this analysis to determine the capabilities the unit must have to accomplish the unit's mission in support of the higher headquarters. Mission analysis helps commanders select the few—the most important—collective tasks on which the unit must train. Commanders do not attempt to train all the tasks and supporting collective tasks that support their unit METL, or all the capabilities specified in the unit's table of organization and equipment or table of distribution and allowances mission. Commanders at all levels train to master a select few mission-focused collective tasks—even though they know they will probably have to adapt to unforeseen missions.

Chapter 3

Determining the Collective Tasks to Train

3-13. When selecting collective tasks to train, commanders seek the right collective tasks that not only support the mission, but also are more likely to enable the unit to adapt to unexpected missions.

3-14. During mission analysis, the commander also considers—
- The unit's current readiness assessment of the collective tasks to train.
- The higher commander's guidance.
- The unit METL.
- Time available to train.
- The expected operational environment.
- Risks involved in not training collective tasks that the mission might require.
- Any resources needed for training that are not readily available at home station.
- Input from subordinates.

Commanders' Dialogue

3-15. The mission analysis is complete when commanders are prepared to discuss the following topics with their higher commanders in a one-on-one discussion:
- The collective tasks the unit should train during the upcoming Army force generation (ARFORGEN) force pool or similar training cycle.
- The commander's assessment of the collective tasks to train.
- The amount of time a commander expects the unit requires for proficiency in the selected tasks.
- Potential risks with not training other tasks that could be used in the mission—and intended mitigation measures.
- The training environment the commander will create to replicate an operational environment and any required support to achieve that environment.
- Significant unit readiness issues.

3-16. The commander coordinates a dialogue with the higher commander to discuss the topics to gain guidance, gain support, and set expectations for developing the unit training plan. Formal dialogues occur at company level and above. If feasible, the dialogue includes the gaining commander if the unit commander is deploying. For brigades, the dialogue includes any units that will be part of the deploying force.

Course of Action Development

3-17. Given the results of the commanders' dialogue, the commander determines the best training plan for the unit. As with planning an operation—which involves the analysis of several suitable, feasible, and acceptable courses of action (COAs)—the commander and staff assess different ways to achieve task proficiency for the unit in the time available before developing the final training plan.

Determining and Sequencing Training Events

3-18. Using the list of approved collective tasks from the commanders' dialogue, the unit commander develops the training events (for example, field-training exercises, situational training exercises, and terrain walks) that will support task training to proficiency. Given the visualized end state, the commander backward plans the training events needed to achieve task proficiency. To help determine the right events, the commander consults various references such as doctrinal training templates, event menu matrixes, and unit-specific and functional CATS. These resources, located on ATN, can inform the development of the unit training plan (UTP).

Time for Subordinate Training Management

3-19. While developing the training plan, the commander ensures it allows subordinates adequate time to plan their own training events. Commanders select the few, major training events necessary for the unit to attain intended MET proficiency levels. Leaving time between these events is essential, since it allows subordinate commanders the ability to accomplish the training necessary to support the higher unit's mission and achieve their own training objectives. Adequate allocation of time at each echelon facilitates training down to individual Soldier tasks. Commanders and staffs leave ample time available for company and below training without designating a separate, special event.

Time Management

3-20. Senior mission commanders use time management cycles—such as red-green-amber and training-mission-support—to manage access to training capabilities at home station. A time management cycle helps provide some measure of predictability for commanders as they develop their training plans. These cycles establish the priority of support to units at an installation. In the past, these cycles have allowed some units to have greater access to maneuver space, ranges, and other training support capabilities, while others focused on training for a potential contingency mission or on providing support to the installation. Time management cycles help reduce the likelihood that nontraining requirements from higher headquarters or the installation affect a commander's UTP.

3-21. Specific training cycles and their lengths vary among installations according to local requirements, such as ARFORGEN pools, unit deployment dates, and installation size and type. No one solution for time management exists. A system that works at one installation may not work at another. Installation commanders develop a system that best suits the installation and the units stationed there.

Leader Development Planning

3-22. Commanders and other leaders plan, execute, and assess leader development objectives. As commanders develop the UTP, they concurrently plan how they intend to develop subordinate leaders by leveraging scheduled training events. Whether the senior leader creates a detailed and formal leader development plan, or a broad and informal plan focused on the basics of leadership, the senior leader sets leader development objectives for each exercise. The commander develops unit leader development plans as part of the UTP.

3-23. A unit leader development plan potentially includes—
- Leadership's expectations of subordinate leaders.
- Leader individual training and certification programs by position.
- Leader development objectives in scheduled unit training events.
- Opportunities for leaders to experience positions of higher responsibility in training.
- Subordinate unit leader development plans.
- Leader professional training and education.
- Retraining until leader achieves task standards.

Course of Action Analysis (War Game)

3-24. During this step, the commander and staff war game the most logical sequencing of training events based on the training time available and the commander's desired end state. Unlike the MDMP for planning an operation, in training, the commander typically arranges and sequences training events in the most effective way possible without devising multiple COAs for consideration. Using a crawl-walk-run approach, the commander sequences events from simple to complex. For example, they plan from small-team or crew events to unit-level events as a command post exercise. Any COA, however, must account for the unit's current state of readiness as an entry point for training.

3-25. When using the CATS as the means to create a training strategy, the commander and staff must scrutinize the events and their sequencing to meet the commander's intent for training. The commander and staff also provide sufficient unscheduled time between major events for subordinates to conduct their own training, since their readiness is key to the higher unit's readiness.

Chapter 3

Course of Action Comparison

3-26. Commanders can use a variety of events to achieve task proficiency. Based on their experience, time available, and in-depth knowledge of their units' capabilities with respect to the assigned mission, commanders choose the best events and sequence of execution.

Course of Action Approval

3-27. Once the training COA is selected, the commander seeks approval of the COA from the next higher commander during the training briefing. The approved COA becomes the basis for the UTP.

Training Briefing

3-28. Commanders brief the plan to the next higher commander. This briefing formalizes the plan and the resources required to support it. The training briefing focuses exclusively on unit training and leader development planning; it does not cover other administrative matters. The training briefing is concise and focused.

3-29. The training briefing is a contract between commanders. The unit commander agrees to train as described in the plan, and the higher commander approves the plan and agrees to provide resources to execute it. If the subordinate unit is deploying under another headquarters, the gaining commander or a representative participates in the briefing. The installation staff also participates in the briefing, since they manage the training support resources on the installation.

Approved Unit Training Plan

3-30. The written plan resulting from COA development is the unit training plan. The UTP is similar to planning a major operation in that it is aimed at achieving strategic and operational objectives within a given time and space. In training, the UTP aims at achieving unit training proficiency and leader development within a given period. The UTP lays out a series of training events—a roadmap—that leads the unit to achieve the objective of training proficiency in select collective tasks. As part of the UTP, the unit can include a unit training calendar that depicts the unit's major training events and the sequence in which they will be executed.

Orders Production

3-31. After the training briefing and the higher commander's approval of the plan, the unit commander publishes the UTP as an operation order to subordinates via the Digital Training Management System (DTMS).

3-32. The UTP should include as a minimum—
- The training operational environment.
- The higher headquarters' mission.
- The higher headquarters' METL.
- The higher headquarters commander's guidance.
- The unit mission.
- The commander's intent.
- Key collective tasks to train.
- A concept of operations that includes—
  - A collective training plan.
  - An individual training plan in support of the collective training plan.
  - A leader development plan.
- A time management system (see paragraphs 3-20 and 3-21).
- Tasks to subordinate units.
- An assessment plan.
- Resources required.

- Risks and mitigation for key tasks not trained.
- Supporting attachments as required including the unit training calendar.

TROOP LEADING PROCEDURES FOR DEVELOPING A UNIT TRAINING PLAN

3-33. Company-level units develop UTPs using troop leading procedures (TLP) that provide small-unit leaders a framework for planning and preparing for operations. This framework extends the MDMP to the small-unit level, typically company and below for units that do not have a coordinating staff. (See ATTP 5-0.1 for a more detailed discussion of TLP.) Once the company-level UTP is approved, TLP are also used for planning training events, as appropriate.

3-34. Leaders begin TLP for unit training when they receive the initial warning order (WARNO) from their next higher unit.

3-35. Steps of TLP are as follows:
- Step 1 – Receive the mission.
- Step 2 – Issue a warning order.
- Step 3 – Make a tentative plan.
- Step 4 – Initiate movement.
- Step 5 – Conduct reconnaissance.
- Step 6 – Complete the plan.
- Step 7 – Issue the order.
- Step 8 – Supervise and refine.

Step 1 – Receive the Mission

3-36. Receipt of a new training mission may occur in several ways. The primary means of transmission from higher headquarters is a WARNO via DTMS, but the staff can just as easily pass the order by any other communications means. With the receipt of the WARNO, leaders normally conduct a confirmation briefing to the next higher commander. Leaders ensure they understand the commander's intent for training, the implied and specified collective tasks on which to train, the time window to achieve proficiency, and any other clarifying guidance from the higher commander.

3-37. Upon mission receipt, leaders perform an initial assessment of the mission and begin determining the collective tasks the unit will train to meet mission requirements. They also assess the time and resources necessary for the unit to achieve collective tasks proficiency.

3-38. Just as at the battalion level and higher, leaders at the company level ensure that all subordinate elements have adequate training time to achieve task proficiency. Generally, leaders at all levels use no more than one-third of the training time available for planning and issuing their operation order (OPORD). They allocate two-thirds of the time remaining for subordinates to plan their own training.

Step 2 – Issue a Warning Order

3-39. As soon as leaders complete their initial assessment of the situation and available training time, they issue a WARNO to subordinate elements. The WARNO is as detailed as needed. It provides subordinates the unit training mission as well as the collective tasks that the unit will need to train. It will also include the training timeline to attain unit task proficiency. As more information becomes available, leaders may issue additional WARNOs to provide better details to aid in subordinate element training plans.

3-40. WARNOs follow the five-paragraph OPORD format. Normally at company level, the WARNO includes—
- The training mission and the collective tasks to train.
- The time and place for issuing the order.
- Units or elements participating in the training.
- Specific tasks not addressed by unit standard operating procedures.
- The timeline for the training.

Step 3 – Make a Tentative Plan

3-41. Once the initial WARNO has been issued, leaders begin to develop a tentative training plan for the unit. These steps are less structured than for units with staffs. Often, leaders perform them mentally and include their principle subordinates in the process. However, leaders—not their subordinates—select the training COA on which to develop the unit training plan.

Mission Analysis

3-42. To frame the tentative training plan, leaders perform mission analysis. In this case, the objective is to—
- Determine the collective tasks to train (higher commander's intent and mission for training).
- An operational environment to replicate.
- Training resources needed to train.
- Training limitations—constraints and restraints.

3-43. Leaders determine the collective tasks to train from the WARNO provided by the higher commander. This would include the specified tasks to train, including additional implied tasks needed to train to ensure mission success.

3-44. Replicating an operational environment is critical to ensuring that training is as realistic and challenging as possible.

3-45. Leaders also determine the training resources needed to train the unit collective tasks. Some of these resources include unique items not readily available on the installation. In such cases, leaders identify the resources to the next higher commander, and staffs obtain them.

3-46. Limitations may include any other considerations that preclude the unit from training all identified collective tasks to standard. For example, units may lack the training time available or available essential resources to train. Restraints identify actions that prohibit the unit from conducting unit training.

Course of Action Development

3-47. Leaders develop a course action using mission analysis and strategies. Mission analysis provides the information necessary for leaders to develop the single, most logical COA for conducting unit training. The CATS provide proponent-approved strategies on which to base the UTP. The plan is stored in DTMS for record and disseminated to subordinates as needed. Once the tentative plan is ready, the leader dialogues with the higher leader to review the list of key collective tasks to train and the overall unit training plan (same concept as the commanders' dialogue for units above company level). This also includes the higher leader's acknowledgement of the resources that the unit requires to conduct the training. The higher commander then approves or modifies the plan, as required.

Step 4 – Initiate Movement

3-48. Once the higher unit commander has approved the plan, the commander directs subordinates to begin actions that facilitate execution of the plan.

Step 5 – Conduct Reconnaissance

3-49. When creating a UTP or planning for a training event, this step ensures that units have these resources available for scheduling and unit use when required. Resources include maneuver space, ranges, simulations, simulators, and facilities.

Step 6 – Complete the Plan

3-50. Following the higher commander's approval of the plan, leaders make final updates pending any modifications made by the higher leader. Leaders make these updates before providing the final approved plan to subordinates.

Step 7 – Issue the Order

3-51. Normally leaders issue small-unit orders verbally. They write fragmentary orders as necessary. At company level, leaders post approved training plans to DTMS for dissemination to subordinate elements. These orders follow the standard five-paragraph OPORD format.

Step 8 – Supervise and Refine

3-52. Company-level training meetings help ensure both the unit and higher training plans are on track. Leaders use training meetings to review the results of the previous weeks' training and adjust future training planning and preparation, as required. (The *Leader's Guide to Company Training Meetings* on ATN has more information.)

PREPARE

3-53. Once leaders disseminate the UTP OPORD to subordinates, execution of the training plan begins. Leaders adapt to changes, as necessary. Thorough preparation to conduct training is essential. Assessment of unit and individual performance is a continual process. While units execute one event, they plan and prepare another. Plan, prepare, execute, and assess are not performed sequentially, but overlap in a series of dynamic and interrelated processes throughout the life cycle of the UTP until the unit attains the commander's visualized end state for training. Training meetings facilitate this integrated process by assessing the collective tasks trained during UTP execution, as well as coordinating resources and planning for future events. Training meetings provide the necessary course corrections as the UTP is executed.

PLANNING AND PREPARING TRAINING EVENTS

3-54. Because the UTP is executed as a series of interrelated training events, each event builds upon the training proficiencies attainted from the previous events, ultimately leading the unit to the commander's visualized training proficiency. Event outcomes are usually a direct reflection of the amount and quality of the preparation that preceded it. Whether training evaluators, conducting rehearsals, or coordinating resources, quality preparation ensures successful event execution and effective unit training and leader development.

TRAINING OBJECTIVES

3-55. **A *training objective* is a statement that describes the desired outcome of a training activity in the unit**. A training objective consists of the task, conditions, and standard. Units focus their training execution on achieving the standards for these objectives during training events. Units achieve a training objective when they meet the standards. The time it takes to achieve the objective is not the deciding factor. Leaders allow enough time during training execution to retrain tasks if training units did not meet the standards. If necessary, units continue training beyond the scheduled time until the unit meets the standards. Retraining should be tailored to fix the shortcomings. If training units achieve the objectives before the scheduled end of the event, then leaders consider ending the training early or training on tasks that require additional training.

TRAINING SUPERVISION

3-56. The Army commander with administrative control of a unit oversees a unit's training until the unit is assigned or attached to a gaining unit. Once assignment or attachment occurs, the gaining commander is responsible for not only the unit's training and leader development, but also for informing the providing commander about the unit's readiness.

3-57. Training supervision is a collaborative process. For a deploying ARFORGEN unit, the providing commander involves the gaining commander in the training process. The providing and gaining commanders share information, resources, and guidance to ensure the unit trains on the right tasks under the right conditions to accomplish the mission. This mutual involvement begins with the assignment of a mission to the unit and ends when the unit returns from deployment to enter the reset force pool of ARFORGEN.

3-58. The commander providing a subordinate unit to another commander for an operation is ultimately responsible for the unit's training. This responsibility includes approval of METLs and the unit training plan, provisioning of training resources, and assessments of training events. The gaining commander recommends tasks to train for the assigned mission and can help assess the training proficiency of the unit. The gaining commander shares information on the area of operations (which may have an impact on training), provides unit standard operating procedures, and visits key training events—especially during culminating training events.

Training Models

3-59. Training models can provide a framework for planning and managing training events. Training models, such as the eight-step training model, are only guides and not lock-step processes. They can be useful, but they are, effectively, just modifications of either the MDMP or TLP.

Support Requirements

3-60. Providing required resources for unit training and leader development is a shared responsibility between the unit's higher headquarters and the installation. The higher headquarters prioritizes units for training support and provides such resources for exercises. These resources include higher control, evaluators, and equipment and Soldier augmentation. The installation supports all units stationed on the installation through the garrison staff by providing facilities, ranges, maneuver space, ammunition, logistics support, and other training support services.

3-61. Commanders leverage the capabilities offered by mission command training complexes and employ an integrated training environment (known as ITE). Commanders use a combination of live, virtual, constructive and gaming training enablers to create a realistic training environment, optimize training time, and mitigate live resource shortfalls.

Training the Trainer

3-62. Trainers include leaders, evaluators, observer-controller-trainers, opposing force personnel, and role players. Commanders identify these individuals early enough to ensure they are trained and rehearsed before training begins. These personnel not only improve the quality of the event, but these roles offer developmental opportunities since they can observe how other units and leaders operate. Commanders ensure that these personnel are not only tactically and technically competent on the unit's tasks, but also that these personnel understand how their role supports the unit's training.

Pre-Execution Checks

3-63. Similar to pre-combat checks, pre-execution checks ensure that equipment is ready and serviceable, trainers are prepared, training support resources are coordinated and available, and leaders have conducted initial risk management checks. The training plan must allocate time for pre-execution checks.

Rehearsals

3-64. Rehearsals help leaders and subordinates understand the conduct of events and their responsibilities. Rehearsals help the organization synchronize training with times, places, logistics, and training support. A rehearsal of a concept drill helps leaders visualize an event as it unfolds as well as likely branches and sequels if leaders must adjust the training. Commanders and other leaders also use rehearsals to—
- Ensure leaders and trainers understand training objectives.
- Identify shortcomings and deficiencies in the training plan.
- Instill confidence in the training plan.
- Suggest effective training techniques to subordinates.
- Identify and correct potential safety issues.
- Understand how trainers intend to evaluate the performance of individuals and organizations and whether they understand how to conduct effective after action reviews.
- Assess trainer competencies to conduct the training.

Training Schedules

3-65. The OPORD developed for each training event provides enough guidance on preparation, execution, and assessment to leave room for the exercise of initiative. Once the OPORD is published, units develop their training schedules. The schedule normally covers at least one week of training; however, commanders determine how far in advance subordinate commanders must publish their training schedules. Commanders determine the approval authority for changes to the training schedule. Information in training schedules normally includes, but is not limited to, the training audience, the time and place to conduct the training, the individual responsible for the training, the uniform, and the equipment.

EXECUTE

3-66. Leaders must plan, prepare, execute, and assess each training event that supports the UTP. Training meetings and recovery after training are key activities that occur as each training event is conducted. These activities ensure that units execute the UTP and it meets the commander's desired objectives for unit training and leader development.

TRAINING MEETINGS

3-67. Training meetings provide an integrating function to allow the commander, staff, subordinate commanders, and other leaders to manage current and future training events that support the UTP. Training meetings provide commanders with continuous bottom-up feedback on requirements, task proficiency, task performance, and the quality of the training conducted. They give the commander an opportunity to provide feedback to the unit on its unit training and leader development. The meetings allow the commander to allocate resources to ensure subordinates have what they need to achieve their objectives.

3-68. Training meetings are the single most important meeting for managing training in brigades, battalions, and companies. Normally, platoons, companies, and battalions meet weekly. At company and platoon level, training meetings focus on the specifics of assessing previous training events, training preparation, pre-execution checks, and execution. Companies must become proficient in individual skills and small-unit collective tasks to support battalion and brigade collective task proficiency. At battalion level and above, training meetings primarily cover training management—especially resourcing issues—as well as staff training proficiencies. Meeting frequency is a function of command preference, but occurs often enough to ensure subordinate units have what they require to execute training. (See the *Leader's Guide to Company Training Meetings* on ATN.)

RECOVERY AFTER TRAINING

3-69. Recovery after training is part of training. A training event has not ended until recovery is complete. Recovery ends when the organization is again prepared to conduct collective training and operations. Recovery includes—

- Inspecting and maintaining equipment and personnel.
- Accounting for personnel, equipment, training support items, and ammunition.
- Gaining insights on how to make the next exercise or event better.

ASSESS

3-70. Commanders assess and evaluate all aspects of training—planning, preparation, execution, and ultimate task proficiency. Only the unit commander can assess the readiness of a MET. Assessment refers to the leader's judgment of the organization's ability to perform its METLs and, ultimately, its ability to accomplish its mission. Evaluation refers to the process used to measure the demonstrated ability of individuals and units to accomplish specified training objectives and achieve task proficiency. Leaders continuously monitor the unit's METL proficiency and the progress of the UTP.

Chapter 3

TRAINING EFFECTIVENESS

3-71. Commanders assess each training event by focusing on the extent to which the unit achieved the commander's intent, training objectives, and progress towards unit collective task proficiency. The training meeting is the best forum to aggregate evaluations of tasks by subordinates and the commander into the METL assessment. Commanders assess METs as **T**—trained, **P**—needs practice or **U**—untrained. The commander records these assessments in the DTMS and uses these assessments to determine the organization's training ratings for readiness reporting. Training assessments also address such areas as training support, force integration, logistics, and personnel availability. Given these assessments, commanders adjust their future training plans.

ASSESSMENT CONSIDERATIONS

3-72. When assessing training, commanders consider—
- Their own observations and those of subordinate leaders and other individuals.
- Feedback from after action reviews.
- Results of unit evaluations.

AFTER ACTION REVIEWS

3-73. After action reviews provide opportunities for units to develop critical thinking in leaders. **An *after action review* is a guided analysis of an organization's performance, conducted at appropriate times during and at the conclusion of a training event or operation with the objective of improving future performance. It includes a facilitator, event participants, and other observers**. Organizations conduct after action reviews (AARs) to identify unit strengths to be sustained and weaknesses that need to improve. They apply observations, insights, and lessons to future training and operations to improve not only task proficiency, but also the quality of the training event. AARs are best conducted throughout an exercise at appropriate times, rather than just at the end of the exercise, to allow Soldiers and their leaders to take immediate, in-stride corrective actions. AARs are not critiques. They are part of an open learning environment where facilitators, participants, and observers freely discuss successes and honest mistakes. AARs help units and individuals understand what went right and why, what went wrong and why, and what to do better in future training and operations. Units share lessons learned with other units using various methods. They can use the ATN and Center for Army Lessons Learned web sites, video teleconferences, pre-deployment site surveys, right-seat rides, and other collaborative opportunities. Commanders and other leaders integrate these observations, insights, and lessons into their unit training and education to try to prevent their units from committing the same mistakes. (Refer to the *Leader's Guide to After-Action Reviews* on ATN.)

TRAINING AND EVALUATION OUTLINES

3-74. All training must be evaluated. Otherwise, the training time is wasted. Task standards reside in the training and evaluation outlines for each collective task. **A *training and evaluation outline* is a summary document that provides information on collective training objectives, related individual training objectives, resource requirements, and applicable evaluation procedures for a type of organization.** This document provides the task title, task description, the recommended conditions to use in training, the standard to be met and the task steps and performance measures to attain a 'GO/NO-GO' for each step. Trainers access training and evaluation outlines from ATN, through CATS and the DTMS. The training and evaluation outline provides the means to help leaders evaluate task execution and subjectively assess the unit's ability to perform the task.

Glossary

The glossary lists acronyms and terms. Terms for which ADRP 7-0 is the proponent are marked with an asterisk (*).

SECTION I – ACRONYMS AND ABBREVIATIONS

AAR	after action review
ADP	Army doctrine publication
ADRP	Army doctrine reference publication
ARFORGEN	Army force generation
ATN	Army Training Network
CATS	Combined Arms Training Strategies
COA	course of action
DA	Department of the Army
DTMS	Digital Training Management System
FM	field manual
JP	joint publication
MDMP	military decisionmaking process
MET	mission-esential task
METL	mission-essential task list
NCO	noncommissioned officer
OPORD	operation order
TLP	troop leading procedures
UTM	unit training management
UTP	unit training plan
WARNO	warning order

SECTION II – TERMS

*after action review

A guided analysis of an organization's performance, conducted at appropriate times during and at the conclusion of a training event or operation with the objective of improving future performance. It includes a facilitator, event participants, and other observers.

*mission-essential task

A task a unit could perform based on its design, equipment, manning, and table of organization and equipment/table of distribution and allowances mission.

*mission-essential task list

A compilation of mission-essential tasks.

*multiechelon training

A training technique that allows for the simultaneous training of more than one echelon on different or complementary tasks.

*training and evaluation outline
    A summary document that provides information on collective training objectives, related individual training objectives, resource requirements, and applicable evaluation procedures for a type of organization.

*training objective
    A statement that describes the desired outcome of a training activity in the unit.

References

Field manuals and selected joint publications are listed by new number followed by old number.

REQUIRED PUBLICATIONS

These documents must be available to intended users of this publication.

JP 1-02. *Department of Defense Dictionary of Military and Associated Terms*. 8 November 2010.

RELATED PUBLICATIONS

These documents contain relevant supplemental information.

ARMY PUBLICATIONS

Most Army doctrinal publications are available online: <http://www.apd.army.mil/>.

ADP 3-0 (FM 3-0). *Unified Land Operations*. 10 October 2011.

ADP 6-0 (FM 6-0). *Mission Command*. 17 May 2012.

ADP 6-22. *Army Leadership*. 1 August 2012.

ADP 7-0 (FM 7-0). *Training Units and Developing Leaders*. 23 August 2012.

ADRP 3-0. *Unified Land Operations*. 16 May 2012.

ADRP 5-0. *The Operations Process*. 17 May 2012.

ADRP 6-0. *Mission Command*. 17 May 2012.

ATTP 5-0.1. *Commander and Staff Officer Guide*. 14 September 2011.

FM 27-10. *The Law of Land Warfare*. 18 July 1956.

OTHER PUBLICATIONS

Leader's Guide to After-Action Reviews (AAR). Fort Leavenworth, Kansas: United States Army Combined Arms Center –Training, 2011. Available at <https://atn.army.mil/Media/docs/LG%20to%20AAR%20(MASTER%2030%20Aug%2011).pdf>.

Leader's Guide to Company Training Meetings. Fort Leavenworth, Kansas: United States Army Combined Arms Center –Training, 2011. Available at <https://atn.army.mil/Media/docs/LG%20to%20Training%20Meeting%20(MASTER%2016%20Aug%2011).pdf>.

WEB SITES

Army Training Network at <https://atn.army.mil>.

Center for Army Lessons Learned at <http://usacac.army.mil/cac2/call/>.

Digital Training Management System at < https://dtms.army.mil>.

REFERENCED FORMS

DA Form 2028. *Recommended Changes to Publications and Blank Forms*.

This page intentionally left blank.

Index

A

adaptability, development of, 2-10
    leaders, 3-53
after action review, 2-8, 2-23
    defined, 3-73
assess, 1-16–1-18, 2-23, 3-70–3-74
    after action reviews, 3-73
    considerations, 3-72
    training and evaluations outlines, 3-74
    training effectiveness, 3-71
assessment, considerations, 3-72
    initial, 3-37

C

collaboration, mission-essential tasks and, 3-6
    training, 3-57
collective tasks, determining, 3-37
    planning and, 3-12
    selecting, 3-13–3-14
    standards of performance, 2-5
collective training, 1-7
Combined Arms Training Strategies, 3-25, 3-47, 3-74
command, art of, 2-24
commanders, assessment by, 3-70
    framework for, 3-2
    responsibilities of, 3-58
    responsibility of, 2-2
    role of, 1-10–1-18
commanders' dialogue, 3-15–3-16
    military decisionmaking process, 3-18
    troop leading procedures and, 3-47
complexity, 1-4, 2-6
concurrent training, multiechelon and, 2-16–2-17
control, science of, 2-24
course of action analysis, 3-24–3-25
course of action approval, 3-27–3-30
course of action comparison, 3-26
course of action development, 3-17–3-23, 3-47
critical thinking, 3-73
cultures, 2-7

D

describe, 1-13
Digital Training Management System, 3-31, 3-36, 3-74
direct, 1-14

E

environment, learning, 1-9, 2-22, 3-44, 3-61, 3-73
    replication of, 2-6, 2-11
    training, 3-15, 3-61
equipment, maintenance of, 2-14
execute, 3-66–3-69
    recovery, 3-69
    training meetings, 3-67–3-68

F

feedback, 2-3, 3-67
fundamentals, 2-9

I

individual tasks, standards of performance, 2-5
individual training, 1-6
institutional training domain, 1-8
integrated training environment, 3-61

L

lead, 1-15
leader development, 1-8–1-9
    feedback, 3-67
    operations process and, 3-1–3-7
    planning, 3-22–3-23
    principles of, 2-18–2-28
    resources for, 3-60
leaders, adaptive, 2-25, 3-53
    development of, 1-1–1-4, 2-21, 3-22–3-23
    imitation of, 2-20
    principles of development, 2-18–2-28
    relationships of, 2-27–2-28
    responsibilities of, 2-27
    subordinates and, 2-21, 2-27–2-28
learning, growth, 2-22
learning environment, 1-9
    creating, 2-22–2-23

M

maintenance, training, 2-13–2-15
military decisionmaking process, 3-9–3-32
    collective tasks and, 3-13–3-14
    commanders' dialogue, 3-15–3-16
    course of action analysis, 3-24–3-25
    course of action approval, 3-27–3-30
    course of action comparison, 3-26
    course of action development, 3-17–3-23
    leader development, 3-22–3-23
    mission analysis, 3-12–3-16
    orders production, 3-31–3-32
    receipt of mission, 3-11
    time management, 3-20–3-21
    training briefing, 3-28–3-29
    training events and, 3-18
    training management, 3-19
    unit training plan, 3-30
mission, receipt of, 3-36
mission analysis, 3-12–3-16, 3-42–3-47
mission command, 1-10, 2-24
mission-essential task, assess, 3-71
    defined, 3-5
mission-essential task list, defined, 3-5
movement, initiate, 3-48
multiechelon training, concurrent and, 2-16–2-17
    defined, 2-16

N

noncommissioned officers, responsibility of, 2-3–2-4

O

operation order, 3-31, 3-65
    unit training plan, 3-53
operational environment, training for, 2-6–2-7
    understanding, 2-11
operational training domain, 1-8
operations process, training and, 3-1–3-7
orders, issue, 3-51
orders production, 3-31–3-32

P

plan, 3-8–3-52
    complete, 3-50
    framing, 3-42–3-47

plan (continued)
    tentative, 3-41–3-47
planning, leader development, 3-22–3-23
pre-execution checks, 3-63
prepare, 3-53–3-65
    pre-execution checks, 3-63
    rehearsals, 3-64
    support requirements, 3-60–3-61
    training events, 3-554
    training models, 3-59
    training objectives, 3-55
    training schedules, 3-65
    training supervision, 3-56—3-58
    training the trainer, 3-62
presence, 1-15
principles, leader development, 2-18–2-28
    unit training, 2-1–2-17
problems, solving, 2-26
proficiency, sustain, 2-12
    time and, 3-19

R
readiness, unit, 3-56
receive the mission, 3-11, 3-36–3-38
reconnaissance, 3-49
recovery, after training, 3-69
refine, supervise and, 3-52
rehearsals, 3-64
resources, maintaining, 2-15
    training, 3-60

S
self-development training domain, 1-8–1-9
standards, leaders and, 2-21
    training, 1-3
standards of performance, training to, 2-5
stewardship, 2-15
subordinates, development of, 3-3
    environments for, 2-22–2-23
    initiative, 1-10, 1-18
    leaders and, 2-27–2-28
    responsibilities of, 2-15
    training management, 3-19
    training of, 1-9, 2-2, 2-4, 2-14, 2-16, 2-18
supervise, refine and, 3-52, 3-56–3-57

support, requirements, 3-60–3-61
sustain, 2-12

T
tactical, competence, 1-2
tasks, 3-5–3-7
    adapting, 2-25
    determining, 3-4
    mastering, 2-10
technical, competence, 1-2
techniques, training, 1-3
think, critically and creatively, 2-26
time, training management, 3-19
time management cycles, 3-20
trainer, training of, 3-62
training, collective, 1-7
    development of, 1-1–1-4
    effectiveness, 3-71
    endurance, 1-5–
    individual, 1-6
    managing, 3-68
    operations process and, 3-1–3-7
    proficiency, 3-70
    resources for, 3-60
    responsibilities of, 2-2
    selection of, 3-26
    standards, 1-3
    supervision, 3-56–3-58
    synchronize, 3-64
    techniques, 1-3
    times for, 2-8, 3-65
    trainer, 3-62
training and evaluation outline, defined, 3-74
training briefing, 3-28–3-29
training cycles, 3-21
training domains, 1-5, 3-3
training environments, 3-61
training events, 3-18, 3-55, 3-59
    managing, 3-67
    operation order, 3-65
    planning, 3-24
    preparing, 3-54
    support from, 3-66
training management, 3-20–3-21
    subordinate, 3-19
training meetings, 3-52, 3-53, 3-67–3-68
training models, 3-59
training objective, defined, 3-55
training strategy, 3-25

troop leading procedures,
    complete the plan, 3-50
    conduct reconnaissance, 3-49
    course of action development, 3-47
    initiate movement, 3-48
    issue a warning order, 3-39–3-40
    issue the order, 3-51
    make a tentative plan, 3-41–3-47
    mission analysis, 3-42–3-46
    receive the mission, 3-36–3-38
    steps of, 3-35–3-52
    supervise and refine, 3-52
    unit training plan and, 3-33–3-52

U
understand, 1-11
unit training, 1-7, 3-39
    after action reviews, 3-73
    course of action development, 3-47
    operations process and, 3-1–3-7
    planning, 1-11, 3-8
    preparation, 3-54
    principles of, 2-1–2-17
    proficiency, 3-30
    resources, 3-60
    training briefing, 3-28
    training meetings, 3-67
    troop leading procedures and, 3-34
unit training management, 1-4, 3-1–3-74
    mission command, 2-24
    operations process, 3-1–3-7
    subordinate, 3-19
    time, 3-20–3-21
    training meetings, 3-67
unit training plan, 3-8, 3-22, 3-32, 3-53
    approved, 3-30
    operation order, 3-53
    support, 3-66
    troop leading procedures and, 3-33–3-52

V
visualize, 1-12

W
war game, 3-24–3-25
warning order, 3-34
    issuing, 3-39–3-40

ADRP 7-0
23 August 2012

By order of the Secretary of the Army:

RAYMOND T. ODIERNO
General, United States Army
Chief of Staff

Official:

JOYCE E. MORROW
Administrative Assistant to the
Secretary of the Army
1218004

DISTRIBUTION:

Active Army, Army National Guard, and United States Army Reserve: To be distributed in accordance with the initial distribution number (IDN) 111080, requirements for ADRP 7-0.

This page intentionally left blank.